700
4/8

THE
WAKING
DREAM

THE
WAKING
DREAM

UNLOCKING
THE SYMBOLIC LANGUAGE
OF OUR LIVES

RAY GRASSE

QUEST BOOKS
The Theosophical Publishing House
Wheaton, IL, U.S.A./Adyar, Madras, India

The Theosophical Publishing House
P.O. Box 270
Wheaton, IL 60189-0270

A publication of the Theosophical Publishing House,
a department of the Theosophical Society in America

Library of Congress Cataloging-in-Publication Data

Grasse, Ray.
    The waking dream : unlocking the symbolic language of our lives / Ray Grasse —
1st Quest ed.
        p.   cm.
    "Quest books."
    Includes bibliographical references and index.
    ISBN 0-8356-0726-7 (cloth) — ISBN 0-8356-0749-6 (pbk.)
    1. Symbolism.   2. Symbolism—History.   3. Coincidence—Psychic
aspects.   4. Shamanistic symbolism.   5. Symbolism (Psychology)
    I. Title.
BF1623.S9G72   1996
133—dc20
                                    95-48487
                                      CIP

8 7 6 5 4 3 2 1 • 96 97 98 99 00 01 02

Copyright acknowledgment for illustrations: (p. 225) photo by Hans Peter Widmer

Every effort has been made to secure permission to reproduce the images in this book. Any
additional copyright holders are invited to contact the publisher so that proper credit can be
given in future editions.

Book and Cover Design by Beth Hansen
Cover Illustration by Ray Grasse

This book was set in Trump Medieval, Book Antiqua Italic, Herculanum, and Papyrus.
Printed in the United States of America.

TABLE OF CONTENTS

For Judith

ACKNOWLEDGMENTS

uring the more than twelve years spent writing and researching this book, many people provided helpful support and feedback. I wish to here express my deepest gratitude to all of them, including: my parents Catherine and Raymond Grasse, John Kranich, David Fideler, Alice O. Howell, David Frawley, Peggy Firestone, Rick Tarnas, Jody Piro, Shirley Nicholson, George and Linda Gawor, Gary Lachman, Medicine Grizzlybear Lake, Rosemary Clark, and Scott Korn. Thanks also to Scott Sterns, Tom Chapin, and Ruben Cabigting for their technical support during the latter stages. My appreciation to Karen Rybacki for helping me track down the many images which grace these pages.

My boundless gratitude to my editors Brenda Rosen and Virginia Smiley, who proved invaluable in the final shaping and refining of this material, and especially for Brenda's early support in pushing to get it published in the first place. Also, to the many others at Quest who played a role in the production of this work, including Vija Bremanis, Nancy Grace, Karen Yates, Dawn Hicks, Patti Hamilton, Pam Demers, and graphic designer Beth Hansen, who skillfully brought it all together. Last but not least, my deepest appreciation to Goswami Kriyananda of Chicago and Shelly Trimmer, without whose insight and generosity of time over the years this book would not have been possible.

There is a dream dreaming us.

—Kalahari Bushman to Laurens van der Post

The wise say that the two states, dream and waking, are one . . . though in fact the objects of waking experience appear as real, still they are unreal.

—Gaudapada

Recognize this infinite variety of appearances as a dream, as nothing but the projections of your mind, illusory and unreal.

—Tsele Natsok Rangrol

We are such stuff as dreams are made on.

—Shakespeare

(Our dreams), inasmuch as they originate from us, may well have an analogy with our whole life and fate.

—Goethe

Is all our Life, then, but a dream . . .

—Lewis Carroll

Our life is but one of the dreams of that more real life, and so it is endlessly, until the very last one, the very real life—the life of God.

—Tolstoy

Well, yes, one could also say that we are not sitting here drinking tea, but that we're dreaming all that.

—Niels Bohr

. . . the universe begins to look more like a great thought than a great machine.

—Sir James Jeans

INTRODUCTION

Things here are signs.

—Plotinus

hile preparing for his role in the 1939 film *The Wizard of Oz*, actor Frank Morgan decided against using the costume offered him by the studio for his role as the traveling salesman Professor Marvel, opting instead to select his own wardrobe for the part. Searching through the racks of second-hand clothes collected by the MGM wardrobe department over the years, he finally settled on an old frock coat that would eventually serve as his costume during filming of the movie. Passing the time one day, Morgan idly turned out the inside of the pocket of the coat and discovered the name "L. Frank Baum" sewn into the lining of the jacket. As later investigation confirmed, the jacket had been originally designed for the creator of the Oz story, L. Frank Baum, and somehow made its way through the years into the collection of clothing on the MGM lot.

Almost everyone, at some time or another, has experienced extraordinary coincidences or synchronicities so startling they are compelled to reflect upon their possible meaning. Do such occurrences hold a deeper significance? Might they hint at a hidden design underlying the seemingly random events unfolding around us? Or are they, as modern science suggests, merely the expression of chance processes, completely explainable in terms of statistics and probability theory?

One way to begin answering such questions is to consider the insights of an ancient worldview. For thousands of years philosophers and mystics have formulated ideas and esoteric laws that attempted to explain the hidden workings of reality. Seen as a whole, this network of ideas and laws may be designated by the term "symbolist," in reference to the many symbolic systems—astrology, tarot, kabbalah, and others—it has found expression through, and as a reference to the broader symbolic vision of reality it reflects. This symbolic perspective is in stark contrast with the more materialistic and "literal" worldview promoted by contemporary society.

Although this body of thought is complex and multifaceted, it is nevertheless possible to identify certain recurring themes among its expressions, which through different times and cultures have displayed remarkable consistency. A brief list of these includes the following:

- The world reflects the presence of a greater regulating intelligence, or Divine Mind, that both permeates and transcends material reality.
- All things partake in a greater continuum of order and design; consequently, there are no coincidences or truly random events. In turn, any chance event or process can divulge greater patterns of meaningfulness within the life of an individual or society.
- Reality is multileveled in character, involving phenomena and experiences across a wide spectrum of frequencies or vibration.
- The world is interwoven by a complex web of subtle correspondences or affinities, secret connections that link seemingly diverse phenomena through a deeper resonance of meaning.
- All phenomena are governed by processes of cyclic change, according to which things arise, grow, and decay.
- All forms can be reduced to a basic set of universal principles or archetypes. Described in various ways by differ-

ent traditions, these principles reflect the underlying language of both outer and inner experience.

• Understood at their subtlest level, these archetypes reveal themselves to be an expression of deeper numerological or geometrical principles, also explainable through the concept of proportion or ratio.

In short, the symbolist standpoint considers life to be a living book of symbols, a sacred text that can be decoded. Through applying the proper key, the patterns of the world reveal hidden resonances and levels of information overlooked in our contemporary preoccupation with literal meanings and surface interpretations.

This book takes a deeper look at the symbolist worldview and its aspects. It explores the philosophical implications of many of its key ideas, and how these ideas have been understood and employed by men and women throughout history. On a more personal level, it offers a number of practical suggestions and examples to help the reader understand the teachings and messages encoded within the people, places, objects, and events experienced each day. Taken together, these approaches provide readers with a set of tools by which to revision their world. It is ironic, perhaps, that our culture accords great honor and prestige to the individual who devotes long years to acquiring higher degrees, while granting none whatsoever to the person who devotes even one day to studying the symbolic language presented by daily experience—the most important and profound text in anyone's world.

There is profound value in recovering this traditional perspective. The symbolist way of thinking has deep roots in the human psyche; its persistence through millennia speaks dramatically to what one writer has called the common human passion for meaning.[1] In an age when many people question seriously whether life may be empty or without significance, the symbolist perspective tells us life is not empty, but is in fact rich in meaning, purpose, and archetypal resonance. Through a study of the varied systems of this ancient way of looking at the world, we can discover the different ways humans have sought to find meaning in their environment and, in turn, learn to unearth the treasures hidden within the seemingly mundane events of our daily lives.

SOURCES

Rather than codified in any single text or tradition, the insights of the symbolist worldview are found within the oral and written teachings of esoteric schools around the world, both in the yogic traditions of the East and the hermetic and kabbalistic traditions of the West. In addition to a broad study of the published literature in this field, my own work with this subject over the years has led me into discussions with figures from various traditions, some of them well-known (Chogyam Trungpa, Joseph Campbell), but most of them relatively unknown or even obscure. Of particular value in this process has been my sixteen years of study with two American-born teachers affiliated with the Kriya Yoga tradition, Goswami Kriyananda of Chicago and Shelly Trimmer, a direct disciple of Paramahansa Yogananda. Through them, I was afforded access to an oral tradition of great richness and complexity, with roots deep in the esoteric systems of both East and West.

The insights of the symbolist worldview in somewhat subtler and more implicit form are encoded within the great esoteric systems of antiquity, such as astrology, tarot, numerology, and other forms of divination and mantic inquiry. As anyone who has ever worked with these systems knows, each of them contains a unique array of overt and covert insights regarding reality and the psyche, insights that divulge themselves only after extensive use of these systems over many years. This book extrapolates from these systems to provide a broader illumination of the essential principles of symbolist thought.

Symbolist ideas can even be detected within the superstitions and folk beliefs of traditional and modern societies. Cultures throughout the world, for example, emphasize the number seven (sometimes called the perfect number) and believe in the reality of omens and portents. Crude as their external form may be at times, such recurring motifs reflect deep-seated patterns of the psyche, and to that extent can sometimes be read for the insight they provide into the greater universe of which the human mind is a reflection.

Yet the interest of this book is not simply to provide an objective survey of symbolist thought; rather, it is to offer a creative synthesis, drawing together many of its wide-ranging themes with extrapolations and reflections from my own experience, toward the end of imparting a broader sense of its essential vision.

A LOOK AHEAD

This book has been structured so each chapter unlocks a different door onto the symbolist point of view.

Chapter one begins with a look at some of its essential principles, focusing especially on the universal laws described by mystics and philosophers since antiquity as governing the universe. Just as the modern worldview is supported by certain hidden presuppositions which guide and inform it, symbolist philosophy conceals its own underlying presuppositions which characterize its far-ranging beliefs and are therefore essential to a broader understanding of its implications.

Chapter two steps back to reflect on the historical context of symbolist thinking and its development through time. It points to why such thinking was critical to past cultures and why it has largely disappeared from our own.

Chapter three presents a way to categorize symbolist events and argues that meaning is not an isolated occurrence in our lives, limited only to the strange and unpredictable coincidence, but extends across the entire horizon of personal experience.

Chapter four examines one of the most popular forms of meaningful event identified by traditional societies: the omen. It includes a discussion of divination and the practical ways men and women have sought to harness the symbolic dynamics of nature to understand and influence the future.

Chapter five looks at human relationships. Like an ingeniously conceived script written exclusively for ourselves, when seen through the eyes of symbolist thought, ordinary interactions present us with a rich and multifaceted mirror of our own inner growth. Friend, enemy, spouse, parent, even the nameless passerby on the street—all can be profound teachers in our quest to understand ourselves.

Chapters six and seven take a close look at the broader forces propelling the unfoldment of our destinies, from both the past and future. In these chapters is a discussion of the Eastern notion of *karma* (or spiritual cause-and-effect) and the evolutionary principle of *telos* (purpose). In the dialectic tension between these two principles lies the most eternally gripping questions of the human experience: Is the world a reflection of our current thoughts or desires? Do we create our reality, as many claim? Are the fortunes or tragedies of our lives a form of reward or punishment for our actions in the past? Or are they the result of natural cycles which govern the unfoldment of nature in all its manifestations, regardless of merit?

In chapter eight, attention turns to the most deeply practical aspect of symbolist philosophy, the role of ritual. We will discover ritual to be far more pervasive than we had ever imagined and learn that all activities are magic of a sort.

The last third of this book looks more closely at the theoretical dimensions of the symbolist worldview, centering on the quintessential symbolist art, astrology. Chapter nine asks, what possible mechanism underlies the operations of astrology? The symbolist perspective hints at a possible answer to this question, and this in turn provides a point of departure for revisioning our relation to the universe. Could it be, as is commonly held in New Age and even new science circles, that everything is instantaneously connected to everything else? Additionally, this chapter examines the possibility that astrology may be properly understood only as part of a broad network of interconnections, in which the stars and planets are but small parts.

Chapter ten starts with a discussion of archetypes. If life is indeed a living book of symbols, then what is the language of that book? And what are the components of that language? Here also is an examination of astrology's symbols and those found in another of antiquity's great symbolic systems, the yogic philosophy of the chakras. Astrology and the chakra system, this chapter shows, are not truly separate, but deeply entwined in meaning and message. Together, they offer a way of unlocking symbolic clues and provide the foundation for a sacred psychology based on archetypes and universal processes.

But what lies behind the archetypes? Chapter eleven introduces the principle of proportion, or subtle geometry, as the source of meaning underlying all universal patterns. It examines the classical notion of the elements, and the intriguing possibility that symbols may arise out of the architecture of consciousness itself.

Finally, chapter twelve reflects on the interconnections between symbolist ideas and contemporary culture. It begins with a look at Carl Jung's theory of synchronicity, and how it contrasts with perennial symbolist ideas. It explores the ambivalent relationship between symbolist principles and modern science and examines the implications of the symbolist worldview in our continuing quest to understand and relate to the physical universe.

Let us begin our exploration. Behind the door of coincidence is found a world of archetypal presences and magical connections, a dimension of meaning that extends to every aspect of ordinary experience. With a subtle shift of vision, we can become fluent in a symbolic language both ancient and new, which emerges from our own personal waking dream.

Chapter 1

The World as Dream

To the magus, there exists no accidental happening . . . everything is established solidly by that law which the wise man discerns in happenings that appear accidental to the profane. The curve observed in the flight of birds, the barking of a dog, the shape of a cloud, are occult manifestations of that omnipotent coordinator, the source of unity and harmony.

—**Kurt Seligmann**, *Magic, Supernaturalism, and Religion*

uring a trip through the Southwest in 1982, I spent an afternoon with a Native American medicine man, a figure respected and feared by fellow villagers for his medicinal and magical knowledge. After talking for several hours about his practices and beliefs, he suggested we carry our conversation outside and take a walk along the edge of the village looking out over the desert.

As we made our way along the sandy pathway, he asked about my life and interests back home in the Midwest. I started telling him about a project I was scheduled to become involved in. Exactly at the moment I related my suspicions that this effort appeared to be taking a much different direction than I had originally intended, a bird conspicuously darted in front of us letting out a sharp cry, only to change direction abruptly and make a sharp right turn.

Noting this event, my companion cheerfully remarked, "See! There you are! Like you thought, things are going to turn out quite differently than you originally planned." When I asked him to explain himself, he told me the signs around us indicated this. The winged apparition at the precise moment I spoke provided a message about what would transpire for me. He went on to say such messages are around us all the time, but nowadays we have forgotten how to read them. "We have lost the capacity to interpret the signs from nature," he said.

To the contemporary mind, the notion there might be messages or signs within random events seems strange, even absurd. Yet for millennia, such perceptions were commonplace in societies around the world. Whether we read stories of Chinese scribes seeking guidance by interpreting sticks thrown randomly on the ground, or hear tales of ancient Romans scrutinizing omens in the entrails of sacrificed animals on the eve of battle, or study accounts of Tibetan priests searching out candidates for the position of high Lama by gazing into a sacred lake, we find ourselves confronted with a way of viewing the world profoundly different from our own. As seen from this ancient perspective, reality is pregnant with hidden meanings and connections waiting to be unlocked by the discerning mind.

Symbolist thinking regards the world as a kind of *language,* with the people, animals, and events representing elements of a living vocabulary; a flower may be linked to a distant star, or an animal's movements entwined with the thoughts of a passing observer. Nowadays, we dismiss such notions as little more than remnants of a primitive age with a misguided predilection for confused categories and magical thinking. We tolerate that a dancer might have a pair of lucky shoes, but for most of us, the objects and random events of our daily life have no inherent meaning or significance.

But are such ideas *only* superstition, with no validity or importance? Or, can it be that in our wholesale rejection of the symbolist worldview, we overlook a level of insight hidden beneath the patent foolishness this way of looking at the world seems to imply?

It is curious, despite the rising tide of scientific and secular thought, that many of the greatest creative and philosophical minds of recent centuries have continued to find value in symbolist ideas. Consider Emerson's statement, "Every natural fact is a symbol of some spiritual fact."[1] In a well-known essay, the German philosopher Schopenhauer reflects upon the curious design that underlies the apparent accidents of our lives, as if to suggest a deeper organizing principle beyond the range of conscious perception.[2] In a related vein, the philosopher and mathematician Gottfried Wilhelm von Leibniz developed a theory to explain how the outer events in our lives coincide with our inner development in a grand expression of "pre-established harmony";[3] while his contemporary Isaac Newton privately entertained deeply occult notions concerning the subtler forces and laws that underlie the phenomena of nature. As economist John Maynard Keynes observed, Newton "saw the whole universe and all that is in it *as a riddle,* as a secret which could be read by applying pure thought to certain evidence, certain mystic clues which God . . . hid about the world to allow a sort of philosopher's treasure hunt to the esoteric brotherhood."[4]

In more recent times, psychologist Carl Jung coined the term *synchronicity* to define the puzzling sense of design that lies behind coincidences in our lives;[5] while his Austrian forerunner in the study of coincidence Paul Kammerer used the term *seriality* to describe his own unique theories of this same phenomenon. On studying Kammerer's research concerning coincidences, Albert Einstein concluded it was "original and by no means absurd."[6] And recently, a man regarded by millions around the world to be among the leading spiritual figures of our times, the Dalai Lama, openly professed a belief in omens and oracles.[7]

In the field of literature, we likewise find many of the greatest writers drawing inspiration from this same stream of thought. In his epic work *Ulysses,* Irish novelist James Joyce crafted a vision of reality underscoring both the archetypal undercurrents of ordinary experience as well as the intricately coincidental nature of events in our lives. In an article commemorating the centenary of Joyce's birth, Dan Tucker offered the following comments on Joyce's symbolist perspective:

> *There is something inside-out about Joyce's books compared to other writers': messiness and jumble and horseplay out in the open, the shape buried deep. What at first looks like a hodgepodge or a joke turns out to be all interconnected, laced together with hundreds of tiny threads . . . insignificant scraps of memory and association. They keep popping up just often enough to imply some sort of design. Do you notice something about that comment? It applies to our own lives. Life is like* Ulysses *that way, full of haphazard, pointless events and coincidences, variations on silly themes. But every so often they hint at connectedness, structure, hidden meanings; often enough to keep us looking for those things. We don't want the things that happen to us to be meaningless—a mere succession of events. And just by their shape and texture, Joyce's books keep telling us that they aren't meaningless.*[8]

In his book *Coincidance*, Robert Anton Wilson cites the following dramatic example of synchronicity from Joyce's life. Joyce once made a trip to visit the grave site of a former romantic rival, Michael Bodkin, who had earlier courted Joyce's wife-to-be. Paralleling the events in Joyce's short story "The Dead," Bodkin died of pneumonia after singing love songs to his beloved in a rainstorm. On finding Bodkin's grave, Joyce was startled to discover the headstone immediately next to it bore the name "J. Joyce"—an incident which, Wilson suggests, left Joyce with a lifelong preoccupation with synchronicity long before Jung had himself labeled this phenomenon.[9]

A continent away during an earlier century, the grandfather of modern literary symbolism, Herman Melville, composed *Moby Dick,* one of literature's most enduring and insightful testaments to the traditional symbolist worldview. Not only the white whale but every event and person in Melville's story operates on multiple levels, as he writes, "Hark ye yet again—the little lower layer. All visible objects, man, are but as pasteboard masks" (Chapter 36).

Symbolist thinking also captured the imagination of Goethe, Germany's greatest writer. In the closing lines of his life work, *Faust*, he declared, "All that is transitory is but a metaphor." Goethe too was intrigued by the sense of patterning which seemed to characterize many life events and speculated as to the possible source of this design. Aniela Jaffé writes:

> In Goethe's view there exists an ordering power outside man, which resembles chance as much as providence, and which contracts time and expands space. He called it the "daemonic," and spoke of it as others speak of God.[10]

What intrigued these masters of philosophy, science, and literature? To begin to understand their fascination, we need to familiarize ourselves with the essential presuppositions which underlie the symbolist outlook.

A   M E A N I N G F U L   U N I V E R S E

Those who believe that the world of being is governed by luck or chance and that it depends upon material causes are far removed from the divine and from the notion of the One.

—**Plotinus,** *Ennead VI.9*

To step into the worldview of the man or woman for whom the universe is meaningful is to enter a way of thinking that views all events and phenomena as elements of a supremely ordered whole. Like the intricately arranged threads of a great novel or myth, so the elements of daily experience are seen as intimately interrelated, with no situation or event out of place, no development accidental. In this way, even a seemingly trivial occurrence may serve as an important key unlocking a greater pattern of meaning. The passage of a bird through the sky, the appearance of lightning at a critical moment, or the overhearing of a chance remark—such things are significant to the degree they are perceived as interwoven within a greater tapestry of relationship. Unlocking their significance requires an ability to perceive holistically how an individual event or detail fits into a larger set of experiences and developments.

Underlying this view is a deep conviction that all events are themselves the manifestation of a greater, more fundamental ground of being. In contrast with the modern mechanistic viewpoint, which regards nature as an essentially physical phenomenon with no inherent meaning or consciousness, traditional symbolic thought perceives the world as suffused with mind, with all events and perceptible forms representing facets of a spiritual intelligence made visible. As the Swedish mystic and scientist Emmanuel Swedenborg commented in *Heaven and Earth,* "There is a correspondence of all things of heaven with all things of man." All things reflect the deeper ideas and esoteric principles of which they are a visible expression, or "signature," and can thus be deciphered for their higher significance.

For many cultures, this same idea found a more poetic expression in the belief that the world represents a kind of dream, similar in many respects to our fantasies during sleep. In Taoism, for example, there is a story of the man who dreamt one night he was a butterfly, only to discover upon waking he was a man. How could he be certain, he now wondered, whether he was a man who had dreamt he was a butterfly, or a butterfly who was now dreaming he was a man? As the Buddha said,

> *Thus shall ye think of all this fleeting world; A star at dawn, a bubble in a stream, A flash of lightning in a summer cloud, A flickering lamp, a phantom, and a dream.*

For the symbolist, the recognition of the essentially dreamlike character of reality carries with it a series of far-reaching implications. For instance, if experience is a kind of dream with its own symbolic dimension of meaningfulness, then it must also be possible to interpret it like a dream. Events and circumstances unfolding outwardly are reflections of developments occurring on deeper levels of our own consciousness. As in the myths and sagas of antiquity in which the important developments and beings encountered along the hero's or heroine's journey are ultimately recognized as guides and initiators in the unfoldment of a greater spiritual quest, so in our own life the people, events, and creatures encountered can be seen as messengers bearing important clues into our own unfolding inner processes.

In this way, a randomly observed auto accident may hold a clue to understanding some inner conflict or problem; an unexpected gift of flowers may reveal a subtle shift of fortunes; or a job application lost in the mail or other recurring obstacle in the pursuit of a goal may be interpreted as reflecting a deeper lesson needing to be learned. Read as dream symbols, ordinary occurrences yield depths of information and teaching completely unsuspected by the untrained observer.

A DIFFERENT WAY OF SEEING

Yet to unlock the symbolist worldview, the individual must enter into a completely different way of thinking. Our contemporary tendency, based on the scientific model, is to view the world as composed of literal facts, best understood through the lens of mechanistic rationality. But for ages prior to our own, esotericists and mystics perceived the world through the lenses of *metaphor* and *analogy*. Like a parable or myth that on subtler reflection is found to contain dimensions of meaning beyond the obvious, so through this shift of perception, ordinary experience is transformed to reveal levels of information inaccessible to the rational mind.

Viewed in a purely literal or materialistic way, for example, the bird I saw while taking my walk with the medicine man held no relevance to anything else occurring in my life; but when seen in terms of its subtler level of meaning, the abrupt switch in the direction of its flight was now analogous to the sudden switch of direction about to occur in another area of my life. Hence, an event may be seen as suggesting something deeper only when viewed metaphorically, in terms of its inner dynamic *process.*

While largely dormant in the modern psyche, the ability to think metaphorically lies just below the surface of ordinary rational consciousness, as evidenced by our capacity for metaphor in ordinary conversation. Within the picturesque turns of speech we conjure up to describe situations and states of mind ("This job is like a millstone around my neck"; "Meeting you has been a breath of fresh air"), we witness the psyche's intuitive capacity for perceiving the metaphoric subtext unfolding through our lives, a capacity innately rooted within the symbolic language of the human soul.

This shift of perception holds profound implications. In recognizing the metaphoric dimension of experiences, one steps from a framework of purely personal concepts and associations into one of objective, or universal meanings. Like a Copernican revolution of the psyche, one's understanding shifts from the localized viewpoint of the ego to a more galactic, transpersonal point of reference. Having peeled away the layers of subjective notions and awakened to the archetypal drama underlying ordinary experience, immediate situations and objects are broken open, exploded by the infusion of cosmic significance. No longer at a remove from direct experience, the sacred or archetypal is recognized as residing within the mundane, the general within the particular.

At the same time, paradoxically, this awareness of the archetypal dimension of events in no way lessens or negates their concrete or mundane significance. Indeed, to the traditional esoteric mentality, there may be no clear-cut separation between the levels of "spiritual" and "material." As the religious historian Mircea

Eliade has pointed out, the fact that one's house holds archetypal importance (as, say, a reflection of the entire cosmos) does not make it any the less a construction which answers to the specific needs of its inhabitants in all the normal practical ways, and which, in turn, demands the customary maintenance.[11] Or, as psychologist Sigmund Freud more prosaically put it when told that his cigar might be a phallic symbol, "That may be true, gentlemen, but sometimes a cigar is just a cigar."

THE LAWS OF SYMBOLIST THOUGHT

A series of principles or "laws" are traditionally associated with the symbolist worldview, which are seen as governing the unfolding of events on all levels of phenomenal reality. Let us begin by focusing on three of the most important: *correspondence, contagion,* and *condensation.*

CORRESPONDENCE

A man must become a psychologist and a philosopher before he can ...

understand correctly the Great Law of Universal Sympathy. Not only

astrology but ... theosophy and every occult science, especially that

of attraction and repulsion, depend upon this law for their existence.

—H. P. Blavatsky

As many anthropologists and philosophers have pointed out, the traditional symbolic worldview believes all things and events are linked by a hidden network of secret relationships, referred to by such terms as affinity, correspondence, analogy, sympathy, or similarity. Whereas classical mechanistic physics regards diverse phenomena as related to one another principally in terms of linear cause-and-effect (as classically illustrated in the interaction of billiard balls on a pool table), the esoteric view holds that phenomena can also be related through a subtler form of vibrational resonance or meaning. For the philosopher Plotinus, this was comparable to the way a note struck on one musical instrument causes a similarly tuned note on another instrument to vibrate sympathetically in unison. In a similar way, all things possess their own rate of vibration or tuning and are entwined with all other things by means of either *sympathy* (harmonious accord) or *antipathy* (inharmonious accord). For instance, while the elements of earth and water are compatible by merit of harmonious sympathy, water and fire are incompatible by merit of an innate discord.

In its most infamous form, the concept of correspondence is familiar to us in sympathetic magic, as when a sorcerer or magician uses a drawing or effigy of an enemy to affect that individual for better or worse. The essential belief underlying this practice is that a hidden thread of connection exists between any thing or person and its representation. Examples of this sort can be technically classified as a correspondence of outer form, what some have called *resemblance*, or which I prefer to call "literal" (or obvious) correspondence.

Beyond this more obvious expression, however, the principle of correspondence may assume subtler forms, in which one finds a resonance not of outer appearance but of inner meaning, or quality. Here, the connection between separate events or objects is not readily visible, as in the case of the "voodoo" doll and the person it is modeled after, but is rather analogous in nature, perceptible only through a metaphoric shift of perception. An example of this type of correspondence can be seen in the way such seemingly diverse ideas as fire, knives, the color red, athletes, and all forms of combat can be classified under the category of Mars, the archetypal and astrological principle of force. While having little or no obvious connection, these varied ideas share an affinity of archetypal resonance, or what may be called "metaphoric" (or subtle) correspondence. Over time this belief in subtle relationships gave rise to the elaborate tables of correspondences utilized by esotericists and magicians to both understand nature and work actively with her dynamic energies.

In addition to this distinction between literal and metaphoric correspondence, traditional esoteric thought also proposes a distinction between *horizontal* and *vertical* forms of correspondence. Horizontal correspondence can be described as the subtle relationship or affinity between two or more things on the same plane of experience, such as we find among fire, knives, war, the planet Mars, and the color red—all distinctively physical, all occupying the same plane of reference. Vertical correspondence, on the other hand, refers to the subtle relationship between symbols across entirely different planes of being—as we find, say, between the physical symbol of fire and the higher psychological state of passion or anger; or between the physical symbol of a circle and the higher principle of spiritual wholeness. This is the form of correspondence specifically referred to by such hermetic sayings as "as above, so below," or the kabbalistic statement "there does not exist the smallest thing in the world which is not itself attached to something on High, and is not found in dependence upon it."

Ultimately, all physical forms and phenomena partake simultaneously in both orders of correspondence, vertical and horizontal. That is, every thing or event on the physical plane is related in subtle ways to other physical phenomena as well as to higher patterns on subtler levels of existence. For this reason, the estericist might well conclude there is no event which is not in some way "coincidental," insofar all things ultimately *co-incide*.

CONTAGION

You are standing on the sea-shore and the waves wash up an old hat, an old box, a shoe, a dead fish, and there they lie on the shore. You say: "Chance, nonsense!" The Chinese mind asks "What does it mean that these things are together?"

—**Carl Jung**, *The Symbolic Life*

The principle of correspondence describes the relationship between phenomena arising from a subtle resonance of form or meaning. By contrast, the principle of contagion describes the link existing among phenomena by means of proximity, as when two things once in contact retain a connection after being separated, even when far removed from one another in time or space. As in the case of correspondence theory, the most familiar example of this principle is in sympathetic magic, as when a magician or sorcerer works ritualistically with an article of clothing or bodily part acquired from another person (such as hair or fingernails) in the belief it somehow retains a connection with the person to whom it belonged.

Here, too, we must distinguish between such crude examples of contagion and more subtle forms. The following is an example of subtle contagion. In his book *Sacred Places,* environmental psychologist James Swan tells of being unexpectedly given a suit of clothes once owned by the singer Dean Martin. Because of the timing of this gift in relation to career decisions he was pondering, Swan chose to interpret this event as informing him symbolically to move his work into a more public arena, rather than continuing in a private, almost reclusive direction. In this case, the gift was significant not because it somehow linked Swan tangibly with the famed performer, or even because of some subtle energy transmitted to him from the singer via the medium of the clothes. Rather, because of a previous association with a famous entertainer, the acquisition of these clothes at this precise moment suggested a proximity—or contagion—to the symbolic *principle* of public exposure.

Examples of this sort illustrate the principle of contagion in terms of a proximity through space, involving elements that have been in touch with one another physically. Yet this principle has a temporal expression as well, in which two or more phenomena occurring within the same moment of time may be subtly linked to one another long afterwards. For example, a man opens a business and discovers that his brother has won a million dollars in a lottery on the very same day. While these two events are in no way physically connected, nor do they share a relationship of similarity or correspondence, the fact of their having occurred (or touched) within the same moment of time would be deemed significant by the symbolist, and might be read as reflecting positively on the impending fortunes of the man's business. This same idea can be seen in the belief that the circumstances of an individual's birth in some way foreshadow the character and impending destiny of the child—a notion explored in greater detail in chapter four.

The principle of contagion also addresses the way forms or phenomenon exert a subtle influence upon each other by merit of their closeness. For this reason the ancients believed that a sacred relic was capable of affecting the environment and spiritual state of those who drew close to it; while the presence of an evil or unlucky person could rub off on the fortunes and moral character of the community around them.

By way of contrast, modern science can accurately measure the electromagnetic fields generated by household appliances or power lines, or gauge the radiation emitted by bodies of various kinds. Such forms of influence are tangible and easily analyzed using purely empirical methods. But how are we to measure in strictly quantitative terms such influences as described in the Chinese geomantic philosophy of *feng shui,* in which it is thought a mountain or rocky outcrop bearing the features of a particular animal can affect the destinies of nearby inhabitants in accord with the symbolic properties of that particular animal? Or the notion that the pollution of the water near a famed seaside gambling city portends that much of the money pouring through the city will likewise be "dirty," or illegal—as one practitioner of this ancient art contended?[12]

To comprehend examples like these we must turn not to concepts of force or energy but to notions of symbolism and the belief that forms and phenomena affect one another in terms of their deeper archetypal meaning. According to this outlook, all things are embedded within a larger symbolic field, in which each part exerts its own unique influence upon that greater continuum of meaning, less in quantitative than qualitative terms. Such qualities are not susceptible to empirical measurement, since they can be apprehended only through a metaphoric mode of consciousness.

CONDENSATION

> *To see a world in a grain of sand*
>
> *And a heaven in a wild flower,*
>
> *Hold infinity in the palm of your hand*
>
> *And eternity in an hour.*

—**William Blake**

Usually described as a subset either of correspondence or contagion theory, condensation is distinctive enough to merit discussion as a category unto itself. Simply defined, the principle of condensation (a term commonly associated with the theories of Freud) describes the way one thing or part encapsulates a larger whole or entity. Indeed, this principle may be seen as the defining concept of symbolism itself, with every symbol serving as a form which expresses a larger body of meaning. Like a convex (or fish-eye) mirror which reflects a much larger field of imagery, so through apprehending a symbol one can comprehend a far greater set of ideas or states of consciousness of which it is only a distillation.

In Eastern literature, this concept finds eloquent expression in the mythical image of Indra's net, a cosmic web of gems in which each distinct part reflects all other parts of the web. In the occult tradition, this idea is also seen in the doctrine of the *microcosm*, the belief that each human being encapsulates the entire cosmos. It is this philosophical principle that underlies the ancient system of astrology, which holds that the universe outside of us is a reflection of the universe within. As Herman Melville expressed it in *Moby Dick*, "O nature and O soul of man; how linked art thy analogies; not the smallest atom exists in matter that does not have its cunning duplicate in mind" (Chapter 70).

In fact, the principle of the microcosm can manifest itself in a great many ways. For instance, just as the human body can be seen as a microcosmic reflection of the entire universe, so in turn are various parts of the body condensations, or microcosms, of the entire body and personality. We are most familiar with this idea in the system of palmistry, which regards the hands as symbols of the entire individual; though for the esotericist, there are many parts of the body which encapsulate the entire body, including the face, eyes, mouth, feet, and even the ears, to name the most obvious. Even in mainstream biology we find a similar idea in slightly different form, in the underlying structure of DNA, in which every cell of the body encapsulates the genetic instructions for the entire body, within proportions defined by the chemical components of the genetic strand.

On a collective level, traditional societies viewed certain individuals as microcosms of the entire society; for example, the pharaohs of Egypt and the emperors of ancient China. Accidents, illnesses, or abrupt shifts of fortune in the lives of these figures were scrutinized for clues or omens to the fortunes of the greater nation. In the Arthurian tale of the Fisher King, whose illness mysteriously entwines with the desolate condition of his entire kingdom, it is ultimately his cure which serves to restore harmony to that greater kingdom. In its most degenerate form, this idea is also reflected in the notion of the scapegoat, in which one individual or animal is singled out as the embodiment of all the ills and misfortunes befalling a society—and treated accordingly.

Just as certain points or persons in space may encapsulate a larger reality, so certain moments in time can condense temporal trends or developments beyond the scope of a given moment. Consequently, an unexpected crisis may reveal itself as encoding a larger set of issues or archetypal dynamics taking place in one's life; or the events around a person's birth serve as a condensation within a single moment of time of the trends to unfold over the course of the individual's entire life. The principle of condensation likewise underlies most divinatory systems, in the way a chosen action, in a given moment of time (such as the casting of runes, the random selection of tarot cards, or the vision seen when gazing into a crystal) is seen as offering a glimpse, in miniature, of a larger pattern in the life of the inquiring individual.

As with correspondence and contagion, it is necessary to distinguish between literal and more metaphoric forms of condensation. For instance, a microfilm copy of the Bible may be described as a condensation of the larger Bible it reproduces, but in a very straightforward, photographic way. Compare this with the manner in which the physical body is esoterically said to condense the solar system and universe, with each organ relating in a subtle way to a particular planet in outer space. An individual may thus be said to contain the Sun; yet this does not take the form of an internal ball of hot gas but rather of the physical heart, which in an analogous way serves as the center and regulatory life-center of the human body. In such cases, the microcosmic connection between inner and outer, between the very small and the very large, is metaphoric, different from the photographic reduction seen in the example of the microfilmed Bible.

With this basic philosophic vocabulary established, we turn now to the broader role the symbolist worldview has played in the historical unfoldment of human thought.

CHAPTER 2

THE FORGOTTEN LANGUAGE

It should be said at once that the completely profane world, the wholly desacralized cosmos, is a recent discovery in the history of the human spirit.

—Mircea Eliade, *The Sacred and the Profane*

 hat follows is a brief look at the origins, growth, and eventual decline of the symbolist tradition, along with some of the ways it has expressed itself within various cultures and eras. Though not intended to be exhaustive, this overview will help provide a valuable perspective by which to evaluate its legacy for today.

ORIGINS

It is impossible to determine exactly when or where the symbolist worldview began, but it is exceedingly ancient, with roots in the earliest awakenings of religious thought. Whether inspired by encounters with lightning, the natural mysteries of death, or the infinity of the night sky, the religious urge was, at its most fundamental, an awakening to the symbolic dimension of reality and the depth aspect of ordinary experience. No longer a purely physical

phenomena, reality was perceived as pointing beyond itself, as mediating a deeper, more mysterious ground of being. This primordial
insight transformed the phenomena and events of everyday life into
vehicles of meaning. As Mircea Eliade has said,

> *What we find as soon as we place ourselves in the perspective of*
> *the religious man of the archaic societies is that . . . the existence*
> *of the world "means" something, "wants to say" something, that*
> *the world is neither mute or opaque, that it is not an inert thing*
> *without purpose or significance. For religious man, the cosmos*
> *lives and speaks.*[1]

From this awakening emerged a progressively more complex
array of beliefs and practices. These ideas were at every stage shaped
and informed by the prevailing mythic framework. Thus, what had
probably begun for many societies as a vaguely defined set of beliefs
and superstitions, through time, gave rise to an increasingly refined
body of theory and ideas, in some cases even quasi-scientific systems of thought concerning the hidden workings of nature and everyday life.

For instance, employing a basic understanding of correspondences, a tribe or culture might link the cycles of the moon, death
and resurrection, vegetation, rain, menstruation, femininity, snakes
(who shed their skin as the moon changes phases), and the principles of time and change. This understanding of life's affinities aided
early humanity both in the interpretation of phenomena as well as
in the practical, or "magical" manipulation of natural forces towards
desired ends. This two-fold emphasis is sometimes described by
modern writers as the distinction between "theoretical" and "practical" occultism.[2] The foremost specialist in this knowledge in early
societies was the shaman, who possessed the most refined understanding of hidden laws and their effects, and who was called upon
in situations requiring interpretive insight or practical expertise.

But what began with the isolated shaman as an eclectic body of knowledge incorporating a broad grasp of many different areas, from reading omens and dreams to the magical employment of symbolic principles in rituals, became specialized, with the rise of higher civilizations, into many separate fields of knowledge, each with its own trained specialists and set of rules. Out of this splintering process arose highly complex disciplines in astrology, *haruspicy* (the reading of animal entrails), palmistry, dream interpretation, and the important skills of magic and healing (which for prescientific cultures were largely based upon deeply symbolic principles).

SYMBOLISM: PERSONAL, COLLECTIVE, AND UNIVERSAL

In most traditional societies, symbolist ideas were applied on three levels: personal, collective, and universal.

At the personal level, symbolist thought was applied to the circumstances and needs of specific individuals—the level we are largely concerned with in this book. Here, emphasis was on discerning personal fortunes through study of the omens or symbols of daily life, casting divinatory horoscopes for individuals (in early times, usually rulers of countries or other important officials), interpreting personal dreams, and similar concerns.

On the collective level, symbolist principles were applied to the subtle dynamics of entire societies or civilizations. Here, practitioners interpreted trends or developments in politics, the arts, sports, warfare, or Earth changes—all with an eye to understanding how each reflected changes of fortune in the life of the community. For example, a fire destroying the house of a prominent citizen might be read as an omen for the entire city; or an eclipse or other unusual celestial phenomena might be seen as portending a political crisis. Astrologers at this level cast horoscopes for the entire nation or for a mass event such as a battle, in the hope of fathoming the deeper patterns governing the collective destiny.

At the universal level, the symbolist perspective was directed toward understanding and deciphering nature's patterns. Here, the universe in all its forms revealed itself as a great book encoding the truths of spiritual reality. Through a study of the symbolic meaning of the human body, the forms and processes of plant life, animal behavior, or the vast cycles of the seasons and the planets, the symbolist hoped to glimpse the workings of the Divine Mind. Practitioners of this approach ranged from classical thinkers like Pythagoras to more recent mystic-scientists like Kepler or Newton, for whom discoveries into nature's laws held spiritual rather than strictly physical significance.

The important point here is that virtually every civilization in history actively subscribed to the essential tenets of the symbolist worldview, on one or more of these levels. And while most clearly apparent in an obsession with divination, superstition, and magic, such expressions reflected a more implicit, all-encompassing symbolic vision that extended to all aspects of experience, at varying levels of subtlety. Following, in broad outline, is an overview of some of the more distinctive expressions of symbolic thinking in ancient cultures.

MESOPOTAMIA

In ancient Mesopotamia, preoccupation with symbolic events and omens unfolded in a systematic way, leading to what some have called the birth of the modern scientific method. Over hundreds of years, priestly chroniclers methodically cataloged thousands of unusual events of various types towards the end of establishing a body of data which could be used to interpret or predict future events. Importantly, this record was periodically updated or modified in keeping with changing observations, strongly suggesting this was not simply a rigid body of beliefs but a vitally evolving—and empirically based—system of thought. For example, if a three-legged calf or other malformed animal was born in a city and shortly afterward a disaster befell that city, this would be duly noted. If this same combination of events continued to occur over time, this would likewise be recorded, with a formal notation that any future appearances of this circumstance (or set of circumstances) could reasonably be considered an omen heralding a similar outcome.

Termed the "Babylonian Omen Series" by historians, the clay tablets recording these observations fall into several broad classes. On one set of tablets concerned with terrestrial (earthbound) omens called "If a city is set on a hill," we find a concern with such events as the birth of monstrosities, the movements of animals, the significance of chance or overheard remarks and sounds, or the omens drawn from a person's behavior during sleep, to name only a few. On another class of tablets focusing on omens and symbolic events of a celestial, or skyward nature, are detailed records of phenomena related to the appearances of planets, the Sun, the Moon, and meteorological events, with these primarily used to explain and predict developments within the society. It is in conjunction with this latter category of observations that many contemporary scholars believe Western astrology had its origins during the first and second millennia B.C.[3]

INDIA

In some respects the belief in life's dreamlike character could be viewed as the cornerstone of India's mystical, or yogic worldview. As W. Y. Evans-Wentz wrote, "By a careful analytical study of dreams and psychological experimentation on himself as the subject, the yogin at last comes actually thus to realize, and not merely to believe, that the total content of the waking state as well as of the dream state is, in fact illusory phenomena."[4]

This essential perception made possible the development of a far-reaching and vitally symbolist view of life, as expressed in a variety of sources. In India's ancient mystical text the *Artharva Veda,* for example, a chapter is devoted to the interpretation of nightly dreams. The immediately adjacent chapter is on the interpretation of waking omens or portents; in other words, what happens outside of us was seen as carrying the same symbolic weight as what happens inside us in dreams and could be interpreted within the same symbolic framework.[5] On a collective level, this sensibility gave rise to a keen sensitivity toward the occurrence of significant omens and symbols in society in general—an attentiveness that, as everywhere else, took on heightened importance during times of war and crisis. India's great religious epic *The Mahabharata*, for instance, contains the following account of omens presaging the fortunes of the two great warring factions, the Kurus and the Pandavas:

> *Many horrible dreams are being seen by the Kurus, and many terrible signs and gruesome omens, predicting victory for the Pandavas. Meteors are falling from the sky, and there are hurricanes and earthquakes. The elephants are trumpeting, and horses are shedding tears and refusing food and water. Horses, elephants and men are eating little, yet they are shitting prodigiously; wise men say that is a sign of defeat. They say that, by contrast, the mounts of the Pandavas are quite happy and that wild animals are circling their camp to the right, a good sign, while all the wild animals are circling the Kurus' camp to the left. Peacocks, wild geese, and cranes follow the Pandavas, while vultures, crows, kites, vampires, jackals, and swarms of mosquitoes follow the Kurus.*

While the development of symbolist thought in India generally mirrored that found in other cultures (as for instance in its emphasis on astrology, magic, and omens), two systems of esoteric thought arose within Indian society exhibiting a depth of sophistication and complexity unparalleled in the world. These were the doctrines of *karma* (or spiritual cause-and-effect) and the *chakras* (or subtle psychospiritual centers of consciousness along the spine). Later chapters show how these doctrines contribute to the broader understanding of key facets of symbolist philosophy.

EGYPT

Arguably the most profoundly symbolist civilization in history,

Egypt was regarded throughout much of the ancient Western world as the source of all philosophical and esoteric wisdom. For the Egyptians, the world was regarded as a repository of hieroglyphic messages, with all phenomena representing reflections of higher principles. This analogy with language is vital for understanding pharaohonic culture, since in ancient Egypt, language was invested with a deeply spiritual significance and was seen as nothing less than the key to reality itself.

Hieroglyphic images held several levels of inference at once: phonetic (in which an image or mark represents a particular sound), pictographic (in which an image directly depicts the phenomenon it represents), and symbolic (in which an image subtly infers multiple ideas and levels of meaning). In this way, a given word composed of hieroglyphs was able to convey various nuances of meaning simultaneously, a tendency most clearly reflected in the great Egyptian fondness for puns. This multileveled feature of language in turn reflected a multidimensional view of life itself, with all events or forms having the potential for interpretation on many different levels simultaneously.[6]

As writers like R. A. Schwaller de Lubicz, Robert Lawlor, and John Anthony West have argued, Egyptian society was based on a sophisticated foundation of sacred science, which informed the most diverse aspects of life, from architecture and the arts to the common system of weights and measures employed by merchants and engineers.[7]

CHINA

To the ancient Chinese mind, the world was the expression of a vast web of harmony, extending from the smallest blade of grass to the movements of the stars. This orderly conception of reality reflected a deeper play of universal principles, the interaction of which produced the varied forms of change governing all phenomena, both inwardly and outwardly.

Most fundamental of these principles were the essential polarities of *yin* and *yang*, the cosmic feminine and masculine, which gave birth to the phenomenal realm and its "ten thousand things." Just as all images can be seen as the interplay of light and dark, so all experiences reflect varying degrees of balance between these two cosmic principles. The goal of the sage was to attain a proper balance of these qualities in all activities and thoughts.

All of China's esoteric systems in one way or another reflected an alignment with this philosophical notion of polarity, as seen most dramatically in the great Chinese "Book of Changes," the *I Ching*. This work describes the sixty-four archetypal patterns of existence, or "hexagrams," which express the variations of relationship between yin and yang. Through the use of chance-based divinatory techniques, such as observing the patterns made by sticks cast on the ground, individuals were able to determine the underlying archetypal dynamics at work in any given circumstance, and thus understand the mode of action which best served to establish harmony with the order of the universe itself.

On the collective level, the Chinese conception of harmony was intimately associated with the role and person of the emperor. As in the case of the Egyptian pharaoh, the emperor was understood to be the mediator or conduit between Heaven and Earth, who acted as the harmonizing principle for the greater kingdom. Any omens or anomalous phenomena throughout the kingdom (whether earthbound or celestial) were carefully observed as potential warnings or expressions of the will of heaven relative to the emperor and his rule.

GREECE

In epic tales like the *Iliad* and the *Odyssey*, we find many examples of the symbolist view among the early Greeks. Homer's description of bird omens at the palace of Menelaus when Helen has been restored after the victory at Troy, or Odysseus hearing thunder from a clear sky when he prays to Zeus for a sign on his return to Ithaca, to cite two examples, testify to the important role symbolist thought played in ancient Greek culture.

Yet even in the rational fifth century B.C. Athens of Pericles, the symbolist imagination continued to shape the Greek mind. Cicero tells us the Athenians called in *manteis* (interpreters of signs and symbols) for consultation in all important deliberations. The great importance accorded this knowledge by the Greeks is also reflected in the story (come down to us through Aeschylus) that among the arts brought from heaven by Prometheus was divination. This art was positioned midway in importance between medicine and mining. Through this gift humans could determine the obscure import of omens and voices, wayside signs, and the flights of taloned birds. Astrology also played a vital role in Greek society, where the now-common practice of "personal" (or *genethlial*) horoscope interpretation was pioneered.

Among the most important expressions of the symbolist tradition in Greek culture was the towering figure of Pythagoras. Part mystic and part scientist, he established a body of esoteric and mathematical ideas that influenced Western thinking for the next two thousand years. While little is known with certainty of his life or teachings, it is safe to say Pythagoras's vision of the world was characterized by a perception of mathematical harmony. Like the Egyptians, from whom he likely drew much of his knowledge and inspiration, Pythagoras believed everything in the world—including our personal experience—was an expression of geometry and number, a concept which he illustrated by reference to the numerical properties embodied within musical harmonies. Reflecting the influence of Pythagoras, Plato later taught a similar doctrine stating that all manifest forms in our everyday world were reflections of divine principles (or "ideas") upon subtler planes of experience.

ROME

A blend of Etruscan, Greek, Babylonian, and indigenous elements, the symbolist practices and beliefs of ancient Rome represented a pervasive—if sometimes obsessive—influence at all levels of its society. A priestly college of *augurs* (interpreters of signs and symbolic events) was officially consulted in all important matters of state or religious life.

Writers like Cicero and Livy recorded many colorful examples of symbolist thinking in the lives of ancient Romans. One famous case involved the omens and portents recorded in conjunction with the Second Punic War. In the winter of 218 B.C., Romans were startled by the following extraordinary series of events: "In the Picenum, a rain of stones fell," while "in Gaul, a wolf carried off the sword of a sentinel by pulling it out of its scabbard." The following year at Falerii, "the sky split open as if torn, and from this opening a great light surged forth; the divinatory tables shrank spontaneously, and one, bearing the inscription 'Mars shakes his lance' fell." Through Suetonius we also learn of the dramatic omens said to have preceded the murder of Julius Caesar: horses Caesar had previously consecrated to the river Rubicon refused all water and wept copiously; the *haruspex* (oracle) Spurinna warned Caesar to beware the Ides of March; on the eve of the Ides, a wren carrying a laurel branch flew up toward the curia of Pompey (the Senate) where it was pursued by birds of every species; in the curia itself, the bird was torn to pieces; and finally, the night before the murder, Caesar dreamed he was flying above the clouds, sometimes shaking the hand of Jupiter, while his wife Calpurnia dreamed that the peak of the roof caved in and her husband was pierced through by the debris as he lay in her arms; then suddenly the door of the bedroom opened by itself.[8] Thus for the Romans, animal behavior, prophecies and omens, and dreams were all regarded as accurate predictors of events.

THE CHRISTIANIZED WEST

Though organized Christianity attempted to banish many of the pagan beliefs and practices associated with earlier traditions, many of these principles simply were pushed underground, or recast in specifically Christian form. On the universal level, for example, the traditional symbolist belief that the universe encoded divine truths was used by Christians in medieval times to examine nature for clues and signatures of biblical principles: The cycle of life, death, and regeneration in the plant kingdom was read as an allegory of the death and resurrection of Christ, while the descriptions of the varieties of animal life in books called *bestiaries* were read as encoding spiritual lessons for aspirants in their journey to salvation. This approach found support from St. Paul, who wrote: "The invisible things of Him from the creation of the world are clearly seen, being understood by the things that are made, even His eternal power and godhead" (Rom 1:20). On the collective level, historic events could similarly be viewed in terms of Christian beliefs: the great fire of London in 1666 was seen as a sign from God underscoring the religious shortcomings of its citizens, and the fall of Rome in 476 was interpreted by Augustine as a symbol of the preparation of a new Christian order across the world.

In contrast to the frequently simplistic character of medieval symbolist thinking, the intellectually rich environment of the Renaissance made possible a complex new wave of symbolist philosophizing. Precipitated in large part by the translation of ancient esoteric texts (believed at the time to derive from Egypt) by the Florentine scholar Marsilio Ficino, ancient hermetic/alchemical ideas eventually merged with Kabbalistic and esoteric Christian streams of thought to produce a unique new synthesis of occult themes which profoundly influenced European thought for centuries. Among the foremost figures in this "esoteric Renaissance" was the Italian metaphysician Cornelius Agrippa, whose encyclopedic *de Occulta Philosophia* synthesized many of the more important ideas and themes of this evolving tradition into one work.

This uniquely Christian approach to symbolist thought was brought to the colonies with the first settlers. In Puritan New England, events and accidents were often interpreted as personal messages from God: tragedies implied God's disapproval or Job-like tests of piety, while success and good fortune implied divine approval or reward. Puritan minister Cotton Mather, an early American evangelist, kept what might today be called a "synchronistic diary," carefully detailing all unusual or coincidental events with an eye toward their religious import. A snake appearing in church one Sunday might be interpreted as a lesson for the congregation about the temptations of the devil; a near-drowning or other serious accident would likewise have been read for the personal warning it conveyed from God.

THE ISLAMIC WORLD

As in Christianity, the Muslim tradition underwent considerable change in its attitude towards omens and divinatory practices. Beneath all the changes, however, lay an unchanging symbolist vision of reality, grounded in the teachings of the Prophet himself. The Koran declares: "Nothing is, that does not proclaim His praise." The entire world was the expression of the Divine and could be read as its conscious handiwork. Indeed, complementing the written Koran was what Muslim sages saw as the "cosmic Koran"—the manifest world itself. Within every creature or phenomenon of nature were written the living letters and words of the great holy book. All things were recognized as "signs" (ayat), interpretable by the sage.[9]

Arab astrologers.

In this spirit, the great Muslim thinkers came to regard science as an essentially sacred activity, capable of revealing the divine qualities of existence. Through understanding the laws of nature, one could draw closer to realizing the presence of God in the world. As with the Mayans of Central America, this process of discovery revolved primarily around mathematics and astrology. In Cairo,

Baghdad, Aleppo, and Mosul, the legacy of the ancient Greek astrologers was kept alive by Muslim thinkers until its eventual rediscovery by Europeans, an event which rekindled Western culture and served as a prime catalyst for the European Renaissance. Muslim astrologers regarded their discipline not merely as a method of prediction but as a tool for spiritual growth. Through astrology, as writer and teacher Anthony Aveni has noted, the Muslim "could discover his or her true cosmic dimension and know how this most lofty aspect of existence influenced daily life. Here was another way to achieve unity and order in the universe."[10]

THE JEWISH ESOTERIC TRADITION

While more conservative to all outward appearances in its attitude toward symbolist beliefs and practices, within Jewish culture an important body of esoteric thought developed that shared much with other great symbolist traditions. Known as the Kabbalah, Jewish esoteric thought included a doctrine of universal principles which underlie all existence, seen specifically in the twenty-two letters of the Hebrew alphabet and the ten *sephiroth* or energy principles of the Kabbalistic Tree of Life. Jewish esoteric thought also included a powerful—if considerably more discrete—science of magic and the occult, heavily influenced by Egyptian and Babylonian sources, as well as a decidedly providential or synchronistic view of everyday experience.

For instance, Kabbalist thought holds that individuals possess their own spiritual destiny, or *tikun*, and can learn to discern the hidden patterns and workings of the divine wisdom through a careful observation of events in ordinary life. In the teachings of Rabbi Luzzatto, for example, are stories in which individuals discover that behind the accidents or misfortunes in their lives are messages which hold a deeper meaning or blessing. Several generations later, this idea was likewise emphasized by the Hasidim for whom all unusual or odd turns of events were seen as highly meaningful and read on several levels.

By way of illustration, a story tells that the Hasidic founder Baal Shem Tov and his disciple were walking down a hot and dusty road one day. When the disciple complained of bitter thirst, the Baal Shem Tov asked him whether he believed in divine providence. When the disciple replied yes, a person suddenly appeared offering him a drink of water from a pail. When the Baal Shem Tov asked this person how he had come to be in such an out of the way spot, the man replied his master had just fainted nearby and he was compelled to bring water from a spring several miles distant. The Hasidic founder turned to his student and said, "You see, there are no coincidences in the universe."[11]

THE AMERICAS

Despite the scarcity of written records among the tribes and civilizations of the new world, there is little doubt the symbolist view of life was pervasive in both North and South America. From the time of the earliest European explorers, observers have noted the extreme importance native inhabitants conferred on signs and messages in the environment, especially the movements of the heavenly bodies and the activities of animal life—with a special emphasis upon birds. Among the most famous (if tragic) examples of this general understanding can be seen in the great attention accorded the startling omens and portents witnessed by Montezuma and his priests immediately prior to the destruction of the Aztec empire by Cortez. Archaeologists have shown that the Mayan civilization possessed a school of augurs similar to those of ancient Rome. The Native American view of the meaningfulness of the environment is summarized in a passage by the contemporary native shaman Medicine Grizzlybear Lake, in his book *Native Healer:*

> *The Creator can and does talk to you through anything if he or she so chooses, a rain cloud, a burning bush, a whirlwind, or a high mountain. He talks to our Native American medicine people the same way it has been from the beginning, for all races. He*

sometimes talks to us through dreams, visions, an eagle, hawk, raven, wolf, coyote, deer, buffalo, snake, rock, bear, lightning, and thunder.

THE DECLINE AND FALL OF THE SYMBOLIST WORLDVIEW

After thousands of years, a profound change took place in humanity's way of thinking about the world. Initiated in the scientific speculations of ancient Greece but reaching its fullest development in seventeenth-century Europe, allegiance began shifting from the older, symbolist perspective to a more secular and materialist way of perceiving reality. Though the underlying causes of this shift are complex, two elements stand out as critical: the emergence of scientific empiricism and the advent of printing and literacy.

Even before the birth of Christ, humanity had engaged in a form of rational scientific speculation regarding the nature of reality; yet in the seventeenth century such speculations were finally welded to the hard methodologies of experimentation and verifiability, giving rise to the modern scientific method. When Galileo looked through the telescope at Jupiter and its moons, he wanted to see beyond what everyone believed was there to what really *was* there; likewise, instead of blindly accepting the prevailing notion that heavier objects fell faster than lighter ones, he decided to test this out by ascending the tower of Pisa and dropping differently weighted objects to the ground. From this point forward, scientists undertook a process of verifying knowledge through increasingly rigorous forms of experimentation.

Over time, however, the success—and usefulness—of this approach gave rise to a tendency to view nature *only* in terms of what could be known through rational and quantifiable methods. This led eventually to a reductionistic philosophy in which anything that did not submit to standards of scientific verification was deemed not only unimportant but, perhaps, nonexistent. The world had become, in the eyes of the scientists, a great, soul-less machine, devoid of meaning, consciousness, and purpose, in which the hypothesis of God was (as Laplace remarked to Napoleon) no longer necessary. Along with the divestment of spirit and intelligence from nature departed any possibility for symbolic meaning in either nature or personal experience. In a dead world, surface phenomena could no longer be seen through toward a deeper ground of archetypal significance.

This change in the collective perception was reinforced by the rise of widespread printing and literacy. As writers like Marshall McLuhan have argued, our modality of language, whether written or oral, may itself be a significant factor in shaping our collective thinking and worldview.

For instance, whereas the symbolist mentality could be seen as involving a holistic, right-brained, and metaphoric cast of mind, the printed word is conducive to a way of perceiving that is left-brained, analytic, and fragmentary. This is further underscored by Western styles of script which are decidedly nonsymbolic or opaque in form, as compared with pictographic or hieroglyphic language systems like old Egyptian or traditional Chinese. These ancient languages, by merit of their visual-symbolic natures, engage more symbolic aspects of thinking. Through representing the world with a set of finite, closed notations, Western forms of writing, by contrast, have acted to seal off the innate transparencies of the world from poetic inference.

Additionally, by segmenting the world into verbs and nouns, actions and things, European languages predispose people to see certain phenomena as alive and others as dead—in stark contrast with the symbolist mentality which views all things as living processes and dynamic elements within a universe of flux. As the linguist Benjamin Whorf has pointed out, such languages as Hopi tend not to make such presumptions, depicting the world as a place of ongoing events and processes rather than of solid things. For such a culture, consequently, it would more fitting to say "the sky blues" or "bluing sky" than to say that "the sky is blue"—a phrase which has the effect of separating the quality of "blue" from the sky, while at the same time isolating the sky as a discrete object of thought. It may be instructive here to recall a story related by nineteenth-century writer George Borrow. Borrow lived for a while among the gypsies in Europe and wrote about his experiences and observations in two books, *Lavengro* (Word Master) and *Romany Rye* (Gypsy Gentleman). Concerned by the almost one hundred percent illiteracy among the gypsies, Borrow tried to convince them of the value of learning how to read. They protested, saying if they did so, they would soon forget to read the stars and the weather, the marks of birds and animals and the cryptic symbols of warning or direction they scrawled on trees, stones, and fence posts; and they would soon forget to tell fortunes in palms, tea leaves, and crystals.

As literacy increased and people began to think scientifically, the symbolist view of reality increasingly disappeared from the collective psyche, surviving largely in vestigial form through folk superstitions or the modern popular fascination with newspaper horoscopes, fortune-tellers, and religious signs. Whatever meanings may be found in nature are now seen as projections of the human psyche rather than as inherent features of the world itself. Hence, what had once been a reality transparent to the presence of the archetypal and symbolic has now become opaque—a world divested of enchantment and closed to any deeper interpretation.[12] As Carl Jung said, as scientific understanding has grown, so our world has

> become dehumanized. Man feels himself isolated in the cosmos, because he is no longer involved in nature and has lost his emotional "unconscious identity" with natural phenomenon. . . . Thunder is no longer the voice of an angry god, nor is lightning the avenging missile. No river contains a spirit, no tree is the principle of life in man, no snake contains the embodiment of wisdom, no mountain cave is the home of a demon. No voices now speak to man from stones, plants or animals; nor does he speak to

them believing they can hear. His contact with nature has gone,
and with it has gone the profound emotional energy that this sym-
bolic connection supplied.[13]

THE RE-EVALUATION

How then, shall we best assess the implications of this vast
tradition of thought and its shifting place in history? Should we
side with writers like Morris Berman who, in *The Reenchantment of
the World,* argues that the traditional, enchanted worldview represented a more spiritual and participatory way of perceiving life, and
its loss constitutes a lamentable step backwards in our collective
evolution? Or shall we instead concur with writers like Ken Wilber,
who eloquently argues in books like *Up From Eden* and *Sex, Ecology,
Spirituality* that the ancient worldview was a decidedly less enlightened one, born of confused categories and primitive mythic-magi-
cal notions of reality? The emergence of rational/empirical thought
in recent centuries, Wilber says, signifies an important step forward
in our evolution toward spirit.

I propose that in a certain sense both perspectives are valid; the
advent of modern rationalistic thought represents simultaneously
a gain *and* a loss in our collective evolution. This point becomes
clearer when we remember that the traditional symbolist worldview
is not a single, homogeneous entity existing at all times and places
at a consistent level of sophistication, but rather a multifaceted
phenomenon with widely varying degrees of subtlety, ranging from
the crudely irrational up to the profoundly subtle. For example, the
way this worldview existed for the yogis of India or the priests of
ancient Egypt cannot rightly be compared with how it expressed
itself among the rural villages of medieval Europe, or within the
stone age tribes of South America. Even in the context of individual
cultures or communities we might reasonably expect to find vastly
different levels of expertise in this knowledge among the members
of society, as between the average individual and the resident sha-

man or priest. Even specific individuals can exhibit dramatically varying levels of sophistication in their symbolist ideas, as seen in the writings of Renaissance metaphysician Cornelius Agrippa.

In short, symbolist thinking has a great many facets, some more valid and important than others. Yet in most conventional discussions of the subject, these varied forms are lumped together as if constituting a uniform body of thought, with no distinction between the layers of subtlety—a generalization akin to categorizing all religious experiences as being of equal value, thus equating the German mystic Meister Eckhart with evangelist Jimmy Swaggart, since both fall under the heading "Christian." Predisposed by such loose generalizations, we can more easily dismiss the symbolist tradition in its entirety, assuming all its elements to be equally worthless.

Yet as we learn to become more sensitive to the distinctions which characterize this tradition, we begin to see that while humanity has indeed taken a collective step beyond the cruder levels of this worldview, it has done so at the expense of virtually all sensitivity to the subtler levels of symbolist thought. The challenge, therefore, is to review the many aspects of the symbolist view and determine which elements hold lasting value. Towards this end, we might divide symbolist ideas into three categories describing their relative levels of sophistication: the superstitious, the religious, and the mystical.

(1) SUPERSTITIOUS (OR MAGICAL)

This term refers to all symbolist notions of the crudest and most primitive sort, in ancient or modern societies. At this level, events are viewed as meaningful or symbolic to the extent that they reflect the influence of hidden spirits or the workings of vaguely defined laws and forces. An accident might suggest the intervention of hidden beings working against one's benefit, or simply the influence of ill fortune. Notions of correspondence and sympathy are generally of the most literal and simplistic sort, as when an individual employs the powder of a rhinoceros horn to enhance virility because of its obvious phallic shape, or eats walnuts to increase brain power because of the resemblance between walnuts and the folds of the brain. In short, there is at this level little sensitivity to the metaphoric elements involved in these associations. All beliefs and interpretations at this level are perceived in dualistic, black-or-white terms. A setback in one's material fortunes is thus interpreted as bad luck, brought on by magical forces from an adversary or evil source, while finding a valuable object would be interpreted as good luck, indicating one's destiny is now favored or that some form of positive magic is being directed on one's behalf.

(2) RELIGIOUS (OR THEISTIC)

At the religious level, symbolic thought is in many respects similar to that expressed at the superstitious level, except with a theistic or divinely personified twist. Here, events are meaningful specifically to the extent they serve as vehicles of communication from an overseeing God (or in polytheism, gods). As with the superstitious level, all interpretations are viewed against a highly dualistic framework of good and bad, right and wrong, such that all seemingly negative or difficult developments are automatically read as indications of divine disapproval or tests of spiritual worthiness, while all seemingly positive or fortunate developments take on significance as signs of divine favor or approval. To this way of thinking, for example, AIDS can be construed as God's punishment of promiscuous sinners, while victory in warfare is read as verifying God's providence.

(3) MYSTICAL (OR ARCHETYPAL)

Symbolic interpretation that is mystical or archetypal differs notably from both previous levels. Here events are meaningful not because they refer to some hidden realm of mysterious beings or magical forces outside oneself, but because they ultimately reflect an inner field of consciousness with its own laws and principles of meaning. For this reason, mystical or archetypal interpretation is generally more psychological. In contrast with cruder forms of symbolist thought, at this level the sense of connection between the outer and inner is characterized not by confusion or an erroneous sense of *participation mystique,* in which external events hold personal significance simply because of a blurred or undeveloped perception of the relation between inner and outer. Rather, the archetypal symbolist sees the realm of outer events as holding inner significance because of a keenly developed sense of unity between these realms that simultaneously remains fully cognizant of the differentiation between the two. For the true primitive, by contrast, no such distinction exists, since an inner world, egoically, has not yet developed; for all intents and purposes, the outer world *is* the inner world, with no internal self-sense whatsoever. Or, to draw on an observation by Colin Wilson, Wordsworth in his nature poetry is "at one" with nature in a quite different sense from the hippopotamus dozing in the mud.[14]

Paradoxically, the mystical perception shares a similarity with the superstitious level in one respect: both may invoke the operation of impersonal laws or hidden principles. Yet for the primitive, this characteristically involves a far more simplistic—and poorly defined—sense of occult mechanics, with a starkly literal version of correspondence and magical causality. Additionally, as opposed to the dualistic way of thinking found at both the superstitious and religious levels, the mystical level involves a genuinely open-ended sense of archetypal symbolism that transcends limited notions of good and bad, right and wrong, embracing instead a multivalency of meanings more in keeping with the true spirit of symbolism. What might be perceived as a tragedy or run of bad luck at the lower levels might be interpreted mystically as an expression of the archetype of transformation or rebirth in one's life, without moralistic connotations attached; or winning a contest be viewed as an activation of the archetype of expansion, without connotations of good or bad luck. For this reason, both the superstitious and religious levels may be more accurately classified as belonging to the category of sign rather than symbol—the notion of *sign* denoting a narrow, one-to-one relationship (as seen in a company logo or trademark, in which the image denotes a specific and singular reference of meaning); *symbol* implying many levels of possible inference.

No less important than the content of the ideas expressed at these different levels of belief, however, is the manner in which they are held. For the religious or superstitious thinker, beliefs are accepted uncritically and anecdotally from the larger culture without any thought of personal verification (black cats are bad omens not because I have actually tested this out, but because it has always been said to be true). At the mystical level, on the other hand, beliefs are either derived from direct observation and introspection, or drawn from traditional sources but validated by personal testing and experimentation, in other words, a decidedly more scientific form of symbolist attitude. Additionally, at the less developed levels of thought, beliefs are frequently held in a spirit of obsessive dependency or fearfulness, as when an individual is unable to act without first learning what the omens say or believes the answers lie in the symbols outside. The mystic, by contrast, is neither dependent upon nor controlled by external symbols and signs but simply uses them as aids to inner resources of intuition and knowledge.

A simple illustration here may help convey the distinctions between the three levels. Imagine a person driving down the road when the car engine suddenly malfunctions and bursts into flame. Such an event would be interpreted in entirely different ways from each of the three levels of symbolic thought. For the superstitionist, the burning of the car's engine could be read as the work of unseen evil spirits, or bad magic directed by enemies, or simply as an expression of decidedly bad luck. For the religionist, the same failure of the car might be seen as holding significance within a specifically theistic framework; the event was meant either to indicate divine punishment for some transgression on the part of the driver, or to convey a message from God about something needing to be learned from this situation. Perhaps the driver was destined to preach the gospel to the auto-repair person appearing on the scene, or simply to learn something about the nature of patience.

To the symbolist, however, the same event may not even possess any clear-cut single meaning, but instead connect to a larger gestalt of symbolic patterns unfolding in life. Value judgements of good or bad are rejected in favor of archetypal subtleties of interpretation. For example, instead of seeing the engine fire as an expression of bad luck, the driver might reflect on the subtle ways it connects to other developments taking place in his or her life. For instance, the engine might be seen as a symbol corresponding to the driving force or power in terms of physical health or career. The malfunction in the engine could therefore reflect a broader heating up or fieriness occurring in these areas as well. The underlying causes of this event are in turn understood not in terms of hidden spirits or some mechanism of luck but more commonly in terms of an impersonal (though spiritually grounded) law, such as described in the yogic doctrine of karma or the classical principle of *telos* (or purpose). All that occurs is orderly, with each event reflecting this all-embracing order.

Most important, the engine fire is at this level seen as symbolic not in terms of pointing toward some reference point or hidden meaning outside the driver's own experience, but in the sense of reflecting an inner state of consciousness. Hence, to understand this event the driver might need to reflect upon what thoughts were passing through his or her mind at the moment the engine went out or even during the broader course of that day. Were they likewise volatile or fiery? Nor does this awareness of the deeper dimension of meaning blind a person to the purely practical dimension of the event; that is, while at one level the engine may be an archetypal symbol, on a more down-to-earth level, the engine on fire is simply an engine on fire and needs to be doused as rapidly as possible!

Looking back, it is clear that the symbolist mentality has expressed itself through the ages mainly as superstitious or religious thinking, in other words, almost entirely at the crudest and most simplistic levels. Yet this fact should not prevent us from recognizing the possibility of subtler levels of insight which this tradition stands to offer. In the words of Mircea Eliade, "Symbolic thinking is not the exclusive privilege of the child, of the poet or of the unbalanced mind; it is consubstantial with human existence, it comes before language and discursive reason."[15] Or, as Herman Melville expressed this perception in his description of Starbuck, the first mate, in *Moby Dick:*

> *Uncommonly conscientious for a seaman, and endued with a deep natural reverence, the wild watery loneliness of his life did therefore incline him to superstitions; but to that sort of superstition, which in some organizations seem rather to spring, somehow, from intelligence than from ignorance. Outward portents and inward presentiments were his. (Chapter 26)*

With these thoughts in mind, let us continue the exploration of symbolist thought with a look at a further system of classification of meanings contained in the living book of symbols.

CHAPTER 3

A LANDSCAPE OF SYMBOLS

The whole outer world and its forms are a signature of the inner world.

—Jacob Boehme, *The Signature of All Things*

The signatures of all things I am here to read.

—James Joyce, *Ulysses*

n 1798, Napoleon and his army of soldiers and scholars entered Egypt, initiating the first large-scale investigation of ancient Egypt in modern times. Imagine the reaction of these early explorers setting foot for the first time among the sand-drifted ruins of this ancient civilization. Everywhere about them, on the archaic walls and monuments looming up from the surrounding desert, are mysterious images, hieroglyphs, which hold the secrets to that distant world. Yet because they do not know how to decipher these strange symbols, that world remains unknown to them, even though its secrets are at their fingertips. Not until the later discovery and decoding of the Rosetta stone (a granite slab containing the same text in Greek, Coptic, and hieroglyphic scripts) would Western scholars get their first look into the beliefs and ideas of the ancient Egyptians encoded in these images.

By analogy, this is the predicament of the average man or woman today as perceived by the symbolist. We are each surrounded by a vast landscape of symbols, encoded within the events and phenomena of our daily lives; collectively, these experiential patterns contain a wealth of information about ourselves and the world. Yet because we have forgotten the language of these symbols—our *personal* hieroglyphics—this vast dimension of knowledge remains closed to us, even though it, too, is at our fingertips.

Throughout history, cultures have developed different methods of unlocking the information encoded in the living book of symbols, some of which are explored in the chapters to follow. This chapter proposes a broad framework of interpretation to provide a context in which to orient these ideas and methods.

THE VARIETIES OF EXPERIENTIAL SYMBOLISM

As an aid to a systematic study of personal symbols, we can begin by identifying several broad categories of symbolism from which to elaborate more specialized branches of study. The focus here is on five of these categories: environmental symbols, the body, actions, dreams, and attitudes.

ENVIRONMENTAL SYMBOLS

The first and broadest category, environmental symbols, is the primary focus of this book. Here I refer to all forms of information perceived in the immediate external world, including what is drawn from interpersonal encounters, found or presented objects, encounters with animals, environmental changes, as well as more abstract patterns like numerological relationships or name symbolism—in short, all external events.

From the symbolist standpoint, these patterns can be viewed as reflections of inner states of consciousness, interpretable in the same way as nightly dreams. When viewed through the eye of analogical or metaphoric thought, ordinary situations are revealed to possess levels of significance beyond their prosaic or everyday meaning. Subtle cross-connections between different events are perceived through a recognition of similarities. For example, the bird which changed direction in mid-flight during my conversation with the native healer in Arizona could be read as mirroring a similar shift of direction unfolding in my larger life at that time. When I perceived the bird's flight as a metaphor, I was able to discern a deeper connection to broader trends in my own life.

THE BODY

A second category widely recognized as a vital source of esoteric information is the body. As the sixteenth-century Christian mystic and occultist Jacob Boehme wrote, "There is nothing in man that is not marked in his exterior, so that by the exterior one may discover what is in the individual who bears the sign."

The esoteric study of the body is classically subdivided into several categories, any one of which represents a field of study unto itself. These include the markings and shape of the hands, the features of the face and head, the eyes, as well as the overall shape and size of the body, to name the most prominent. On a broad level, the entire body is divisible into left and right halves, with the markings and features on each side possessing different symbolism. For example, if the hands symbolically mirror the psyche and destiny, the left hand specifically concerns all inherited traits as well as the emotional, reactive disposition of the person, whereas the right hand reveals what the person has achieved with those potentials, as well as revealing his or her more rational side. Thus according to this system, someone whose left hand has relatively weak markings but whose right hand has strongly defined markings has probably developed relatively meager capacities to the greatest possible advantage. Moreover, all changes anywhere on the body suggest important changes in one's personality and destiny.[1]

ACTIONS

Another category of symbolism concerns the subtler meanings associated with an individual's actions—what Boehme called "customs and usages." Simply by observing a person's movements, gestures, and general behavior, sages have claimed that a great deal may be learned about his or her inner disposition. In the third-century Buddhist text the *Visuddhimagga,* an individual's spiritual growth is revealed by the way the person stands or moves, his or her footprints, and even in the way the person gets out of and into bed. In recent decades, this ancient belief has been echoed in the complex theories about body language developed by psychologists.

Yet for esotericists, human movements yield not only psychological but metaphysical information as well. To the ancient Pythagoreans, for instance, a person's behavior upon awakening on the first day of the year revealed important omens about the rest of the year for that individual. We all are familiar with superstitions and folk beliefs of this sort, ranging from notions about walking under ladders to spilling salt and breaking mirrors. Indeed, to the esotericist *all* behavior, from the patterns of one's speech and handwriting to the way one moves one's body on a particular day, potentially encodes larger bodies of symbolic meaning.

DREAMS

As with the events of waking experience, the images of our dreams offer an important glimpse into the workings of the deep psyche written in the language of symbolism and analogy. According to some traditions, however, dreams issue from a subtler level of consciousness than the phenomena of everyday life, and for that reason offer a decidedly more fluid look into the changing psychological condition of the soul than do waking events. Yet dream symbolism should not be thought of as more accurate than waking symbolism; rather, each type provides a glimpse into a different part of human nature. According to esoteric Hindu teachings, dream symbolism offers insight into the emotional dimensions of our being, while the symbolism of waking events reflects the underlying aspects of our rational or analytic nature.

ATTITUDES

Even more intangible than dreams, our shifting moods and attitudes contain a rich wealth of meaning. Because of their proximity to everyday consciousness, we often find in our emotional patterns types of information difficult to discern through other sources. By way of illustration, we might outwardly experience what is commonly considered a tragedy, say, the loss of a house, all the while remaining in a state of great joy or tranquility. While the outer event may hold an important message about an inner psychic or karmic pattern unfolding at that time, the state of mind brought to bear on the event symbolizes our inner level of development (in this case, emotional maturity or harmony). Similarly, an individual may externally possess great wealth, while internally experiencing profound guilt regarding money. Without negating the symbolic importance of the outer condition, the inner attitude qualifies the external symbol in a significant way. In this case, guilt implies a constriction regarding the symbol of wealth on a more profound level of personality than suggested by the physical condition of having a great deal of money.

Many methods can be employed to explore one's attitudes and moods, among them word association exercises, in which one allows thoughts to arise in response to proposed words or phrases; Rorschach tests, in which an abstract image serves as the point of departure for spontaneous—and highly symbolic—reflections from the unconscious mind; personal mythology, or the study and exploration of mythic themes or archetypes underlying one's drives and feelings; and psychological questionnaires, with questions like: If your house were to catch fire, what object or possession would you save? What are your greatest fears or desires? What is your most vivid recollection from childhood?

From an esoteric standpoint, attitudes toward any one symbol can provide enormous insight into a person's relationship with entire classes of symbols and internal energies. Using astrological terminology, for example, a person's attitude toward authority figures reveals his or her deeper relationship with the entire network of energies relating to Saturn, the planet which most directly rules authority symbols. In addition, attitudes toward religious figures reflect a person's relationship with Jupiter, the planet ruling such figures; and a person's attitude toward the mother can yield subtle insights into his or her relationship with the inner Moon. Through such a process of investigation, one can begin to grasp the essential core patterns or archetypal roots underlying a diverse array of thoughts and moods.

THE THREE RINGS: CLASSIFICATION BY TIME

Onto these five basic areas of experience it is possible to superimpose another framework of classification based not on types of symbolism but on increments of time, or duration.

For example, some esoteric systems, such as astrology, divide individual experience into short-term events, longer-term trends, and life-long patterns or themes (in astrology these are termed tran-

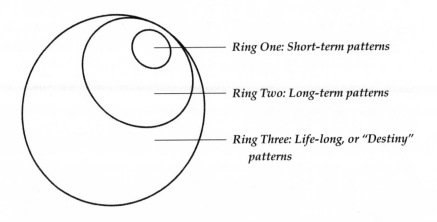

Ring One: Short-term patterns

Ring Two: Long-term patterns

Ring Three: Life-long, or "Destiny" patterns

sits, progressions, and the natal horoscope). While intimately inter-twined, each level reveals a different type of information. To illus-trate this concept, the globe pictured here represents the experi-ence of an entire life. The first ring, covering the smallest area on the globe, relates to life-events of the shortest and most transitory nature. The slightly larger ring relates to more long-lasting condi-tions and events. The third ring, associated with the surface of the entire globe, relates symbolically to the destiny patterns of an en-tire life.

Each kind of symbolism explored earlier may be looked at from any one of these three levels of duration. For example, in discussing the symbolism of the body, we can speak of short-term transitory changes taking place with a person's health or physique, such as common illnesses, cuts or bruises of any kind, and simi-lar occurrences. We can also speak of longer-term conditions as-sociated with the body, such as chronic illnesses or trends in one's style of dress. Finally we might reflect upon life-long physiologi-cal features, as symbolically expressed in a person's general body shape, size, or features. In the category of actions, we may de-scribe short-range symbols, such as individual gestures or situa-tion-specific body language; those of a longer-range significance, such as jobs, hobbies, or habitual activities of a personal or pro-fessional nature; or life-long actions, such as basic patterns of walking, self-expression, or career activities. In these categories, each of the three levels of duration reveal different meanings. Consider, for example, how this scheme applies to the category of environmental symbols.

RING ONE:
TRANSITORY SYMBOLIC EVENTS

At any given moment, people are engulfed by a constantly chang-ing ocean of information from the environment, ranging from back-ground noises of traffic and overheard conversations to changing images, odors, and sensations. But if everything is in some sense meaningful, there must be some practical way of sifting out what is truly important, of distinguishing "signal" from "noise." Towards this end, consider the following broad guidelines.

Traditionally, the single most dramatic indicator of importance in any event is unusualness: to what degree is an event out of the ordinary? What tends to happen on a consistent or repetitive basis may not suggest anything of significance to the mystic or symbolist, yet the event or situation that is unusual implies a rupture or break with the established order, and therefore holds broader implications of meaning.

Suppose, for example, that you had the newspaper delivered to your front door every day. In this context, the appearance of a newspaper on the porch would not hold any deep importance as a symbol. But suppose you never had the newspaper delivered to your front door, when suddenly, one morning, there it is, today's edition on the doorstep. This simple event, while hardly earthshaking, out of sheer unusualness takes on potential significance as a symbol of larger developments in your outer or inner life. As to the specific meaning of the symbol, you might look at what headline appears on its front page and consider how it literally or metaphorically connects with what is happening in your life. Does it read "Opposition Leaders Meet"? Or "Strike Reaches Deadlock"? Or "Flood Ravages City"? In a more fundamental way, newspapers are symbols of communication and mental concerns: compare, for instance, the very different meaning implied by an accidental delivery of flowers or a pizza! At this level, the appearance of a newspaper may suggest a larger trend taking place in your life toward greater communication or social interaction.

Needless to say, an event of this sort would rank fairly low on virtually anyone's scale of unusualness. As a general rule, one might conclude *the more unusual an event is, the more importance it takes on as a symbol of change or transformation in one's life.* For instance, suppose a fire breaks out in your basement, causing extensive damage. As in the interpretation of a dream, you might ask how this event reflects some inner "fire" or outbreak of energy in your life, possibly at the level of the emotional subconscious (since basements commonly symbolize that which is "down below" in the psyche). Or imagine you wake up to find a bat flying through the darkness of your bedroom, as happened to a friend of mine. Not surprisingly, this event occurred during a period of great emotional turmoil in my friend's life.

In this vein we might also include what became for Carl Jung the primary focus of his work with synchronicity: extraordinary coincidences between events that display a striking quality of meaningfulness. Coincidences fall into several different categories. Early in this century, Austrian biologist Paul Kammerer focused his attention on coincidences of a more sequential kind, in his aptly named theory of "seriality." Examples of sequential coincidences include an individual encountering the same number several times in a row during a short period, or being locked out of buildings in separate incidents during the course of a single day.[2] Carl Jung, by contrast, focused his attention largely on coincidences of a more simultaneous or synchronous sort—as in the case of someone stumbling across a photo of a friend from grade school who happens to call precisely at that moment, or an appropriate book that falls off a shelf just as one needs the answer to a problem.

In a general sense, coincidences may be thought to represent a kind of heightened punctuation relative to a lesson or message one is dealing with at that time. For actor Frank Morgan, finding the name of author L. Frank Baum sewn into his coat during the filming of *The Wizard of Oz* no doubt seemed a confirmation from the universe of the rightness of his involvement in the movie. In many cases, however, the key to interpreting a coincidence lies in taking a more metaphorical approach and connecting the unusual occurrence with what is happening in your personal life. Take the case of the recurring locked doors: in what way are you feeling blocked in your efforts to make changes or transitions? Or in the case of the childhood classmate calling just as you stumble across his or her photo; what does this person represent or embody for you? Think particularly of his or her traits or your childhood connection to this person. Or with the book that fell off the shelf: is the topic the plight of captive animals? Or is it the life story of an eccentric and socially distant artist from the nineteenth century? We must remember that such instances, from the mildly unusual occurrence to the most extraordinary, are neither positive nor negative in nature, but simply neutral vehicles through which different types of meaning can arise.

RING TWO: LONGER-TERM SYMBOLIC EVENTS

At this point we must pull back to include larger trends or phases which unfold over longer periods of time. Like the stage sets in a given act which frame the scenes of a play, these broader trends may be less obvious and constitute the invisible environment of daily life; nonetheless, they represent important keys to understanding the larger contexts against which the more transitory events of life draw significance.

For instance, aside from whatever unusual or extraordinary events may occur in one's home environment over the course of a day or week, where one is living—next to a church, an ocean, or a toxic dump, for instance—may be significant from a broader perspective. Likewise, one's job might seem relatively uneventful during a given period, yet in a larger context, the nature of the job could itself be an important symbol in one's life. For example, I knew a woman who found temporary work at a county flood control department exactly at a time she was trying to stem the tide of turbulent emotions following a bitter divorce.

In addition to one's job or home environment, clues may also be found in such areas as health, relationships, family, and neighbors. One useful way of clarifying these broader patterns is by keeping a diary, with a focus on larger trends rather than individual days. In other words, every month or two, put aside some time to reflect on what larger developments have been taking shape in your life, with an eye to any longer-range inner trends connected with the period in question. Broader patterns of this sort can be easily overlooked in the narrower focus of a daily diary.

While most second-ring patterns express themselves in terms of long-range developments, in some cases, however, even shorter, more transitory events may be important enough to jump rings into this second and broader category by merit of their long-range effects or implications. This can include major accidents, unexpected changes, or events of extreme unusualness, or what some call "high strangeness." A classic example of this is an individual getting struck by lightning—a fleeting event, to be sure, yet with far broader implications. In traditional societies, individuals who survived direct lightning strikes were seen as singled out or chosen by the gods or fate for some unusual destiny. Even more unusual would be experiences of a paranormal nature, such as the sighting of ghosts, strange animals, or unidentified lights in the sky.

This second category of symbolic patterning also includes all of life's archetypal or threshold events, such as deaths, divorces, marriages, graduations, domestic moves, the birth of children, leaving home, job changes, or even falling in love. Such developments are significant in at least two respects: first, as symbols in themselves which express in microcosm larger changes unfolding in the life of the psyche. Hence, the loss of a cherished friend could reflect a deeper transformation being experienced, or the act of getting married might correspond to some "union" taking place in other areas of one's life. Secondly, these archetypal events are significant as hubs through or around which other important symbols and synchronicities may constellate. As numerous writers on synchronicity have noted, such points of change in our lives are often accompanied by powerful symbols or synchronicities in our environment. In turn, these events frequently reveal important clues concerning the broader transition being experienced.

As an example, a woman approached me after a lecture one evening and told me her father had died on her wedding day. She wondered whether this might hold symbolic or synchronistic meaning. Rather than view the event in terms of positive or negative implications, I told her the sheer momentousness of such a symbol in conjunction with her wedding day underscored the magnitude of the step she had taken by entering married life, leaving her youthful identity behind her. Needless to say, in no way should the marriage be viewed as having caused the father's death, but simply as being conjoined with it.

Of all the archetypal events or turning points in our lives, perhaps none is as significant as our own near-brushes with death. After all, what could be more unusual or out of the ordinary than stepping to the brink of mortality? Having had a few such experiences, I have been struck by the way they seem to occur at times of great psychological transition or intensity, with the circumstances of the near-fatal encounter encoding the larger issues being confronted. Hence, my near-drowning in a hidden whirlpool on a river many years ago mirrored a period of considerable emotional turmoil precipitated by a family crisis. A near collision, in which a car from an opposite lane suddenly hurdled toward my own, exactly coincided with a heated confrontation taking place with a coworker that same week. Ironically, the home state of the other driver was the same as that of the individual causing me difficulties in the personal sphere. On a subtler level, such close calls with death can also signal profound changes in an individual's destiny or karmic "program," with the events serving to redirect a person into a different life direction.

Though it is associated almost exclusively with shorter-term events, Jung's notion of meaningful coincidence may be applied to this second level of magnitude, in the form of recurring events or situations unfolding over many months or years. Consider the case of an aspiring actress who over the course of a month was offered virtually identical roles in totally unrelated plays or television shows. The roles were different from anything she had done before. In a recent book, a writer described the unsettling experience of seeing fire imagery repeatedly crop up in her life over a six-month period: the plane she was on caught fire, the hotel she walked into one day burst into flames, and she had close-calls with bomb scares on a London street.[3] Or consider the businessman who, over the course of several years, found himself repeatedly running up against the same obscure problem at work. Here as well, the challenge lies in being able to grasp the symbolic or metaphoric dimensions of such events rather than their purely literal interpretation. For example, was the recurring role offered the actress that of a high-powered businesswoman? If so, perhaps there was something she could learn from this character about becoming more practical and assertive in her life. If the characters emphasized the more negative side of this career orientation, maybe the actress needed to be less ambitious or driven in her attitudes. Likewise, did the problem repeatedly confronting the businessman concern blockages in the plumbing of his various office buildings? Possibly in his own life at that time there were issues of unresolved emotionality, or "clogged plumbing" needing to be looked at. In other words, upon further reflection, such situations can shed much insight into the broader lessons being confronted in one's life.

THE THIRD RING:
LIFE-DESTINY PATTERNS

This level of personal experience involves neither short nor long-term symbolic patterns but rather the broader design or theme of an entire life. In a famous passage from his essay "Transcendent Speculation upon an Apparent Intention in the Fate of the Individual" (1850), the philosopher Arthur Schopenhauer muses how the unfoldment of seemingly unintended events and accidents in one's life give the appearance of a carefully constructed novel, as if all that ever happened, whether intended or not, represented integral elements of a larger unfolding destiny.[4] Indeed, just as a book may fall under a particular category (fiction, nonfiction, romance, mystery, adventure), so we often note a similar unifying pattern to our own lives which serves as the guiding principle informing individual events or trends. Unlock this pattern and we unlock the guiding symbols of an entire life.

This theme, or what might be called a meta-pattern, can be discerned in several different ways. For example, we find it within long-term conditions or patterns that extend for the duration of an entire life, as in the symbolism of a life-long profession, hobby, struggle, or behavioral pattern. A person whose entire life is associated with books, from a childhood in the family bookstore to an adult occupation as a writer, is dominated by the archetype of Mercury (in Greek, Hermes), the god of intellectual and communicative interests. Someone whose life is continually preoccupied with battling social injustice, on the other hand, may be seen as being governed by the archetypal pattern of justice, law, or what might be called "crusading for the underdog."

Another source of insight into one's life-destiny pattern is the human body. In addition to those more transitory marks or health conditions relating to the first two levels of symbolism we have been looking at, one's essential body shape and facial features can hold profound clues to one's overall state of consciousness and "karmic inheritance" for this lifetime. Occultists and astrologers have long theorized about the ways body or facial types relate to various planetary or archetypal qualities governing different individuals. They classify certain bodies as Saturnine (long and thin), Martian (athletic, fierce-looking, or commanding), Mercurial (short and wiry), Venusian (sensual), and so forth. In turn, each individual part of the body can be seen as encoding some facet of one's inner or outer life, with particular attention paid to any unusual or prominent features, such as birthmarks, deformities, scars, or areas of abnormal strengths or handicaps. Again, none of these signs are either positive or negative, but are to be viewed simply in terms of their symbolic implications. Such features assume either constructive or destructive expressions depending on the will of the individual.

Still another approach to this question (dealt with in greater depth in the next chapter) involves the careful examination of the very first moments of life. It is ironic that one of the briefest periods of an entire life should also reflect the longest term dimension of meaning for that life; yet for many cultures the symbols and cir-cumstances surrounding birth are seen as being a microcosm or blueprint of the greater themes and conditions of an entire lifetime. Perhaps the most obvious example of this practice is the astrologi-cal horoscope, which symbolically encodes the grand overarching patterns of an individual's life. Yet as I show in chapter four, horo-scopes are by no means the only example of this practice employed by traditional cultures.

We saw earlier how certain short-term events can overlap onto second-ring magnitude patterns. It is even possible for some singu-lar events or accomplishments to assume so much importance they jump across both first and second-ring categories to become third-ring, or life-long symbols. For Sir Edmund Hillary, climbing Mount Everest became a key symbol reflecting the destiny pattern or karma of his entire life. For Richard Nixon, the Watergate scandal was an important key to the meaning of his life-long destiny, both in re-gard to the elements of criminality and deception this event signi-fied, as well as the symbolic imagery of the name itself: a "gate holding back water," one could argue, was an appropriate psycho-logical description of Nixon himself. In terms of your own personal experience, look back to those key situations that embody either the highest pinnacles or lowest depths of your life, and by reflecting on these, come to better understand the further extremes of your own karmic spectrum of destiny.

We saw earlier how the idea of coincidence may be understood not only in terms of transitory, short-term events, but in connec-tion with longer periods of time. Extending this idea one step fur-ther, we might also note the presence of coincidences which tran-spire over many decades and which therefore hold significance in relation to an entire lifetime. For example, we may notice uncan-nily similar situations recurring in connection with domestic envi-

ronments, such as successive neighbors all sharing the same obscure hobby, or consistently purchasing houses with faulty founda-
tions. I am reminded of a woman I met who had been struck by
lightning not once but three times over the course of her life. Once
she was hit directly in an open-air strike, a second time indirectly
by lightning traveling through a phone line, and on the third occasion, she was struck through a fireplace. To the astrologically
minded, such clusters of symbols in a life are readily comprehen-
sible through an analysis of the archetypal patterns indicated in the
individual's horoscope. In this woman's case, her horoscope revealed
an intense configuration centering around the planet Uranus, the
planet most often associated with lightning, which was positioned
at the top of her chart. In astrological terms, this would indicate a
person who might experience "lightning-like" shifts of fortune in
career or reputation, as well as a powerful need for freedom and
independence in life generally. Her unusual relationship with lightning symbolized a broader destiny and personality that permeated
many other areas of her life.

Approaching this idea from a slightly different angle, it is possible that each area of one's life conceals long-term recurring patterns of one type or another, whether in the area of relationships,
work, money, body and health, schooling, or friendships, to name a
few. For example, all of the long-distance journeys one has ever taken
may have been characterized by unexpected meetings with religious
figures who subsequently had an important impact on one's life. In
astrology, such conditions would be seen as relating to the karmic
energies of the Ninth House—that sector of the horoscope relating
to philosophy and one's Higher Mind. Indeed, none of the various
areas of one's life truly exist in isolation, but entwine to comprise a
greater whole, much in the same way the various instruments of an
orchestral piece come together to form a great symphony. For this
reason it is more accurate to speak of an individual's destiny-pat-
tern less as a singular, uniform entity than as a complex chorus of
elements or themes.

For the average person, this basic symbolic template runs through the various stages of an entire life, periodically shifting in the subcategory or octave of symbolism expressed, or even in the changing combination of areas and subelements emphasized, yet remaining essentially similar throughout. This consistency of symbolism is visible in the way archetypal situations or interests experienced in childhood will tend to recur in seemingly very different ways and levels through an entire life. During his childhood, for instance, Bulgarian-born spiritual teacher Omraam Mikhael Aivanhov (1900-1986) exhibited an inordinate fascination with the phenomena of fire and water, along with a passion for climbing trees. As his biographer Georg Feuerstein suggests, these interests foreshadow his later concern with the cosmic principles of masculine and feminine, universally symbolized by the elements of fire and water, as well as his adult interest in attaining a transcendent perspective on life, a process symbolized in many traditional sources by climbing a great tree.[5]

To summarize, we have seen how the problem of meaning in our lives can be approached from several different perspectives simultaneously. In this chapter, we have explored two complementary systems which help map the primary categories of symbolism in our life, as well as the contexts of time. A simple analogy would be the way a novel can be studied on several different levels at once: most minutely, in terms of its individual sentences or grammar; more broadly, in terms of its chapters or narrative scenes; or, in the broadest possible sense, in terms of its greater overall theme or message. At each of these magnitudes of focus, a different type of information concerning the book and its ideas presents itself. So it is with our own life. Depending on which level of focus one chooses to emphasize, entirely different symbolic patterns can be studied or emphasized. Using this three-fold structure, there is virtually no detail or aspect of a person's life—be it fleeting or long-lasting— that does not have its place within the overall framework of symbolism in the person's experience. Meaning is not limited to the rare and extraordinary event but permeates the landscape of our lives in a rich variety of ways.

In the chapters that follow, we look at other ways of approaching and classifying the patterns of our world, beginning with a look at the most popular and intensely scrutinized of all traditional symbolic events, the omen.

CHAPTER 4

OMENS AND DIVINATION

Coming events cast their shadow before them.

—Ancient proverb

he symbolist worldview encompasses a wide range of symbolic patterns in our lives. Yet one class of symbol in particular, the omen, has captured the imaginations of both individuals and societies around the world. Through the study of omens, men and women have sought to glimpse future possibilities and shifts of fortune and thus prepare themselves for the challenges and opportunities they may bring. In his symbolist masterpiece *Moby Dick,* Herman Melville provides a series of vivid glimpses into the omenological imagination at work. After setting out on his fateful voyage to hunt down the white whale, Captain Ahab spots a passing ship and attempts to make contact across the turbulent waters to learn the whereabouts of the great whale:

> *"Ship ahoy! Have ye seen the White Whale?"*
> *But as the (other) captain, leaning over the pallid bulwarks, was in the act of putting his trumpet to his mouth, it somehow fell from his hand into the sea; and the wind now rising again, he in vain strove to make himself heard without it. Meantime his ship was still increasing the distance between. While in various*

silent ways the seamen of the Pequod were evincing their obser-
vance of this ominous incident at the first mere mention of the
White Whale's name to another ship, Ahab for a moment paused;
it almost seemed as though he would have lowered a boat to board
the stranger, had not the threatening wind forbade. But taking
advantage of his windward position, he again seized his trumpet,
and knowing by her aspect that the stranger vessel was a nan-
tucketeer and shortly bound home, he loudly hailed— "Ahoy there!
This is the Pequod, bound round the world! Tell them to address
all future letters to the Pacific Ocean! and this time three years, if
I am not at home, address them to—"

At that moment the two wakes were fairly crossed, and in-
stantly, then, in accordance with their singular ways, shoals of
small harmless fish, that for some days before had been placidly
swimming by our side, darted away with what seemed shudder-
ing fins, and ranged themselves fore and aft with the stranger's
flanks. (Chapter 52)

Here, Melville deftly illustrates how such apparently random
events as the rising of the wind, the accidental dropping of a trumpet into the sea, and the movement of fish at a key moment can
together impart an important message about an impending crisis—
a message seemingly apparent to everyone except the person most
needing to heed it.

As with all aspects of symbolist thought, the omenological sensibility has traditionally expressed itself at widely varying levels of
sophistication. At the most subtle level, omens exist in a world in
which the boundaries between past, present, and future are perme-
able. Influences of past conditions or events still echo in the present,
while from the other direction, what is to come sends ripples into
the now, like the bow waves preceding an advancing boat. Hence
the phenomenal play of each moment represents the complex blending of symbolic influences from all three dimensions of time, with
those from the future designated as omens.

Following a distinction suggested in the earlier discussion of correspondence theory, in classifying omens it is useful to distinguish between literal and symbolic forms. Literal omens require little translation. For example, during an interview the South American novelist Gabriel Garcia Marquez recalled the time he answered his doorbell to find a stranger saying, "You must change the electric iron's cord—it is faulty!" Then, realizing he had come to the wrong house, the stranger promptly apologized and left. A half-hour later, Marquez's iron burst into flames—the result of a faulty cord. Here, the apparent omen foreshadowed the later event in a straightforward way.

Far more common, however, are those instances in which an omen takes on more metaphoric clothing, appearing in ways that, like dreams, require greater skill and intuition to interpret. In the British television production of Robert Graves' story of Imperial Rome *I Claudius,* the death of a central character (Herod) is foreshadowed by an owl landing on his chair during a public ceremony. The owl hoots several times, the number of hoots corresponding to the number of days before his death. The relationship between the omen and what is signified by it was entirely symbolic and involved several levels of meaning. To make sense of such an image, we must perceive it with a discerning eye for similarities.

As creatures of flight, birds are metaphorically associated with the soul's flight at death. Moreover, the owl is specifically a night bird, emphasizing even more dramatically the principle of otherness, and the negative (or passive) half of the day/night polarity, and by analogy, the opposing side of the life/death polarity. The number of hoots emitted by the bird represents a proportional reference to the number of days until the individual's death. In this way, a single and seemingly simple event encodes several dimensions of information and meaning at once.

In ancient times, birds represented one of many different types of omens. Other notable areas of study included the behavior of snakes, randomly situated pieces of wood along the road, patterns on bodies of water, omens derived from celestial phenomena of any sort, and even moles on the human body.

Yet we don't need to turn to ancient history for examples of omens. In the days immediately before and after the inauguration of Bill Clinton, news sources reported four head-on train collisions in separate parts of the country—a news oddity I interpreted as suggesting that Clinton's presidency would be anything but smooth. Within the first two weeks of his term, for example, Clinton's advocacy of gay rights provoked an unprecedented firestorm of controversy both on Capitol Hill and around the country, an event some newspapers referred to as a "butting of heads" or "collision" between political opponents. Subsequent controversies during Clinton's term only underscored the acrimonious quality of those initial months.

IDENTIFYING OMENS

Is there any way to determine whether an event is an omen? While such events do not always lend themselves to easy classification, there are several broad guidelines which can be held in mind when approaching this subject.

The first of these is the quality of unusualness discussed in the previous chapter. For ancient cultures, those events somehow out of the ordinary were frequently looked to as providing insight into possible future trends. This is to say, some events can serve as mirrors to current states of mind (reflective symbols) or reveal impending developments in one's life (predictive symbols), though precisely how one determines which is which may be a matter more of intuition than any systematic rule of thumb. Hypothetically, it is even possible for certain events to contain both aspects at once, since a current state of awareness can simultaneously represent the "entering wedge" of a developing future trend as well.

In this vein, societies have paid special attention to the appearance of bizarre weather conditions, unusual dreams, the birth of malformed children or animals, or major accidents, in the belief that the extraordinary quality of such events portends change in the individual or collective destiny. This preoccupation with anomalies, in part, led ancient cultures like the Babylonian and the Mayan to chart the movements of heavenly bodies as precisely as possible, to determine which movements or phenomena were exceptional or out of the ordinary, and thus of

Babylonian astronomers atop a ziggurat.

consequence to society. The more irregular an astronomical occurrence was, the greater its significance as a portent of social change. For the Chinese astrologers of antiquity, such unusual sights as the daytime appearance of Venus would be regarded as highly significant omens, pointing to an imbalance of forces within the kingdom at large.

However, contrary to popular belief, omens are not always negative in nature. Several years ago, the international media reported the story of three whales trapped beneath the ice off the coast of Alaska. Although probably not a rare occurrence for that part of the world, its prominent exposure in the media certainly was. As millions of viewers watched, Russian and American naval icebreakers converged upon the scene to join in a cross-cultural attempt to save the rapidly tiring whales. The two countries working together eventually freed the two surviving adults. More than one observer remarked on the uncanny timing of this event relative to the political "thaw" gaining momentum between Russia and America. Symbolically, it reflected a "breakthrough" in world politics which accelerated in subsequent months and years. In a similar vein, Native Americans were excited to hear news of the birth of a white buffalo in Wisconsin in 1994. This exceedingly rare phenomenon was widely seen as a profoundly important omen for such tribes as the Lakota. For many Native Americans, this unusual occurrence was regarded as heralding a new era for all native peoples.

A more systematic method employed by traditional cultures to foretell the future is the careful observation of any symbols or events occurring around a beginning, be it the birth of a project, business, relationship, trip, or idea. This belief might be called the "Law of Conception." Esoterically understood, the context surrounding a phenomenon's birth holds the seeds of its unfoldment and eventual outcome—providing one knows how to interpret their symbolic language. In the passage from *Moby Dick* quoted earlier, the mishap involving the voice trumpet occurred in conjunction with the first mention of the white whale, investing it with importance as an omen. Likewise, the highly improbable run of head-on train accidents was important for Bill Clinton's presidency because they happened at the start of his term in office.

In many ancient cultures, great attention was paid to events on the first day of the New Year (or, in some cultures, the first day of the winter solstice or spring equinox). A similar notion is echoed in our custom of the "Twelve Days of Christmas," each of which was traditionally seen as foreshadowing the weather to be expected in the corresponding month of the New Year. The events seen on a person's birthday likewise assume significance as possible omens of the person's upcoming "new year."

Regarding this general principle, the Renaissance mystic Cornelius Agrippa remarked: "All the auspicia [omens] which first happen in the beginning of any enterprise are to be taken notice of . . . if going forth thou shalt stumble at the threshold, or in the way thou shalt dash thy foot against anything, forbear thy journey."[1] With this in mind, it is interesting to recall what happened to Darwin's great contemporary Alfred Wallace as he was about to begin a sea voyage returning him home to England after an exploratory trip through South America and the Pacific Ocean. Just as the ship was to set sail, his pet toucan plunged into the ocean and drowned, a fact Wallace dejectedly made note of in his journal. Within weeks, the ship was destroyed by fire at sea, resulting in the loss of almost all his research. Again, the timing of this event at the start of the trip is the key element conferring omenological importance to it.

When applied to the area of personal relationships, this principle can frequently yield intriguing, if sometimes comical, results. A friend once related to me the problems she was encountering in a current relationship. "He used to seem like such a nice guy," she sighed, "but this last year he's been a real monster." I asked her if she recalled their first meeting or their first time out together. Yes, she said, they went to a movie. Could she recall the name of the movie? "Let me think," she strained to remember, "Oh, yes, *Dr. Jeckyll and Mr. Hyde!*"

I recall one especially dramatic situation which struck many of those present as having the quality of an omen. A couple I had known slightly were getting married. On the day of their wedding, one of the worst storms in many years struck the area. As the ceremony got underway, winds and hail began buffeting the church. People started whispering about the possibility of finding cover in the event of a tornado. Then, as the moment of exchanging vows drew near, the storm subsided with startling rapidity. At the very moment the groom placed the ring on his bride's finger, the clouds parted momentarily to allow a shaft of sunlight to shine down through the stained glass window onto the man and woman at the altar. Subsequent years have revealed the marriage to be not particularly easy, in respect to the external problems challenging the couple; yet despite it all, the emotional bond between them has proven to be a deep one, even in the face of hardship.

One of the most pervasive expressions of this principle in traditional cultures involves carefully noting the symbols arising around a person's birth. We are most familiar with this practice in the form of astrology, which looks at the positions and relationships among the celestial bodies at the moment of birth. Yet in a broader sense anything in the environment during these critical moments can serve as a symbolic clue unlocking an individual's destiny. In many Native American tribes, it was common to look for unusual events or symbols in the immediate environment at the moment a child was born for indications of his or her future character and to suggest the child's name. A deer seen running by might suggest the name Running Deer, indicating that the child would be particularly swift or graceful. Native American lore likewise tells us of the dramatic omens accompanying the births of powerful leaders, such as the great shooting star seen at the birth of Tecumseh, or the winds, lightning, and hail said to coincide with the birth of Pontiac.

An interesting account of this belief in another culture is seen in Plutarch's description of the birth of Alexander the Great. Plutarch says that when Alexander's father, Philip of Macedon, first heard of his son's birth, the birth announcement was accompanied by two other important pieces of information: Parmenio had overthrown the Illyrians in a great battle, and Philip's race horse had won in the Olympics. Sensing this to be a powerful juxtaposition of symbols, Philip sent for augurs trained in the interpretation of such events, who told him his son would attain unusually great success and far-reaching victory in life.[2] While Plutarch does not provide us with a detailed reason for this interpretation, it is not difficult to understand the symbolic logic. The two events connected with Alexander's birth pointed to movement and conquest, in association with victory. Taken together, these omens marked Alexander as a child whose life would be characterized by travel, militarism, and victory in battle—all of which came to pass in later life.

A third source of potential omens is our dreams. Reflecting the widespread belief that dreams precipitate from a higher sphere of reality, the study of dreams yields glimpses into the underlying symbolic patterns of daily life before events crystallize into concrete manifestation. Dream symbols are generally regarded as occurring prior to physical, waking reality. The question of how much time must pass between a dream experience and its manifestation in waking reality is often debated. For some esotericists, dream symbols find expression in waking reality almost immediately, with dreams foreshadowing waking events to occur on the following day. For others, however, the period of time varies considerably; in the Kriya Yoga tradition, among others, this process is commonly said to take around seventy-two hours.

However long this crystallization takes, dreams tend to foreshadow the ensuing physical situation in largely symbolic rather than strictly literal terms. For instance, a dream of falling down the stairs may not herald an actual accident, but rather an emotional fall from grace, such as might accompany a romantic rejection; similarly, a dream of death may symbolize the closing off or transformation of some outworn habit pattern, such as quitting smoking, rather than an actual death.

The belief in the predictive nature of dream reality has led some mystics to believe that working with dream symbols can influence the course of a person's waking life. Suppose a person dreams of a tidal wave crushing his house; if this person can attain lucidity, that is, wakeful awareness within the dream itself, he might redirect or work constructively with the dream symbol. He might, for example, will that the tidal wave be directed elsewhere or, perhaps, transformed into a cascading wall of flowers or gold dust. The impending real-life crisis foreshadowed by this symbol, whether physical or psychological, might be transformed or circumvented entirely.

Some critics of this approach contend that such active control of one's dream state seems an unwise interference with forces of the psyche which are better witnessed than tampered with. After all, some would argue, how can we know what secondary effects might be set in motion by altering the dream? Similarly, if the symbol indicates an imbalance in one's life, such as the danger of being overwhelmed by a tidal wave of addictive behavior, then changing the dream symbol without fully understanding its message may simply be a superficial solution to the deeper problem. In either case, a keen sense of discernment is necessary for any practical application of symbolist principles.

DIVINATION

Though useful when they happen, one can never be sure when an omen might take place. One can't very well wait for a comet to blaze through the sky or an animal to appear at one's window before making an important decision. Consequently, humans have developed an assortment of methods to induce omenological messages at will. Given the order and harmony seen as underlying all events, it was believed that the inherent meaningfulness of the universe could be tapped whenever desired to obtain answers to specific questions. Thus arose in classical times the distinction between natural omens (in Latin, *omina oblativa*) and artificial omens (in Latin, *omina impetrativa*), in other words, omens that naturally presented themselves and those humanly provoked. This latter category is conventionally known as *divination*. Technically speaking, divination may be used to uncover information concerning any situation, past, present, or future; conventionally, however, we associate it almost entirely with foretelling future trends.

As in the case of natural omens, the ancients developed an astonishing array of methods to ascertain the future, including watching the shape of smoke rising from specially tended fires, examining animal or human entrails, opening Scriptures or other books at random, gazing into crystals, and studying the pattern of tea leaves.

In the category of divination, we can also place seeking prophetic advice from an oracle, a man or woman thought to have the ability to speak of past, present, or future events while in a trance state. Such human "mediums" are still around; today we call them "channelers." Whether we look at the ambiguous pronouncements uttered in poetic meter by the famed oracle of Delphi in ancient Greece, or the inspired prophecies of indigenous shamans in trance, societies across the world have drawn on the internal psychic capacities of the human mind for insights regarding the future as an alternative to (or in conjunction with) the purely external sources we have been considering thus far.

Throughout history, oracles were consulted to address a wide range of concerns, from finding lost objects to learning the outcome of battles during wartime. In one of history's most infamous cases, Herodotus tells us that Croesus of Lydia asked the Delphic oracle about his plan to attack Persia and was told that by doing so he would "destroy a great empire." As it turned out, the fallen empire proved to be his own. Yet oracles could be called upon to answer religious inquiries as well, as when seeking a blessing from the gods, or in requesting advice on a spiritual problem.

The problem with human-based divinatory methods, of course, is potential distortion by the human source. Just as a radio broadcast is only as clear as the equipment being used to receive it, so mystics have long realized that the validity of an oracle's message is a reflection of the person channeling the message. Because of this, spiritual traditions have placed enormous emphasis on physical and moral purification as a prerequisite for the position of oracle. Interestingly, because of the perceived connection between spiritual purity and oracular accuracy, some cultures like the ancient Jews viewed the fulfillment of prophecies as an indication of the prophet's spiritual attainment. If a prophet's prediction came true, it was a sign that his insight had penetrated to the highest levels of the divine mind from which all flowed. A failed prophecy would suggest that the prophet had succeeded in ascending only as far as his own subjective imaginings.

DIVINATION: SUBJECTIVE OR OBJECTIVE MEDIUM?

In discussing the mechanism of omens or divinatory techniques, the question is often asked whether the genuinely predictive aspects of these processes are the result of the techniques (or events) themselves, or simply a reflection of the intuitive capacities of those interpreting them. According to this latter view, an event or technique provides a neutral screen onto which the unconscious, or more accurately the superconscious, projects its own insights concerning coming events, which the conscious mind then interprets as having derived from a source outside itself.

While undoubtedly true in many cases, projection does not explain the full range of examples which characterize the classical understanding of omens. For instance, a meteorite plunging into one's neighborhood would, to the traditional mentality, be viewed as a deeply meaningful omen; yet one could hardly classify this as just another event onto which has been projected omenological significance; it is, by any standards, a genuinely unusual occurrence.

For this reason, it may be more helpful to speak instead of a *spectrum* of omenological systems, ranging from those involving relatively little intuition to those requiring a great deal. At the far end of the spectrum are such "low data/high subjectivity" systems such as crystal gazing or tea-leaf reading, in which the mind has a minimal amount of information to work from; while at the other end are "high data/low subjectivity" systems such as astrology or the tarot, in which the system itself provides a relatively high level of information from which the individual can proceed. Even in the case of such highly methodical and data-rich systems, it must be stressed that personal intuition always remains important, since the essentially symbolic nature of the information lends itself to interpretation on many different levels.

THE RITUALIZING OF BEGINNINGS

Along with the belief in omens, and the subsequent development of divinatory techniques to invoke them at will, humans went a step further in their attempt to gain control over the uncertainties of the world. In the case of natural omens, observers had to wait passively for an event to present itself; through the use of divination, they could actively draw out the needed information from the environment when and where they desired. But this led some to wonder: if the symbols around the beginning of an undertaking or birth reveal the outcome of that new beginning, what would happen if they were to implant their own symbols into the fabric of the moment? Would it be possible to modify the eventual outcome in some intended way?

Thus arose the practice of consecrating significant beginnings with symbolic rituals designed to influence future developments in auspicious ways. In traditional societies, rituals were conducted for both public and private events, including marriages, births, the building of new structures, or the start of wars. This sense of control was achieved through a variety of methods; commonly, such rituals involved the presence of a priest or priestess, whose participation not only insured the invoking of beneficent beings or forces to provide assistance, but served in a subtler way to inject the proceedings with a symbolic element of divinity and good fortune. In marriage ceremonies, for example, the priest not only served to formalize the vows, but acted as a spiritual symbol by which the duality of the Two was joined into One and through which the blessings of higher beings or states were symbolically invited into the union.

Through history, this general practice has expressed itself in a variety of ways. In ancient Rome, for instance, generals would choose a soldier with the name Victor to lead soldiers in an advancing attack to help assure victory in battle. Similarly, the ancient Pythagoreans knew that it was important for people to utter only positive words as they were beginning any important venture, such as setting off on a journey to a sacred site. Well-omened words not only promoted confidence but were viewed as helping ensure a positive outcome for the pilgrimage.

Of the many rituals used in connection with beginnings, one of the most common is a symbolic "breaking open," or "opening up," representing freedom and transcending limitations. For instance, in traditional Hindu weddings, the couple breaks open a coconut and drinks the milk. In the Jewish marriage ceremony, a wine glass is broken by the groom to shouts of *"Mazel Tov,"* or good luck. In many traditional cultures, it was customary to open all the windows in the house at the moment of a child's birth and just before the new year. There is an echo of this idea in the modern custom of christening a ship by breaking a bottle across its bow. To be sure, each of these customs holds several possible interpretations simultaneously; for instance, opening windows at childbirth was also intended to facilitate the easy passage of the child through the birth canal, and even to help release evil spirits from the household. Whatever their origin and interpretation, the worldwide persistence of rituals of conception in so many areas fundamentally suggests an intuition as to the sacredness of all beginnings and a perception of the need to accompany them with symbols of liberation.

THE SYMBOLOGY OF ENDINGS

Traditional societies also placed great emphasis on endings and conclusions. Like births and marriages, deaths have always been accompanied by symbols which reflect the crossing of thresholds— what might be called the "Law of Completion." For example, it is said that at the moment of Carl Jung's death, a bolt of lightning hit the tree Jung frequently sat beneath. In *Grace and Grit,* transpersonal psychologist Ken Wilber described the unusually intense windstorm which blew through Boulder, Colorado, where they lived, at the precise moment his wife Treya died. Checking the newspapers the next day, Wilber was intrigued to learn that this meteorological quirk did not seem to extend outside this locale.

Among the most common phenomena associated with death is clocks stopping at the moment of their owner's death—an explicit metaphor, one may presume, for "time running out." History informs us such a timely malfunction occurred at the passing of Frederick the Great. I once witnessed a possible example of this phenomenon in Chicago. On the way to class, I had to pass the famous Wrigley Building on Michigan Avenue, atop which stands the best-known timepiece in the Chicago area. Having seen this clock in perfect working order literally hundreds of times over the course of several years, I noticed one day that the hands on the clock were missing. Though I assumed that the clock was being cleaned, I still wondered if there might not also be a synchronistic dimension to this event because of its unusualness. I went home that night wondering if I might see the TV news announcing that the city's mayor had died (the most likely possibility, I thought) but the news unfolded that night revealing no such story. However, as the newscast drew to a close, the reporter respectfully noted that there had in fact been a death that day involving another prominent Chicagoan: William Wrigley, Jr., the founder of the famous gum company and owner of the building sporting the giant clock!

Because of their high visibility, the lives of celebrities seem to provide an unending source of symbolically provocative anecdotes and a rich assortment of death-related synchronicities. For instance, in 1928 the humorist Will Rogers died in an airplane crash along with aviator Wiley Post; amid the wreckage was Rogers' typewriter, showing that the last word he had typed was "death." Film director John Huston's last completed directorial effort was prophetically titled: *The Dead.* When actress Natalie Wood died during the early

1980s, she had been working on a film titled *Brainstorm* in which death figured prominently. Also during the early 1980s, actor Jon-Eric Hexum died from an accidental gunshot wound to his skull, inflicted upon himself during a moment of off-screen horseplay. Several days after his death, an interview conducted with Hexum shortly before his death was published in the magazine *Playgirl,* bearing on its cover the prominent headline "TV's Sexiest Body Bares His Mind." Before her death in 1985, actress Anne Baxter played her final role in an episode of the TV series *Hotel,* her last on-screen lines being "Shall we have one last waltz?" At the time of his death, *Star Trek* producer Gene Roddenberry was at work on his last film subtitled *The Undiscovered Country*, a Shakespearean allusion to death. When Francis Ford Coppola's son died in a tragic boating accident, the famed director was directing the film *Gardens of Stone* concerning a cemetery. And when martial artist Bruce Lee's son Brandon died during filming of the fantasy drama *The Crow,* many viewers were later startled to discover how explicitly the film centered around the theme of death; indeed, Lee's resurrection from the grave in the opening shots was viewed by more than one critic as uncannily analogous to the renewed popularity the actor experienced during the posthumous release of this film.

A similar pattern of meaningfulness is visible in the uncanny timeliness of song titles or lyrics surrounding the deaths of many famous singers. When he died, Hank Williams' most popular recording was "I'll Never Get Out of This World Alive." At the time of his death in 1960, rock and roll singer Eddie Cochrane was beginning to enjoy the popularity of "Three Steps to Heaven." Pop music legend Buddy Holly died in a plane crash in 1959; at the time, his song "It Doesn't Matter Anymore" was experiencing wide popularity. When ex-Beatle John Lennon was murdered in 1980, he was witnessing his first top-ten single in many years, with the appropriate title "Starting Over." At the time of his death, rhythm and blues singer Chuck Willis had two songs on the charts, titled "Hang Up My Rock and Roll Shoes" and "What Am I Living For?" Otis

Redding's hit single "Dock of the Bay" was ascending the charts at the time of his death, including among its lyrics the plaintive lines, "I have nothing to live for; looks like nothing's gonna come my way . . ." Singer Marvin Gaye's music experienced a posthumous resurgence of popularity with the re-release of his song "I Heard It Through the Grapevine" as part of the soundtrack to the movie *The Big Chill,* which went into nationwide release a day after his death—his song being chosen by the filmmakers to play over the film's opening funeral sequence.

This awareness of the symbols surrounding death is important in the mythologies of virtually all religions. In the New Testament account of the Crucifixion, we learn of the natural wonders, including earthquakes and the darkening of the sky, that took place at the moment of Christ's death. At the death of Krishna, we are told a black circle surrounded the Moon, the sky rained fire and ashes, and spirits were seen everywhere. At the moment the Buddha determined that he too would die, a major earthquake shook the land; three months later he was dead. In a similar vein, many Buddhists contend the deaths or cremations of all great spiritual figures are accompanied by natural phenomena like unusual cloud formations or rainbows.

A more controversial contention held by some is that the actual mode of death contains clues to the life or karma of an individual. Just as the opening moments of a life in some sense preview what is to come, so in a converse way, the specific circumstances of a person's death summarize key lessons or aspects of his or her life story. At first glance, this theory seems especially illogical considering cases in which peaceful individuals died exceptionally violent deaths (as with Gandhi's assassination by a political extremist) or when known criminals died under serene and peaceful circumstances (as in the case of Nazi doctor Josef Mengele dying of natural causes). It may be, however, that it isn't the overt form of death in these cases which contain the relevant clues, as much as the subtler levels of symbolism.

For example, only hours before he died by electrocution while sitting in the bathtub, famed Trappist monk Thomas Merton had proclaimed to an important meeting of world religious leaders that the times ahead were "electrifying." Clearly, it would seem that we should look to the deeper symbolism of Merton's death (a subtle reference, perhaps, to the radical or electrifying nature of his efforts to harmonize Eastern and Western spirituality) rather than its manifestly violent nature. In a similar vein, for many esotericists, drowning in the ocean has been seen as one of the most auspicious deaths possible, due to the mystical connotations traditionally associated with the ocean as a symbol for divine immensity.

Looked at deeply, every death has some significance symbolically. Say a man on his way to church is broadsided by a truck and dies. Here again, the significance of the man's death may reside less in its violence than in the fact that the accident occurred on the way to church. When we examine the patterns in the man's life, we may find that he had continually been "broadsided" by circumstances seemingly beyond his control in pursuit of his spiritual goals. Perhaps he had wanted to be a priest but had to drop out of the seminary to get a job when his father died; perhaps a long-anticipated Easter pilgrimage to Rome many years later was cancelled because of a fire in his home.

As a person becomes more sensitive to the fine shadings of symbol and archetype rather than being limited by simplistic judgments of good and bad, even seemingly negative events reveal deeper (and potentially spiritual) significance. As we see in the next chapter, nonjudgmental interpretations are especially important when looking at the symbolic dimension of human relationships.

4.Gradus.

Chapter 5

A Personal Cast of Characters

We walk through ourselves, meeting robbers, ghosts, giants, old men, young men, wives, widows, brothers-in-love. But always meeting ourselves.

—James Joyce

n *The Aquarian Conspiracy*, writer and futurist Marilyn Ferguson writes of the time in 1962 when psychologist Abraham Maslow was driving down the coast of California in a heavy fog. As visibility grew increasingly poor, Maslow pulled off the main road onto an unmarked driveway in hopes of finding temporary shelter. When he reached the end of the driveway, he found he had stumbled onto the grounds of Esalen, the now famous human potential center. Several people there getting ready for a study group were just unpacking a case of Maslow's books to be used for their discussion.

We are intrigued, or at least entertained, by such uncanny coincidences in our lives, with their hint of an underlying design. But what if all of our relationships or "chance" encounters possess a similarly intricate degree of fatedness, and if everyone we meet is, as Zen writer Paul Reps has said, exactly who we "deserve to meet, or are supposed to meet, or are drawn to meet, like certain water drops down a stream gliding over certain stones on their way to the sea"?[1] The philosopher Schopenhauer speculated that the whole context of world history may be one vast network of interlocking destinies, in which our diverse life-dreams are so artfully interwoven that "while each experiences only what redounds to his own increase, he performs what the others require." Would it not be, he goes on to ask,

> *an act of narrow minded cowardice to maintain it would be impossible for the life paths of all mankind in their complex interrelationships to exhibit as much concert and harmony as a composer can bring into the many apparently disconnected and haphazardly turbulent voices of his symphony?*[2]

Mystics have suggested that each of our ordinary interrelationships conceals a deeper level of meaningful design. Just as the figures we encounter in our nightly dreams are said by many psychologists to represent facets of our own psyche, so each person we encounter during waking life may reflect some aspect of our internal experience. In the timing of our encounters or in the types of personalities we meet, we can, on closer inspection, often detect a certain appropriateness. The Renaissance philosopher and esotericist Cornelius Agrippa reflected this sentiment when he wrote: "amongst all auspicias and omens, there is none more effectual, and potent than man, none that doth signify the truth more clearly. Thou shalt therefore diligently note, and observe, the condition of the man that meeteth thee, his age, profession, station, gesture, motion, exercise, complexion, habit, name, words, speech, and all such like things."[3]

How might this advice help us understand the implications of our everyday interactions? Sometimes, a sense of the design underlying a chance meeting is readily apparent, as in an encounter with an angry stranger on the street just as one is experiencing a surge of deep-seated frustration or rage. Or, one might encounter a respected spiritual teacher in an unexpected location just when one is undergoing an important spiritual transformation. I once bumped into famed yogi Swami Satchitananda in a Texas airport during a particularly significant weekend, spiritually in my own life. For therapists or counselors, this phenomenon is familiar in the uncanny way a client will mirror problems the therapist is grappling with in his or her own life. The insights and solutions found during the session often prove to be ones the therapist also needs to learn.

For one woman I know, this principle materialized in dramatic form. Having suffered the death of a family member, the breakup of her romantic partnership, and the onset of a serious illness, all within a short span of time, the woman began to contemplate the possibility of suicide as a way out of her psychological and physical pain. When her despair was at its most intense, she was taking her accustomed walk across a bridge in her city when she noticed a woman about to commit suicide by jumping into the water below. In compassion for the young woman's plight, she climbed over the railing and talked the woman into changing her mind.

Reflecting on this event in the hours immediately afterward, it became clear to my friend how significantly timed this encounter was in relation to her own dilemma. Not only were the problems affecting the suicidal woman the same as those with which she had been dealing, but the things she found herself saying to the woman on the bridge turned out to be precisely the things she most needed to hear regarding the necessity of "getting on" with her own life. Moreover, the stranger's first name, she learned, was the same as her own. This chance encounter played a critical role in helping the woman turn her own life around.

In ancient times this way of thinking about relationships took on its most extreme form in the notion of *kledonism*, the belief that the most casual and fleeting interactions, including the overheard remarks of passing strangers, hold important insights or clues for one's own life. In *Grand Canyon,* Lawrence Kasdan's wonderful film of synchronicity and survival in modern-day Los Angeles, actress Mary McDonnell's character is jogging down an alley thinking about adopting the abandoned baby she has recently found, when a semi-deranged street person passing by mutters "Take the baby . . . you need her as much as she needs you." This remark, coming at this precise moment and from so unexpected a source, strikes McDonnell's character with the power of epiphany. I am reminded in this context of a writer I met years ago who customarily walked to a nearby restaurant whenever beset by writer's block, hoping that the conversation around him might provide useful synchronistic clues for writing his book. More often than not, he claimed, he found in what he heard the ideas he needed for resolving a problem with the dialogue or action of the book he was writing.

A SYMMETRY OF DESTINIES

Over the course of our lives, this sense of interlocking destinies can sometimes take on a complexity and depth reminiscent of a great novel or play. Consider the curious links connecting the families of Abraham Lincoln and his assassin John Wilkes Booth. When Lincoln's son, Robert Todd, fell in front of a train in Jersey City, the man who pulled him to safety was John Wilkes' brother, Edwin. And when the fatally wounded Lincoln was carried out of Ford's Theatre and into a boarding house across the street, he was placed in a bed where, months earlier, John Wilkes Booth had fallen asleep while visiting a friend. Or consider this story in *Anomalies and Curiosities of Medicine.* A soldier, in the midst of a Civil War battle between Grant's army and a Confederate detachment,

> *staggered and fell to earth; at the same time a piercing cry was heard in the house near by. Examination of the wounded soldier showed that a bullet had passed through the scrotum and carried away the left testicle. The same bullet had apparently penetrated*

the left side of the abdomen of . . . [a] young lady midway between the umbilicus and the anterior spinous process of the ileum, and become lost in the abdomen. This daughter suffered an attack of peritonitis, but recovered. . . . Two hundred and seventy-eight days after the reception of the minie' ball, she was delivered of a fine boy, weighing eight pounds, to the surprise of herself and the mortification of her parents and friends. The doctor . . . concluded that . . . the same ball that had carried away the testicle of his young friend . . . had penetrated . . . the young lady, and, with some spermatozoa upon it, had impregnated her. With this conviction he approached the young man and told him the circumstances. The soldier appeared skeptical at first, but consented to visit the young mother; a friendship ensued which soon ripened into a happy marriage.[4]

From the symbolist perspective, all our long-term or intimate relationships arise out of just such interdependence of life purposes, in which the actions and situations of each life complement the lives around it. Indeed, mystics declare that two individuals cannot even remain in each other's presence for an extended period unless there is some complementary karma linking them. In extreme cases, this sort of karmic symbiosis can manifest as separate lives running along similar tracks over long periods of time, as we see in the lives of some identical twins, in which siblings share not only physical resemblance but often also interests, lifestyles, tastes, and even life events.

More commonly, however, this interweaving of mutual destinies assumes a far less literal form, in which the events or situations of another person's life reflect ours in a purely symbolic fashion. For example, a young woman might experience an emotional breakthrough in therapy on the very same day her mother wins a contest. The developments occurring in the two lives are in some sense parallel in that both express the archetype of "breakthrough" or "abundance," but the connection between them is symbolic rather than overt. In an obverse way, I remember many years ago that on the very day former President Richard Nixon was disbarred as a result of his involvement with Watergate, his wife underwent a mastectomy. In both cases, a profound expression of loss and wounding were present, and each event painfully complemented the other in a precisely timed yet entirely metaphoric way.

Among the more provocative features of this phenomenon is the way a hidden thread of connectedness can seem to link individuals across many decades and many miles. Occasionally, people who haven't been in contact for long periods will discover that fate has continued to shape their lives in remarkably similar ways. Consider this intriguing case related by Jungian psychologist Gerhard Adler:

> *I had started school in Berlin as usual at the age of six. I had quickly formed a close friendship with two other boys, both my age. We had become inseparable, with the intensity and immediacy that boys of that age are capable of. But about nine months later my parents decided to move to a different part of Berlin, almost diametrically remote from their previous habitation. Inevitably I lost contact with my two friends, and I am sure I must have felt the loss strongly for at least some time.*
>
> *However that may be, the story now jumps ahead several decades, when I had been established for quite some time as an analyst. Then I met both friends separately. The one had become a Jungian analyst, the other had undergone a Jungian analysis and was deeply steeped in Jungian thought. In other words, all three boys, now being adults, had made Analytical Psychology the crucial influence and criterion of their lives.[5]*

Though less dramatic than Adler's experience, I have in my own life encountered situations that suggested a similar interdependence of destinies through time and space, often in a subtly metaphoric fashion. Many years ago I presented a lecture to a group of elderly people on Jung's theory of synchronicity, a topic quite unconventional for this rather conservative audience. This being one of the first public lectures I had given, the talk took on a certain importance, and anxiety, for me. Arriving home later that day, I opened my mail to find the current issue of a popular psychology magazine. On the cover, I recognized the picture of a woman I had known quite well in grade school, who had since gone to New York as a model and actress. In keeping with the theme of the issue, she was costumed and posed to depict an eccentric hippie standing in front of a more conservative gentleman wearing a three-piece business suit. He was looking over her shoulder with a vaguely uncomprehending expression. On further inspection, I was surprised to discover several correlations between phrases and ideas in the magazine's lead article and my talk to the group. The article even quoted a line from the poet Emerson that I had used in my talk that afternoon! Because of my previous close link with this woman, receiving the issue at that precise time seemed an intriguing symbolic reflection of what had just transpired in my life: Both my old friend and I were representing an unconventional worldview in a conservative context, both were achieving a new level of public exposure, and both were unsure whether our point of view could be comprehended by our audience. Although separated by many years and over a thousand miles, at that moment our respective lives seemed subtly linked. Again quoting Adler:

> There are these rare moments when the meeting of two fates produces a miraculous illumination, when the veil is lifted and two destinies become visible in their interdependence.[6]

Most of us have experienced examples of this interdependence. I have found myself drawn to an obscure book or topic, only to discover that friends or acquaintances around the country have become interested in this very topic at almost the same moment. Similarly, I once felt an almost overpowering urge to pack up on only forty-eight hours notice and drive a thousand miles to Bear Butte, a sacred site in South Dakota. Later, I discovered that three acquaintances who also lived in the midwest had traveled to that spot, independent of one another, during the same week. Comparing notes after the fact, we were unable to trace our decisions for traveling to this spot to any common source or stimulus, such as television, magazines, or newspaper articles.

Experiences of this sort hint at the Eastern notion of "group karma," the belief that individual destinies are entwined with those of larger groups, such as families, communities, countries, races, or even the entire planet. Under this system, one person's story might act out aspects of a larger archetypal theme or pattern, with the events and situations occurring in separate lives kaleidoscopically mirroring dynamics of a far greater whole. Perhaps my connection with the obscure book or the sacred site reflected my "tuning in" to an archetypal wavelength floating through the collective atmosphere at that time. Likewise, the coincidence of my breakthrough in teaching exactly as my old friend was getting her big modeling break (with the symbols of our experiences complementing one another) might have been dual expressions of a greater trend or energy rippling through one small corner of the collective psyche, affecting many people in distinct yet interrelated ways. In some sense, our actions and thoughts may not fully be our own, but arise from a collective, transpersonal imperative.

RELATIONSHIPS AND THE LAW OF COMPENSATION

Sometimes, the process of interpersonal synchronism may take a compensatory form, in which the traits or circumstances of another person's life and psyche contrast with what is happening in our own. For example, a man lacking in self-confidence may find himself involved with someone possessing a more dominant temperament, which serves to draw further attention to his own sense of inadequacy. Or, a quiet and unexpressive mother who is out of touch with her emotions may find her feelings acted out through the behavior—or even the life-events—of her child. Here the child reflects the mother, but in terms of what she has not faced in herself, rather than in a literal, mirror-image way.

In the movie *Mad Dog and Glory,* this principle is colorfully illustrated in the interpersonal dynamic between the characters portrayed by Bill Murray and Robert de Niro. Murray plays a small-time hoodlum with an active temper, who secretly desires to be creative, as shown in his flirtation with stand-up comedy. De Niro's character doesn't quite know how to express assertiveness or anger, but is actively in touch with his creative side through his work with photography. As different as they seem on the surface, the two complement each other because each represents qualities the other is attempting to integrate and develop in his own life.[7]

The real-life interpersonal dynamic between Adolph Hitler and Charles Chaplin illustrates the same principle. Two of the most recognizable faces of this century, each sporting a similar moustache, Hitler and Chaplin were born the same year, only days apart. Hitler was a tyrant who secretly nurtured a desire to be an artist, while Chaplin was an artist privately capable of being a tyrant. Marlon Brando discovered Chaplin's tyrannical side during the filming of *A Countess From Hong Kong;* Brando was reportedly shocked when he saw how Chaplin treated his own son on the set, barking orders and reprimanding him in front of the crew. Ironically, Chaplin had earlier done a send-up of Hitler in the film *The Great Dictator.*

What shall we make of this pattern? Perhaps opposite personality types are counterbalanced or compensated for within the broader arena of social relationships, similar to the way the creation of matter is compensated for by the creation of anti-matter in physics. It would be only fitting, then, that when this century's embodiment of evil came into the world, its archetypal clown or trickster figure entered as well.

Another historical example suggestive of intertwining destinies between lives that both parallel and complement one another can be seen in the relationship between Thomas Jefferson and John

Adams. The two were opposites in terms of appearance and personality—Adams, short and outgoing; Jefferson, tall and shy. Yet they were close friends for many decades, intimately involved with the founding of the American nation and, most synchronistically, died within hours of each other, fifty years to the day after the signing of the *Declaration of Independence.*

THE ASTROLOGY OF RELATIONSHIPS

The ancient art of astrology offers a systematic way of understanding the symbolism and synchronicities of our relationships and everyday encounters. According to traditional astrological methods, the individuals with whom we come in contact have precise correspondence, symbolically, with the planets and houses of our personal horoscope. Consequently, we associate the religious figures in a person's life with aspects of the astrological chart ruled by Jupiter or the Ninth House (Higher Mind), romantic partners with Venus or the Seventh House, and so forth. Thus our everyday interactions and relationships give us insight into the workings of the universal principles or *archetypes* symbolized in astrology (and in archetypal psychology) by the gods and goddesses of the ancient world. Our ordinary experience, then, reflects a greater drama involving cosmic principles.

If a person suddenly begins noticing dramatic problems in dealing with elderly people or authority figures, for instance, it may indicate challenging energies being activated in association with Saturn or the Tenth House of the astrological chart. This pattern might correspond to a broader set of psychological or karmic issues involving reputation, power, or a person's attitudes toward authority and control—all of which are influenced by the planet Saturn. Significant interactions with women may occur at a time when the Moon is strongly activated in a person's chart. Synchronistically, it is likely that the person's emotions, influenced by the Moon, are being confronted inwardly at that time as well. Theoretically, it should be possible to know what is happening in a person's horoscope by interpreting correctly the symbols expressed by his or her outer relationships or chance encounters.

In fact, according to some astrologers, astrology can shed light on even indirect social connections at the outermost fringes of our lives. For example, the system of houses or areas of the chart referred to above relates primarily to key relationships in a person's environment: father, mother, siblings, spouse, friends. Yet by employing a system of interpretation called "spinning the chart," in which the astrologer looks to the subtle inferences extrapolated from the twelve basic houses, it is possible to find astrological indicators relating to such far-removed figures as the friends of the brother, the siblings of the neighbor, or even the sister-in-law's brother's children! In other words, important events in the lives of these more removed figures show up as planetary activations in the sections of a person's chart that relate to events in his or her own life and psyche.

In its broadest sense, therefore, the astrological view suggests that individual minds are not confined to the space within our heads but extend through the lives of the individuals we encounter over the course of life. In the vast network of people we meet, we witness our own psyches "writ large," as expressed through an extended network of interlocking destinies. Moreover, beyond the sphere of individual relationships are larger webs of societal or national psychology in which our psyches are entwined, and through which we find meaning unfolding within whole systems. Schopenhauer expressed this idea when he wrote, "a vast world-event conforms to the destiny requirements of many thousands, befitting each in his own way."[8]

BIRTHS AND DEATHS

As we examine the dynamics of relationships closely, we notice a subtle grammar encoded in the way events unfold for others in relation to changes in our own life. This is especially evident in the great transitions of birth and death. In the news of children being born, our own or those of people around us, we may recognize powerful signposts of new beginnings taking place in our own lives. News of deaths often carries metaphors of significant closings or transformations in related areas of our experience.

For instance, over a two-day period, I received phone calls from three friends around the country telling me of new babies being born. This same week I began an important new venture of my own. Astrologer Laurence Hillman has described the uncanny way the births of his two children coincided with business projects he had started. We often see the same phenomenon in the lives of prominent individuals, as when an actor's first child is born just when he has made a major new career move, or when an author announces the birth of a child just as she is offered a book contract from an important publisher. Amidst the flurry of biographical trivia to emerge during the trial of O. J. Simpson was the fact that his first child was born on the day he won the prestigious Heisman Trophy.

Deaths are similarly significant. Actor Richard Burton's death, to which his alcoholism and life of general excess contributed, occurred precisely as his long-time lover and ex-wife Elizabeth Taylor was emerging from life-transforming treatment for her alcoholism. In a symbolic sense, Burton had indeed "died" for her. The deaths of parents often seem to coincide closely with major changes or developments in their children's careers, as when George Bush's mother died near the time of his defeat by Bill Clinton; or when Russian leader Boris Yeltsin's mother died just as his authority was seriously challenged by a revolt by political opponents.

CHILDREN, SACRED FOOLS, AND PETTY TYRANTS

While everyone we meet may play a role in the unfoldment of our own life script, children have long been viewed as holding special significance in our lives as messengers of spiritual or prophetic truth. By merit of their innocence and closeness to the source of all life, children have been regarded by esotericists as channels of divine insight. In ancient Egypt, close attention was given to the comments of children playing near the temples, and the Bible tells us to value words which come "out of the mouths of babes."

Great importance has also been ascribed by traditional societies to the remarks of people regarded as insane in the belief that here, too, an impaired rational capacity allows for insights that are normally inaccessible. Unlike the sacred clowns of traditional societies, for whom the balancing act between sanity and insanity was deliberate and more consciously controlled, the true "madman" or "madwoman" was viewed as having completely crossed the threshold from ordinary into nonordinary reality, and could thus serve as a messenger for the energies of unseen realms. For this reason, their oracular gift was double-edged and seen as giving vent to both the highest and lowest and most profane dimensions of spirit. Should a madman or -woman's comments meet with the disapproval of Church or civic authorities, the remarks were deemed the work of evil spirits; if regarded favorably, however, they were seen as channels of divine insight.

The notion of madman-as-oracle has enjoyed a rich presence in the literary traditions of the world. The Fool in Shakespeare's *King Lear*, for example, speaks the wisest truth in the play. In Melville's *Moby Dick*, to cite another well-known example, we see this motif in the figure of Elijah, the deranged man on the dock who utters prophetically cryptic remarks to the first mate Ishmael before he sets out to sea on the ill-fated *Pequod*. Later, the holy fool reappears in the character of Pip, the young black deck hand who goes mad when stranded in the ocean for a time. Musing on the seeming profundities in Pip's mysterious comments, Ahab remarks: "I do suck most wondrous philosophies from thee. . . . Some unknown worlds must empty into thee." (Chapter 127)

We, too, can sometimes access unknown worlds by listening to the words of people who have crossed the threshold of ordinary reality. A friend told me about the curious statements his mother made in the period preceding her death, under the advancing influence of Alzheimer's. Though his mother's rapid deterioration was painful to behold, my friend began to wonder whether her comments might not sometimes conceal a subtler, more psychic sense at work. Once, for example, she made passing reference to a fire having swept through her other son's household. Knowing full well no such fire had in fact occurred, my friend was surprised moments later to get a phone call from his brother, who told him that as a result of a "heated argument," he and his wife had decided to divorce. After this incident, my friend began experimenting with viewing his mother's seemingly nonsensical comments in a more symbolic light, almost like dream imagery, to see if they might hold a similar relevance to events outside her range of conscious perception. On several other occasions, he was struck by an uncanny convergence of statement and fact, a convergence which at one point assumed literal form, when her reference late one night to the arrival of a distant relative was followed by the relative's unexpected appearance at the front door the next morning.

Like the sacred fools in our lives, individuals who in one way or another challenge, hurt, or confront us—our adversaries or "enemies"—can be especially powerful symbolic teachers. When asked who has been the greatest spiritual teacher in his life, the Dalai Lama has often said it was Mao Tse Tung, the man responsible for the murder and exile of millions of Tibetans since 1959. When asked why, His Holiness explains that more than anyone else, Mao has taught him the lesson of compassion and forgiveness. Mystics and teachers from many traditions have extolled the importance of our adversaries as catalysts for personal transformation and growth. They force us to focus on the least developed or most problematic tendencies in our own psyches.

This insight is echoed in the books of Carlos Castaneda. The Yaqui sorcerer don Juan tells his apprentice Carlos of the great value of "petty tyrants" in our lives, those individuals in positions of power who seem to "torment" or restrict us, but who can be used for our own development: "We know that nothing can temper the spirit of a warrior as much as the challenge of dealing with impossible people in positions of power. Only under those conditions can warriors acquire the sobriety and serenity to stand the pressure of the unknowable." Dealing with such figures not only curbs our sense of self-importance, but cultivates such qualities as self-control, will, and patience, teaching us the proper use of personal energy, as well as how to move beyond it. Indeed, don Juan suggests, the true warrior should feel lucky to have such figures around, and might even usefully search for a petty tyrant to help the warrior better "tune" his or her spirit. We should be grateful for such individuals in our lives, don Juan suggests, for helping us to become stronger and more impeccable warriors.[9]

Mythologically, the notion of the adversary-as-teacher finds its most dramatic illustration in the New Testament figure of Judas. Conventionally, Judas has been viewed as the greatest criminal in history. Yet this same Judas made possible Christ's Resurrection; had he not performed the fateful act of betrayal, we might argue, humanity would not have been "saved." In this sense, Judas can be seen not as an enemy of the divine will but as an instrument of it, serving as an agent of transformation and spiritual change. This mythic symbolism suggests we each have "Judas" figures who serve as unwitting agents of personal transformation in our lives. These people challenge and confront us with ourselves. Esoterically understood, such individuals may be regarded as the living embodiments of our most challenging life lessons or karmic patterns. And since every karmic action is connected to larger symbolic patterns in our lives, by coming to terms with the adversarial figure externally, we may resolve a far greater complex of energies within ourselves.

PARENTS

Of all the significant others in our life, perhaps none hold as deeply personal associations as our mother and father. The symbols connected with parents profoundly reflect our psychological or karmic disposition. What follows are a few of the possible ways of interpreting the personal symbolism carried by our parents.

We might start by looking for distinctive or outstanding characteristics associated with our parents. Was a parent intensely devoted to social reform, artistic pursuits, or animal rights? What were our parents' attitudes toward religion or spiritual concerns? Did they get along harmoniously, or fight constantly? What careers did each pursue? Any defining quality or motif that describes a parent's identity or lifestyle can carry symbolic significance when applied to our own life.

Say, for example, that a man's parents were both heavily involved in the martial arts. This could suggest an emphasis in his own life path on issues of control, assertiveness, or defense. He might find himself defending his business from a hostile takeover, or conversely, become a military officer or a contentious trial lawyer. Or suppose one's father was a successful inventor; while this father's offspring may not literally invent things, this symbol could imply a quality of innovativeness or radical thinking in whatever field the person does enter.

As before, however, the challenge here is to avoid applying any judgments of good or bad to parental symbols, thinking instead in terms of the archetypal qualities involved. Parents who are alcoholics do not suggest that a person will become an alcoholic, but rather that there are lessons to be learned concerning sensitivity, responsibility, escapism, or even the quest for inspiration and spirituality. For as some spiritual teachers and psychologists have pointed out, intoxication can sometimes be understood as a misdirected search for higher spiritual experiences, an interpretation suggested by our commonly calling alcoholic substances "spirits." Thus even seemingly negative symbols in a life—like alcoholism—have their positive expressions, which we may choose to actualize if we understand the nature of the energy involved.

Parents may also mirror their children according to the principle of compensation discussed earlier. Conservative parents may have an unruly child, or religious parents may raise a child who grows up to be a staunch atheist. In such cases, the interpersonal dynamic, or dialectic between extremes is significant symbolically, with each family member acting out unresolved issues or challenges on behalf of the other. Yet even in these cases, one notices an underlying archetypal continuity from generation to generation. For instance, while the atheist may not be overtly similar to his or her parents, both parents and child are dominated by the archetypal principle of religion, or dogma. Or, the child might manifest the archetype of religiosity in an entirely different field. A woman whose deeply religious mother has always longed for the far-away perfection of heaven might become a world traveler, with a life-long yearning for far-off or exotic locales.

Another way of approaching the symbolic and synchronistic implications of one's parents involves examining the archetypal meanings associated with the sexes. As the fundamental embodiments of the essential feminine and masculine, a person's mother and father can reveal fascinating insights into a network of subtle connections relating to these principles. Within most esoteric systems of interpretation, women (and the mother) are associated with the symbolic principle of the Moon, while men (and the father) are associated with the Sun. (This is, to be sure, a simplification, but one which is useful for our purposes.) Below is a table highlighting other important associations with the masculine and feminine principles.

Alchemical image of the male and female as the Sun and Moon.

FATHER *(The Sun)*	**MOTHER** *(The Moon)*
outer life	*inner life*
rationality	*emotions*
the future	*the past*
goals/purpose	*karmic legacies*
one's outer persona	*one's private self*
adult life	*childhood*
archetypal masculine	*archetypal feminine*

Holding these basic correspondences in mind, we can deduce many things about our personal destiny pattern. For example, a man's father might be a highly analytic and emotionally reserved scientist, while his mother is an intuitive and spiritually-minded artist. Employing the association of the father to the outer persona and the mother to the inner emotional nature, we might conclude that the parents' occupations and dispositions indicate a dichotomy in the man's personality, such that his public image is conservatism and detached rationalism, while his private nature is one of more poetic or vulnerable. At the very least, the extreme contrast between the father and mother suggests a polarity of interests or temperaments within the man that needs to be reconciled. Or, utilizing the association of the mother with the past and the father with the future, a woman whose mother is a college professor and whose father is a minister may move in her own life from a past phase or career in which the rational element was predominant toward a phase of spiritual or ideological concerns or development.

Divorced, adoptive, or absentee parents also carry meaning, but interpretation of the symbolism in such cases must be approached in an individualized, case-by-case manner. In general, the absence of a given parent may not symbolize the "absence" of a corresponding archetype in one's life, but may simply indicate a greater emphasis, emotionally, on the missing parental archetype in question. The absent parent can also serve to shift the focus of attention to the parental archetype which is present, thus dramatically amplifying that energy in the child's life. For instance, a highly spiritual man who loses his mother at an early age might align himself with a female spiritual mentor or guru later in life. From a conventional psychotherapeutic standpoint, the early loss of the mother might be seen as having created an inner emotional vacuum his later guru devotion attempted to fill. From a symbolic standpoint, however, it is also possible to see the man's earlier wounding as having made possible a heightened receptivity or vulnerability toward the divine feminine in its higher sense. Said slightly differently, it is often through the holes perforating our souls that the divine can most brightly shine through into our lives.

Another intriguing approach I have been working with in recent years involves looking at critical dates or ages in one's parents lives and superimposing these points onto one's own life. For instance, if a person's father began an entirely new career at thirty-nine, look to the life of his son or daughter to see if a major shift takes place at that age. Or, if a mother married for the first time at twenty-five, look to see what happened in her son or daughter's life at the same age in terms of "marriage," either a literal wedding or a symbolic joining, or new venture. This technique may be further refined in terms of the masculine and feminine symbols listed above, such that key dates in the life of the mother can be equated chiefly with changes in one's inner or emotional life, for example, while dates in the life of the father may be more prominently related to changes or decisions in one's worldly or external activities.

For example, a musician's father married at thirty-five; at this same age, the musician signed his first recording contract—a corresponding "marriage" of sorts to a recording company and the public-at-large. The musician's mother was twenty-seven when she married his father; at the same age, the musician experienced an important emotional turning point as a result of intensive therapy, a major breakthrough in facing his fears of performing.

In some respects, the general concept of date synchronicities can be associated with the psychological principle of the "anniversary reaction," in which an individual subconsciously associates a given period or age with a key emotional event in his or her own life or in the life of a loved one. Elvis Presley, for example, had an unusually close connection with his mother. Presley claimed that her death at forty-three was also a "death" for him. Given the synchronicities involved, it should come as no surprise that Presley himself was forty-three when he died.

GENEALOGY: DECIPHERING THE FAMILY TREE

Taking this symbolism associated with parents one level deeper, it is possible to find meanings throughout one's ancestry or genealogy. If parents reveal key insights into the archetypal foundation or "ground karma" of this lifetime, by following back the roots of one's family tree into previous generations, one might uncover even subtler insights into one's unconscious nature.

Here again, the simplest starting point is to consider the most notable features or achievements of one's ancestors, their careers or occupations, unusual experiences, or other distinguishing characteristics. For example, did one's family take part in the Revolutionary War? Does one come from a long line of artists, politicians, or rabbis? As I have stressed, such bits of information may be more accurately seen for the metaphoric meaning they convey than for any literal content. For instance, the fact that one hails from a long line of fishermen probably does not mean that one was a fisherman in past lives, or even that one has a latent passion for fishing in this one. Water is generally seen as a symbol for the emotions or for the deep unconscious mind. Thus it is more likely that "fishing" by one's ancestors symbolizes an involvement in this life with the emotions, or with drawing from the unconscious, which may manifest in a career as an artist, psychologist, or mystic.

Human potentials teacher Jean Houston describes in a recent book her genealogical link to Civil War general Robert E. Lee. The fact that her most prominent ancestor was a famed warrior can itself be viewed as an important symbol, suggesting an alignment with the warrior principle in her present life. Archetypally, this is something which could range in expression from simple assertiveness to a forceful championing of causes. Yet the symbolism of this connection can be refined further. Note, for instance, the association of this historical figure specifically with the Civil War. This clue might symbolize an emphasis in Dr. Houston's work with reconciling "civil wars" or polarities in her own psyche and those of her students, such as conscious and unconscious, rational and emotional, or even masculine and feminine. Here, in other words, the historical symbol suggests involvement in an inner, psychological civil war. Dr. Houston's connection specifically to Lee (rather than, say, Grant) in turn may suggest a partiality to the forces of the psychological "south," which include, by symbolic association, the unconscious, intuitive, and artistic capacities, and the feminine processes of psyche generally.

In short, each individual's genetic makeup is a complex web of lessons and tendencies which encode both constructive and destructive potentials of expression. Imprinted since birth, these family symbols reflect the habitual patterns or conditionings of the past; yet unless they are made conscious, it may be impossible to escape their modifying influences on our personality and destiny. Thus the symbolist endeavor is concerned not only with deciphering the possibilities of the future or the psychological condition of the present, but with modifying the influences of the past as well. The next chapter deals with understanding such past influences.

CHAPTER 6

KARMA AND THE LAW OF CYCLES

All beings who have similar karma will have a common vision of the world around them, and this set of perceptions they share is called "a karmic vision" . . . never forget: What we see is what our karmic vision allows us to see, and no more.

—**Sogyal Rinpoche**

 n the mystical traditions of the East, the understanding of life's symbolic dimensions is inextricably associated with the philosophical notion of karma. The essential principle underlying this idea can be found in many cultures and religious traditions; as, for instance, in the Biblical teaching, "as you sow, so shall you reap." Yet the doctrine of karma finds its most elaborate and sophisticated form in the Hindu and Buddhist traditions of ancient India.

A QUESTION OF BALANCE

Sometimes misunderstood by Westerners as a doctrine of punishment or retribution, karma is a natural law of balance, whereby the effects of all actions or thoughts are ultimately brought to a state of equilibrium, similar to the way a pendulum pushed in one direction will return with equal force in the opposite direction, eventually settling into a condition of stasis. For this reason, the law of karma has been likened to Newton's second law of motion, which holds that for every action there is an equal and opposite reaction.

However, in contrast with conventional theories of cause and effect that operate on a visible level of physical results, karma represents a far subtler form of causality. By way of illustration, say a man is involved in a car accident. He may be able to trace clearly the chain of physical causes leading to this event: the other car hit his after skidding on wet pavement; the wet pavement was caused by a recent shower; the rain was caused by an atmospheric build-up of moisture, and so forth. When looked at in karmic terms, however, the accident may be linked to an entirely different chain of effects extending farther into the past, perhaps even to conditions created within the man's previous life. Some would theorize that the accident served to balance out an occasion either in this lifetime or in a previous one in which the man caused injury to another by his carelessness. However, the Buddhists teach that it is very difficult for us to know the karmic causes of any result we experience with certainty. If we accept the doctrine of karma, our wisest course may be to live now in such a way as to create as few negative karmic results for our future as possible, keeping in mind that every event or action in our lives—physical, emotional, or mental—is linked to both obvious causes and to the subtle, underground influence of the karma we have ourselves created.

THE ARCHETYPAL CATEGORIES OF KARMA

According to Hindu yogic philosophy, a particular action creates a karmic record which is stored as a causal potential in one of several archetypal "compartments," which correspond to aspects of a person's inner soul. The number of these compartments varies in different systems, but they are most conveniently described in terms of twelve areas of karmic concern, which some schools of Hindu esoteric thought see as corresponding to the twelve houses of the astrological horoscope. For example, one aspect of the inner soul may be concerned with family; another with career; others with friends, communications, possessions, journeys, and other major categories of our life experience.

For example, an argument with one's spouse is recorded vibrationally within the part of the soul relating to partnerships. On the other hand, loving thoughts or actions directed toward a friend are registered vibrationally within the soul-compartment relating to friends and associates. Because a given action or thought can partake of several symbolic qualities simultaneously, some activities leave imprints in two or more areas, setting up a complex network of energies among the different aspects of a person's soul.

When the life conditions are right for a karmic imprint to ripen and be actualized as a result, energies are awakened within the corresponding soul-compartment. The result often manifests as an event linked symbolically to the original cause. The results experienced from a stored karmic imprint are generally symbolic rather than literal because what has been recorded on the soul is the deeper meaning or intent of the original action or thought rather than its superficial form. Thus, the same karmic imprint may ripen as results across different centuries, taking on symbolic clothing appropriate to each time and place. For instance, a noble woman who distributed food to the starving peasants of a nearby village in medieval France may perpetuate the karmic pattern of generosity in her current lifetime by donating large sums to an international relief agency. Or a man who created the karmic pattern of killing by serving as the head butcher for the Chinese Imperial court might find himself living in a war-torn city today, in which "butcher-like" atrocities are common.

THE LAW OF CYCLES

To everything there is a season.

——**Ecclesiastes**

The process by which karmic imprints are sown and reaped is not haphazard but takes place according to ordered, mathematically defined cycles known in esoteric thought as the "principle of periodicity." This principle holds that all forms and phenomena are subject to the influence of cycles, with alternating phases of growth and decay, ebb and flow. Karma, too, is susceptible to this rule. How or when a karmic imprint unfolds, therefore, depends in part on the cycle associated with its gestation. By analogy, how a seed grows depends on the season of the year it was planted. A seed sown in mid-winter will take much longer to sprout, say, than a seed planted during the optimal planting period of springtime. Indeed, as many farmers believe, even the phase of the Moon's cycle may make a difference in a crop's growth pattern. Hence, a field of corn planted while the Moon is waxing is said to grow more abundantly and rapidly than one planted while the Moon is waning.

In a similar way, when an action or thought is generated helps determine the intensity, quality, and duration of the karmic result that follows from it. Thus according to some systems of thought, an act of kindness may create a more powerful imprint on the soul if it is "planted" during a sensitive and impressionable period, such as a solar eclipse, than at some other time. Similarly, an outburst of intense anger may create far more lasting karmic damage if it occurs during the start of an important cycle, such as the first day of a new year or on one's birthday.

On the other hand, the activation of latent karmic imprints also takes place in accordance with the astrological cycles unfolding at the time. Like the time-release mechanism on a bank vault, cyclic patterns can serve as the triggering mechanisms by which karmic imprints are released into manifestation. Thus thinking in terms of astrological cycles, karmic imprints related to the physical or earth-based aspects of life may be triggered by an important activation of Saturn in one's horoscope; imprints related to romance may come to fruition during a time when Venus is active in the chart; and spiritual karma by a significant placement of Jupiter or Neptune.

The play of symbols in our lives often reflects a complex blend of many karmic cycles simultaneously. This accounts for the sense of disparity we often experience as various areas of our life cycle pass through positive and negative periods. Just as a woman is experiencing an upswing of positive karmic ripenings in financial dealings, for example, her relationships may be entering a negative downswing, and her work life might be leveling off after a chaotic period. Through a close study of the ongoing planetary cycles in relation to the areas of our horoscope, we can begin to understand the symbolic phases arising in our life to a precise degree.

Importantly, karmic ripenings will intensify, for better or worse, when several cycles overlap or converge—to borrow a gambler's metaphor, when "all the tumblers fall into place"—thus producing an unusually concentrated period of change or psychological transformation. Frequently, periods of great good luck or misfortune in one's life reflect just such a convergence of cyclic patterns, each amplifying the intensity of the other in a cumulative way.

In short, the doctrine of karma suggests events and circumstances of one's life are, to a great degree, influenced by momentums established in the past. Karmic energies unfold according to discernable cycles. To this extent, the symbols that we perceive in the events which occur around us may at times be less representative of our current state of consciousness than the result of states or actions in our past, which are unfolding in conjunction with the cyclic patterns of the planets in our horoscopes. Understanding what is going on during a period of painful ripenings may be at best cold comfort, but a person experiencing a run of bad luck can at least be sure of one thing: temporal cycles are always changing and, in time, the conditions that triggered those difficult conditions will pass away and new and, perhaps, more harmonious cyclic conditions will arise.

KARMA AND THE DOCTRINE OF PLANES

Esoteric traditions have consistently described reality as comprised of several different levels or "planes" of existence, of varying degrees of subtlety. In these systems of thought, the ordinary physical world with which we are familiar is seen as a lower rung on a great ladder of being. For the sake of simplicity, we might divide reality into four essential divisions or planes: the material, astral, mental, and spiritual.

One way of distinguishing the lower planes from the higher is in terms of the duality existing on each plane between the self and the world outside—between inner reality and outer. The highest or spiritual plane is characterized by a sense of undifferentiated unity, with no boundaries between inner and outer reality. Every plane below the spiritual is characterized by a perception of duality, an illusory notion of an independent self set against a seemingly separate outside world. The further down on the scale one descends, the greater the feeling of separation between outer and inner reality. This is most dramatically symbolized on the physical plane by the human body itself, which in one sense is nothing other than the separate self-sense made concrete. Likewise, the higher astral, mental, and spiritual planes are characterized by bodies of varying densities—the "astral body" being less dense than the gross physical body, for example, but more dense than the "mental body." Like the physical body, these subtle bodies are in turn symbolic expressions of the separate self-sense made explicit at each level.

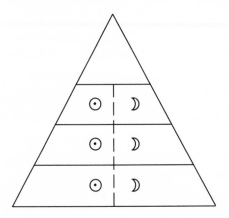

Reality as a four-level pyramid.

This multitiered view of reality is critical for a fuller grasp of the karmic process, since karma operates fully only on the lower levels of the continuum. By its very nature, karma requires a dualistic framework in which to work, because it is based on the duality of cause and effect and on the notion of an independent ego which is separate from the exterior reality it inhabits. After all, in a world of absolute unity without distinctions, what is there to influence or be influenced by?

Moreover, because of the increasing density of the lower planes and their intensifying sense of split between inner and outer reality, more time must elapse on the lower planes between the sowing of a karmic seed and the reaping of its results, or between a thought and its ultimate crystallization. All that happens to us is the result of all we have thought, the Buddha said. However, in contrast with the higher levels of reality where, according to esoteric teachings, a thought may become reality instantaneously, on the physical plane, thoughts and actions which create karma take far longer to manifest their effects in concrete reality. This is not to say a synchronistic link cannot be found between inner states and outer results at the physical level; esoteric traditions clearly suggest there is always a creative interplay between inner and outer reality on all levels of existence, but the inner consciousness is able to affect the outer world to a more limited degree at this grosser level of being.

From the esoteric standpoint, it is also possible to argue that certain events are more fixed, or karmically predetermined, than others, and thus less susceptible to the influence of passing thoughts or emotions. According to some esoteric schools, such life events as death, marriage, illnesses, body shape, and parents may be relatively inflexible when compared with the karma that determines what one's conversation will be with the neighbor on a given day, or which people one will pass on the street on such and such an afternoon. Experiences of this latter sort may thus be more malleable in the form they take in our lives, and therefore more reflective of one's changing inner states at any given time.

P E R E N N I A L   M I S C O N C E P T I O N S

Why are such abstract distinctions important for us to understand? Because the fact that they haven't been clearly articulated or understood has given rise to a wide array of injustices and injurious notions in cultures throughout history. The belief that the outer world is a reflection of one's inner world, or of one's degree of personal merit, has been used in distorted form to justify dubious or immoral actions on the part of many individuals and groups.

Consider, for example, the preacher who tells his parishioners that their material affluence is an indication of the high regard with which the Lord views their work, while the hard times besetting a neighboring congregation reflects God's displeasure with that group's beliefs or level of piety. Similarly, the AIDS epidemic has been viewed by some religious fundamentalists as a sign of God's displeasure with the homosexual lifestyle, and victory in battle has been regarded by warring groups throughout history, as an indication that God is "on their side." This kind of thinking is, at the least, simplistic and disturbing.

The same misconception can be seen in the contemporary New Age suggestion that we each create our own reality, and that what happens to us is a reflection of our inner beliefs or level of spiritual merit. If a woman becomes ill with cancer, according to this notion, she has in some way "created" or "wished for" the illness. Or a man who is forced by circumstances to declare personal bankruptcy is said to have "prosperity issues," while a man who wins the lottery has created the windfall by "abundance thinking." I am reminded of a woman who told me how happy she was about the gifts she had unexpectedly received from people in recent months, since it verified "just how much God really loves me"—leaving one to wonder just how little God must love the starving peoples of Africa or the embattled refugees in any of the world's political hot spots.

Such views result from an inadequate understanding of both the karmic process and its generally overlooked correlate, the law of cycles. While it is no doubt true that we have a hand in creating our own lives—after all, we do plant karmic seeds for the future with everything we do and say—for the average individual, the extent to which we can influence the ripening of karmic seeds is limited by the astrological cycles through which we are passing at any given time. Our state of mind may play a part in unfolding events, but it is not the primary factor.

For instance, a man may suddenly experience a run of good luck in his finances—a stock split, a larger than expected tax refund, and an inheritance from a distant and forgotten uncle, for example—what in astrology would be called a "good Jupiter aspect." As a result, the man becomes more buoyant and prosperous in his general attitudes, which seems to lead to further prosperity. Later, the man's financial weather might take a turn for the worse—the market drops, a client reneges on a loan, and his tax return is audited—and the man becomes negative and depressed. In this state, if the man becomes convinced that his negative thinking is to blame for his shift of fortunes, he may set in motion a feedback loop which reinforces and perpetuates the negative karmic energy several times over. On first glance, it may appear that the ups and downs of the man's finances reflect his shifts of mood. But what is happening to him may really be more akin to taking a roller coaster ride, going up when the financial cycle is high, plunging down when the financial cycle is in a downturn. Though the man's state of mind may have some effect on his financial affairs, the underlying cycles have an even greater influence on the ups and downs of his fortunes.

By the same token, a person's success in utilizing such techniques as visualization or positive thinking to change his or her circumstances will be influenced by the karmic conditions ushered in by the underlying cycles at work. For example, if a woman is at the low point of a difficult romantic phase—what astrologers might call a challenging Venus cycle—it will be exceedingly difficult for her to override the karmic conditions and create a positive romantic situation. On the other hand, a woman in an easy karmic cycle romantically may have to do relatively little in terms of visualization to reap the benefits of these latent conditions. This does not mean that one cannot transcend karmic conditions, but it may take a great deal more work to do so during some phases of the cycle. The best we can do, in many cases, is to track the cycles we seem to be going through—keeping a journal is a valuable aid in this—while keeping in mind that karmic weather changes as often as the seasons. One's astrological chart may not always reveal in detail how a given cycle will manifest—any more than a weather forecast can always tell whether the rain will be heavy enough to ruin a Sunday picnic—but both are good indicators of prevailing conditions and are useful guides to what is to come.

Nor is it only our personal karma and the underlying cycles which constrain an individual's ability to achieve a goal. Collective or group karma also plays a role. An individual woman may have the personal desire to be a priest, but the collective karma prevailing within the Roman Catholic Church at present does not permit that outcome. Collective karma operates within any group of which an individual may be a part—a family, business, community, ethnic or religious group, nation, species—even the whole Earth itself. Like individuals, these collective groups are subject to karmic propensities and to the underlying influence of astrological and other cycles. Thus one's individual karma is always modified by the larger karmic contexts in which it is set, collectively or cosmically.

The relationship between the state of mind of a community or other collective group and the karmic ripenings experienced by that group is complex. Carl Jung used to enjoy relating the following tale to friends and associates, which illustrates one way of thinking about this relationship. Called "The Rainmaker of Kiaochau," it was told to Jung by the famed German sinologist Richard Wilhelm, who supposedly was present at the time of its occurrence.

There was a great drought. For months there had not been a drop of rain and the situation became catastrophic. The Catholics made processions, the Protestants made prayers and the Chinese burned joss-sticks and shot off guns to frighten away the demons of the drought, but with no result. Finally, the Chinese said, "We will fetch the rainmaker." And from another province a dried-up old man appeared. The only thing he asked for was a quiet little house somewhere, and there he locked himself in for three days. On the fourth day the clouds gathered and there was a great snow storm at the time of the year when no snow was expected, an unusual amount, and the town was so full of rumors about the wonderful rainmaker that Richard Wilhelm went to ask the man how he did it. In true European fashion he said, "They call you the rainmaker, will you tell me how you made the snow?" And the little Chinese man said, "I did not make the snow, I am not responsible." "But what have you done these three days?" "Oh, I can explain that. I come from another country where things are in order. Here they are out of order, they are not as they should be by the ordinance of heaven. Therefore the whole country is not in Tao, and I also am not in the natural order of things because I am in a disordered country. So I had to wait three days until I was back in Tao and then naturally the rain came."[1]

This story implies that the disharmony in the environment was actually the reflection of an imbalance within the collective psyche of that region's inhabitants. Through one individual's efforts to bring himself into a state of inward harmony (or Tao), a corresponding harmony was synchronistically achieved in the outer world, and the disordered environment was returned to a state of normalcy. For many Jungian theorists, this story has come to illustrate the mysterious interconnectedness between outer and inner conditions that exists for all of us, and the way outer circumstances can closely reflect our inner state. If our outer lives are disordered (or out of the Tao), then clearly, some have suggested, it is due to an imbalance within ourselves. If we bring ourselves into balance, this line of thinking continues, our outer situation will follow suit.

The view offered by this charming tale is appealing, but it seems to oversimplify what is really happening. For one thing, we must reflect on exactly what constitutes a "disordered" situation—what it means to be out of the Tao. Should we conclude that any situation which feels painful or uncomfortable is a negative or disordered one, and therefore indicates a condition out of the Tao? If one is experiencing difficulty at work, does it mean one is inwardly out of balance, or simply that one is going through a difficult karmic cycle relative to career? Moreover, one's personal difficulties, as we have shown, may be a reflection of a larger karmic condition that affects one's entire company, or type of business, or even the collective economic karma of the country or the world. It would be presumptuous to conclude that one individual's inner state could be "responsible" for such large-scale effects. To cite another example, if a person experiences health problems, is it always a sign of inner imbalance, or simply the reflection of difficult energy being activated in the area of one's health karma, as might be indicated by a challenging phase in this area of the individual's horoscope? There is little doubt one's health can be a reflection of one's emotional or mental state; but it is also possible that poor health simply reflects the natural vicissitudes which befall a body during certain cycles, such as old age.

The same errors in reasoning often occur when thinking on the collective level. It is foolish to conclude, for example, that because the Native American peoples were brutally and convincingly overpowered by European settlers, and their old ways thrown into disarray, the Native Americans must have been less in the Tao than their conquerors. The similar fate suffered by indigenous peoples around the globe indicate that larger collective karmic factors may have been at work. Perhaps, the current movement toward the restoration of native cultures and toward appreciation of their ways and beliefs by many descendents of the former conquerors represents the cyclical movement toward rebalancing the karmic scales on a global level.

To sum up, many situations normally regarded as negative or out of balance may simply be expressions of natural or karmic cycles. Winter may arrive and subject the people of a region to extreme hardship, but this does not necessarily mean they are less balanced or less spiritually attuned than their warmer neighbors to the south. Similarly, it is possible that the difficulties which befall an individual, a community, or even a race could reflect the natural, if painful, cycles of growth and decay which occur for all beings. The Bible expresses this truth in Jesus's remark that the Lord "maketh his sun to rise on the evil and on the good, and sendeth rain on the just and on the unjust." All of life is subject to inevitable phases of increase and decrease, expansion and contraction, ebb and flow. Such variations are natural and inevitable. Balance in the universe requires such changes, and we cannot presume to understand fully the cosmic forces at work in each alteration.

The true test of spiritual attainment is not that one's outer life goes on without any problems, accidents, or tragedies, but that one is able to experience everything that happens—both positive and negative outcomes—as being perfectly whole and luminous, sheared of all judgments, and perceived from a standpoint of balanced equanimity. "If useless thoughts do not hang in your mind," one Zen master has said, "any season is a good season for you."[2] It is easy to feel happy or upbeat when everything is going our way, when the karmic cycles are in an upward cycle and we have no real challenges or problems to contend with. The real test, however, is whether we can retain our sense of humor and inner tranquility even when things are not going smoothly. As the American-born yogi Goswami Kriyananda has expressed it,

> No matter how firmly I keep the "Sun" in my head lit, the Sun out there *will eventually go down. And no matter how tightly I keep the "Moon" in my head full and lit, that other one* up there keeps waxing and waning. I don't know what God is doing; all I have to be concerned with is what I am doing.[3]

FREEDOM FROM THE PAST

Yet if our lives represent a kind of karmic drama, as Tibetan Buddhists have described it, it is natural to question the value of understanding the symbols of our personal play. In other words, if the symbolic patterns arising in our lives are rooted in karmic seeds planted in the distant past, then isn't the effort to understand them a bit like pouring over yesterday's newspapers, or watching reruns of old television shows, which tell us nothing of value about our condition here and now?

While the ideal state of mind may be one of balanced equanimity in the present moment, detached from the karmic energies buffeting our psyches, the fact is, most of us are profoundly affected by the karmic forces at work in our lives. As Carlyle wrote, "By symbols, accordingly, is man guided and commanded, made happy, made wretched." Like actors playing out roles from scripts handed us from offstage, we are generally unaware that we are uttering sentiments we ourselves set into motion in the distant past—often in previous lifetimes—and unaware as well of the hidden cyclical forces that often trigger their ripening. Becoming conscious of these karmic scripts is the first step toward learning to transcend them. Once we accept that everything we say or do creates seeds that will ripen in the future, we inevitably strive to place more positive imprints on our continuum of consciousness. Moreover, knowing that our current state of mind contributes to the ripening of imprints from the distant past encourages us to cultivate a state of inner harmony conducive to the ripening of positive karma. Thus, the process of becoming more aware of the patterns underlying the events in our lives teaches us to navigate better the psychological and karmic seas we are sailing; by becoming more aware of our karma, we take the first step toward becoming free of it.

Traditionally, there are several ways of becoming aware of the karma and cycles influencing one's life. I have already mentioned astrology, with its sophisticated method of calculating subtle energies through a study of the planetary patterns both at the moment of birth as well as throughout one's life. By understanding the cycles of the planets, one is able to better prepare for them both externally and internally.

Another commonly used method in the East centers around the ancient Chinese book of wisdom, the *I Ching*. Also referred to as *The Book of Changes,* this text describes the many archetypal transformations to which all phenomena are subject, and the myriad ways these give rise to the cycles and patterns which govern the unfoldment of life. As mentioned in an earlier chapter, tradition allows for the active invoking of the information contained in this work through various chance-based techniques, such as casting coins or sticks. By interpreting the correspondences set down in this ancient manual of divination between particular coin or stick patterns and the sixty-four patterns of change known to the ancient Chinese, a person can determine and reflect upon the archetypal patterns at work in his or her life and better prepare for the cycles ahead. The *I Ching* expresses the importance of keeping track of the cyclical patterns in life in the following words:

The Superior man or woman
Sets the calendar in order
And makes the seasons clear.

These lines are followed by a paragraph of commentary:

In the course of the year a combat takes place between the forces of light and the forces of darkness, eventuating in the revolution of the seasons. Human beings master these changes in nature by noting their regularity and marking off the passage of time accordingly. In this way order and clarity appear in the apparently chaotic changes of the seasons, and human beings are able to adjust themselves in advance to the demands of the different times.[4]

Other divinatory methods such as laying and interpreting Tarot cards or rune stones work on similar principles. The reason such methods "work"—that is, yield useful information about the karmic patterns and cycles through which we are moving—is that, as I have been showing, everything is connected within a meaningful pattern of design. Interpreting a cryptic passage from the *I Ching* or a particular spread of Tarot cards is a way of linking inner and outer reality. The forces of "chance" which determine which symbols will be turned up in a Tarot spread are, in fact, reflections of the underlying karmic patterns which govern life, as is the mind which interprets these symbols. Keeping track of these symbols in a journal, tracking how they reflect the ups and downs experienced in various areas of life, brings into awareness how much each individual life is a part of all that there is. The more that we are aware of this connection, the more we can use the information provided by the symbols which surround us to live in harmony with the universe.

In the next chapter, we look at another formative principle at work in our lives, one concerned less with the influence of our past legacies and focused more on the potentials of our future.

CHAPTER 7

LIFE AS GURU

There's a divinity that shapes our ends, rough-hew them how we will.

—Shakespeare, *Hamlet*

n the years prior to his enlightenment, the future Buddha undertook a strenuous regimen of asceticism in the hope of attaining ultimate spiritual freedom. Growing weak and feeble from the prolonged disciplines in which he had been engaged, he was sitting one day by the side of a road, when along came a group of singers and dancers. One of them, a woman, sang these fateful words:

> *Fair goes the dancing when the sitar's tuned;*
> *Tune us the sitar neither low nor high,*
> *And we will dance away the hearts of men.*
>
> *The string o'er stretched breaks, and the music flies;*
> *The string o'er slack is dumb, and music dies;*
> *Tune us the sitar neither low nor high.*[1]

Recognizing in these lyrics a timely message about the potential dangers and unhealthy extremism of his spiritual practice, the Buddha came to realize the necessity of exercising moderation in all things, even in pursuing enlightenment. This idea

---

came to be known in Buddhism as the doctrine of the "middle path."

The last chapter explored the idea that our lives are heavily influenced by the actions and thoughts of the past. Many esoteric traditions have described the presence of another force shaping our lives, one oriented less to the actions and influences of what has preceded this life than to the yet unfolding potentials of what is to come. As the Jewish mystic Rabbi Moses Chaim Luzzatto remarked in *The Way of God*, "Things can happen to an individual both as an end in themselves and as a means toward something else." That is, while the principle of karma works at bringing all things to a point of equilibrium or homeostasis, our lives also reflect the influence of a principle whose function appears to be drawing human consciousness into increasingly higher levels of being—as in the coincidental appearance of the singer on the road at a critical juncture in the Buddha's life.

In ancient Greece, this principle found its supreme expression in the concept of *telos*—the tendency of things to progress toward an end goal. An acorn is an excellent illustration of the teleological principle: If we wish to understanding the nature and function of an acorn in its most complete sense, we have to study not only its chemical composition, appearance, and past history, but also its inherent purpose, or fully developed condition as an oak tree. In a sense, the condition of "oak tree-ness" could be thought of as the *telos* or end goal of the acorn, which pulls it forward in its evolution toward higher stages of development.[2]

By the same token, the esotericist would claim that to understand the life of an individual human being, it is not enough to look simply at the past or current causal forces which have influenced the individual, but at the end results toward which the individual's experience may be heading. Like the acorn, human beings are not merely the sum of observable influences and conditions but are the essence of future possibilities as well. While it is important to understand the past, it is just as important to know where human

———

beings, individually and collectively, are heading, in terms of their physical and spiritual evolution.

On a practical level, the principle of telos implies that each of us is subject to a spiritual evolutionary principle which is constantly working to bring us to a realization of our divinity. Toward this end, the evolutionary impetus employs all means at its disposal, including the symbols and circumstances of our waking and dream lives. To paraphrase the first-century Indian master Nagarjuna, the enlightened beings are everywhere, just waiting for sentient beings ripe for spiritual guidance. When an appropriate moment comes, they can manifest as animals, objects, lovers, thieves, spiritual masters, or whatever may be needed to push or pull beings toward a higher state of spiritual development.[3]

One finds expressions of this principle in all major religious traditions. In Buddhism, for instance, we have already seen the example of the Buddha and the passing singer; yet another famous instance of this principle from the Buddha's life occurs in the famous story of the "Four Passing Sights":

Having been born the son of a princely house, the young Gautama's father had wished to see his son grow up to become a great king. Wishing to shield his son from the disillusionments of the outside world, he ordered that his son be kept from beholding any sign of the sorrowful aspects of life. Growing increasingly restless with his sheltered existence, however, the future Buddha decided to venture out into the world beyond his father's walls, where during the course of his excursions, he beheld four sights which changed his life forever. First, he saw an old man; then, a person riddled with disease; then a dead body; and finally, an ascetic-sage who had renounced the world. Witnessing these signs in consecutive order served to awaken him to the transitory nature of life, while simultaneously quickening his desire for spiritual insight and liberation. To the Buddhist, this succession of images was not accidental, but rather a meaningful expression of the all-

pervading Genius of Life, which (as Indologist Heinrich Zimmer put it) is broadcasting all possible initiations, revelations, and messages all the time.[4]

Yet if all beings are being guided, or in some sense "drawn forward" in their evolution, what precisely is responsible for this guiding? And toward what end are they being drawn? For ancient Greeks, this aspect of the cosmic order was explained through the idea of *nous,* the divine principle of rationality which governed and regulated the world, identified by philosophers like Heraclitus and Pythagoras with the related principle of *logos* or Reason. In Hinduism, the teleological principle is associated with the creative power (or *shakti*) of Ishwara, the Divine Lord of existence, comparable to the Western concept of God, considered to be a special Self among the countless transcendental Selves of the universe.

In the nontheistic philosophy of Buddhism, the teleological principle takes on an impersonal cast, with its rejection of both a singular monadic "Self" and of a centralized God-concept toward which all things are heading. On the personal level, our inner potential for enlightenment, termed the Buddha-nature, choreographs all events for the purpose of furthering our awakening. For some Buddhists, as already noted, the presence of symbolic teachings or messages in the environment is explained as the result of countless awakened teachers selflessly operating through the phenomena in our lives to guide all sentient beings toward the manifestation of their innate divinity.

At the other end of the spectrum, life's teleological aspect assumes perhaps its most personalized form in the Christian notion of *providence,* the capacity of the divine intelligence to direct and provide for the welfare of all beings. While the earlier Greek philosophers had described telos largely in relatively impersonal terms, Christian philosophers including Aquinas, gave providence a decidedly personal, even paternal quality. For Christians, providence derived from a benevolent Father in heaven whose concern extended even to the falling of a sparrow, and whose influence upon creation and its creatures was a relatively creative affair, unfettered by the limitations of a universal fate or abstract laws, as had so often constrained the gods of antiquity. For the Christian believer, to say God rules the world by His providence was to say He orders all things in view of Himself, by His knowledge and His love.

In the New Testament, the teleological perspective is glimpsed in various passages, as in the story of Christ healing the blind man. Having encountered a blind man one day, the disciples asked Jesus, "Master, who did sin, this man, or his parents, that he was born blind?" To which Jesus replied, "Neither hath this man sinned, nor his parents: but that the works of God should be made manifest in him" (John 9:3). In other words, the blind man's condition cannot simply be viewed as the result of past causes (karma), but as the working out of a greater, long-range design. As a result of being healed, the man experienced a life-changing conversion to Christ's teaching, with the healing simultaneously serving as a metaphor for others of Christ's purpose in the world. "I have come for the judgment of this world, so that those who cannot see may see," Jesus said (John 9:39). Thus one man's state of health is shown to play a vital role in the spiritual design of his life, as well as in the lives of those around him.

THE TEACHINGS OF ORDINARY LIFE

In our own lives, we can distinguish at least two levels upon which the principle of telos manifests, one immediate and short-term, the other long-range in scope.

In its narrow form, the purposive principle of life can express itself through any events that serve the function of guiding us toward higher levels of learning and spiritual awakening. Who has not at one time or another encountered a situation or person who we later realized had the effect of initiating us into an important new stage of personal growth? These life-initiations can take many forms, even—as it was for the Buddha—as a simple phrase heard in passing.

For instance, a woman who had been searching for spiritual direction in her life contemplated becoming involved with a group of Sufis (a mystical branch of Islam) in her home state of Tennessee. Reflecting on the choice facing her while waiting in the airport to catch a plane back to Nashville, she suddenly heard an announcement over the airport public address system calling to prayer anyone who might be interested in attending Islamic services being conducted in the airport chapel. Never having heard an announcement for Islamic worship in all her years of traveling, the woman thought the announcement might be a hint that she at least give this spiritual path a try. On arriving at her destination, she got together with the members of the Sufi group and had what proved to be one of the most extraordinary spiritual experiences of her life.

The teleological principle may also appear to us on rare occasions through seemingly miraculous events or confluences of circumstance. A man described to me the period in his younger years when he was, in his own words, "unencumbered" by feelings of compassion or sympathy for the underprivileged and less-fortunate of the world, being more concerned with looking out for his own interests. One stormy night while driving through a wooded area, he was startled to see what appeared to be a globe of ball lightning floating across the road several hundred feet ahead of his car. He slowed down and watched as it continued its slow glide off the highway and into an unmarked muddy side road, where it suddenly exploded in a noiseless flash. Surprised, but being of a scientific bent, the man decided to pull off and look more closely at this spot to see if there were any residual traces of this remarkable phenomena. As he drove down the side road, he noticed a car with two occupants, apparently stranded. Inside, he found a woman and her mentally impaired son who was seriously ill at the moment and in immediate need of medical attention. As a result of the light on the road, the man arrived at the most opportune moment for performing a humanitarian service. He drove the mother and her son to the nearest hospital, where the young man received life-saving treatment. This entire set of circumstances—especially having saved a young man's life—had a life-changing impact on the man's attitudes and direction. The event served as a catalyst for his learning to be more compassionate and eventually led to his becoming involved in volunteer work in his local community.

Far more commonly, however, the great initiations in our lives take a more modest or prosaic form, sometimes even as a compelling crisis or tragedy that serves to awaken important insights or dormant abilities. As the poet Rainer Maria Rilke wrote, "the purpose of life is to be defeated by greater and greater things." For some, this can take the form of a failure in one's professional life. Suppose a man has risen to a partnership in his law firm, all the while becoming increasingly filled with pride and self-interest. For such a person, a fall from grace, precipitated by a scandal, might bring about a much needed collapse of the shallow values which had obscured his spiritual vision, paving the way for the birth of a more spiritual sensibility. As mystics have long realized, and as Carl Jung echoed in modern times, a victory of the spirit often takes the form of a defeat for the ego. Many of the greatest advances in the life of the soul arise in conjunction with developments that, by worldly standards, represent great tragedies or failures.

Illness can also be a teacher in the way it redirects people in ways more suitable to their spiritual destiny, or in the way it forces them to take a more reflective look at their inner life. A striking example of this from Western history is the life of Saint Francis of Assisi who, following a severe illness, changed from a secular lifestyle to a more sensitive and spiritual way of perceiving the world. Many of us have heard similar, if less dramatic, stories along this line, in which people in high-stress positions are forced by a heart attack or other health crisis to reexamine their lifestyles.

In this same category we must also include the illness or "wounding" of the shaman, or traditional healer of indigenous peoples, including African tribal groups and Native American peoples. Shamans are frequently initiated into their role by challenging situations, such as a life-threatening illness, which serve to awaken dormant skills and spiritual perceptions. In his book *Native Healer*, Medicine Grizzlybear Lake describes in detail the crises he experienced early in life which prepared him for his calling. These included three near-death experiences—an illness, a car accident, and a near-drowning. These trials equipped him with new strengths and sensitivities and made him more aware of the unseen world. "The calling [to be a Native healer] comes in the form of a dream, accident, sickness, injury, disease, near-death experience, or even actual death," he writes. Such events are a school of shamanic wisdom:

> *In this kind of school we learn about fear, anger, hate, confusion. We learn about other worlds and how to travel between both. We learn about our strengths and weaknesses, power, love, reality, healing and life itself. We learn that there are, indeed, two separate but interrelated worlds of existence, the physical and the spiritual.*"[5]

Another medium through which life as a teacher can reveal itself is the printed word. In our serendipitous encounters with books, magazines, or correspondence, we may find ourselves stumbling onto key insights or lessons that we need to learn. The late poet and Zen writer Paul Reps was fond of relating how his introduction into Eastern mysticism occurred while sitting in the New York Public Library reading a book on Western philosophy. Unexpectedly, a stranger walked up to his table, placed a copy of the Hindu *Upanishads* in front of him, and walked away, never to be seen again. This singular event initiated Reps' lifelong involvement with Eastern philosophy and religion. Writer Arthur Koestler coined the term "library angel" to describe this common phenomenon, in which a book suddenly presents itself in our lives by falling off a shelf or by unexpectedly being given to us, exactly when we are most in need of the information it holds.

Some Christians seek the help of this particular "angel" by opening the Bible at random to get advice on a problem at hand. For instance, a woman I know set out on a trip to do a spiritual retreat in a cabin on private land in Utah, high on a butte adjacent to Zion National Park. On her way, she was stranded for more than two weeks in Oklahoma City waiting for an engine part to be shipped in from out of state. Exasperated and depressed, she opened the Bible in her hotel room one night; her finger alighted on Isaiah 2:2-3: "And it shall come to pass in the last days, that the mountain of the Lord's house shall be established in the top of the mountains, and shall be exalted above the hills; and all nations shall flow into it. And many people shall go up to the house, and he will teach us the way, for out of Zion shall go forth the law." Startled and encouraged by this message, she persevered in her efforts to reach her own mountain in Zion.

A similar but more momentous example occurred in the life of the great Latin scholar Petrarch. In 1336, armed with a copy of St. Augustine's *Confessions*, Petrarch set off to ascend Mount Ventoux in Italy. Upon reaching the top, he opened the book at random to the startling words: "And men go abroad to admire the heights of mountains, the mighty billows of the sea, the broad tide of rivers, the compass of the ocean, and the circuits of the stars, and pass themselves by." Stunned by the coincidence between this passage and his situation, Petrarch was catalyzed into a process of introspection and transformation that led to his influential writings, pointed to by some as a symbolic starting point for Renaissance thought, with its emphasis on the individual psyche and human interiority.[6]

LIFE AS GURU—THE BROADER PERSPECTIVE

Beyond its narrower form, however, the purposive qualities of life's teaching also reveal their effects across the span of an entire life, possibly even several lives. At this level, we see the individual soul guided along in its development not simply by isolated events or symbols, but by means of the shaping influence of experiences transpiring over many years. The philosopher Schopenhauer described how in looking back over the course of one's life, certain encounters and events which seemed purely accidental at the time begin revealing themselves as crucial structuring features of an unintended life story; as a result of these broad changes, the potentialities of one's character are fostered to fulfillment, almost as if the course of one's own biography were a cleverly constructed novel.[7] Of course, this sense of overall design is rarely visible to us as we are living the events and usually presents itself only from the retrospective standpoint of many decades.

Jungian psychologist Edward C. Whitmont has suggested a similar perspective on how we might look at traumatic events in childhood. If we allow the "destiny" concept into our interpretation of life stories, then what we have commonly viewed as traumas which lead an individual to experience mental or emotional difficulties in later life may instead be seen as vital stages within an emergent life-pattern. "Traumatic events of childhood which we associate with the genesis of neurosis or psychosis, and therefore regard as quasi-accidental or avoidable under 'ideal' circumstances, may perhaps be seen as essential landmarks in the actualization of a pattern of wholeness."

He goes on to liken the unfoldment of life conditions to the stages of a Greek tragedy. In Act One, the basic conditions which establish the foundation of the entire story are set. In Act Two, challenges or misfortunes are introduced into the setting, while in Act Three, the challenge is brought to a final resolution. Now, although the misfortunes of the second act can be viewed in terms of cause-and-effect dynamics arising out of Act One, from the standpoint of the greater story line, they may also be seen as necessary stages in a pattern of growth not readily apparent until the final act of the play. Similarly, Whitmont suggests that the challenges which arise early in our lives may compel us toward modes of action whose purpose lies within a broader developmental design, provided we are capable of bringing emotional awareness and insight to the larger issues raised by those earlier stages.[8]

History provides us with many colorful examples which illustrate the influence of teleological principles in action. Recall, for example, the life of the ancient Greek orator Demosthenes, who early in life experienced great difficulty communicating with others. Through the process of struggling to overcome his own inherent limitations (involving such practices as shouting into the surf and learning to ennunciate with mouthfuls of pebbles), he eventually succeeded in becoming one of history's greatest elocutionists. In one sense, the process of having to struggle beyond his limitations became the very thing which made possible his later excellence as an orator. Then there is the case of Helen Keller, whose sensory limitations only served to temper the inherent greatness of the woman in a way that may not have been possible had she been a normally endowed child.

In the annals of spiritual storytelling, I know of no tale which expresses this sense of long-range purposiveness in life more beautifully than in the Sufi tale of "Fatima the Spinner," which is worth relating here at length:

Once upon a distant time there was a young woman named Fatima, who was the daughter of a prosperous spinner. One day her father asked her to go on a long journey to an island across the sea where he was to do business; while there, he thought, perhaps she would find herself a husband. Along the way, however, a great storm blew up, dashing the ship against the rocks and killing the father. Fatima found herself half-conscious, washed up on the shore, with little memory of her past. Destitute and suffering from exposure, a family of cloth-makers found her and, taking pity on her, invited her into their home. There she lived for two years, learning the skills of their trade.

One day, a band of slave traders invaded the family's dwelling, taking Fatima and her new companions to Istanbul, where she was to be sold as a slave. Her world had collapsed for the second time. Among the buyers at the market was a man looking for slaves to work in his woodyard, where he made masts for ships. When he saw the dejection of the unfortunate Fatima, he decided to purchase her, thinking he might be able to give her a slightly better life than if she were bought by someone else by making her a serving maid for his wife. On returning home, however, the mastmaker discovered that pirates had stolen all his money and valuables. Thus Fatima, the man, and his wife were left to run the business by themselves, and Fatima now learned the skill of making masts. She was grateful to the man, however, and worked hard. In return, he granted her freedom, and she became his trusted helper.

One day he told her, "I want you to go as my agent to Java and sell masts." But while sailing off China, a typhoon struck, and once again, she found herself washed up on shore, penniless, and far from home. Feeling confused and despondent over why such ill-fortune had befallen her again, she began walking inland. Now, it so happened, there had been a legend in China that someday a female stranger would come from a distant land and make a tent for the Emperor. And because no one knew how to make tents, everybody looked forward with excitement to this event. Through the years, successive Emperors had sent heralds throughout the land each year asking that any foreigners be sent to the imperial court.

When Fatima stumbled into a town by the Chinese seashore, it was one such occasion. The people spoke to her through an interpreter and explained that she would have to go see the Em-

peror. On reaching the court, the Emperor asked Fatima if she knew how to make a tent. She replied, "I think so." First, she asked for flax, and using the skill learned from her father, she spun some rope. Since there was no stout cloth in the region, she used the skill she had learned from the family of cloth-makers to weave some. And needing tent-poles, she recalled her time spent in Istanbul making masts to make these as well. Putting these elements all together, she was able to make a tent for the Emperor.

Delighted, the Emperor offered her the fulfillment of any wish she might have. She chose to live in China, where she eventually met and married a handsome prince. There she remained in happiness, surrounded by children until the end of her days.[9]

In this tale we see how one individual's repeated encounters with apparent tragedy actually proved essential to the fulfillment of a greater destiny, with each skill or lesson learned along the way eventually serving this final end. Note the close similarity of the lead character's name with our word for "fate." That a specifically *royal* marriage results from Fatima's misfortunes tips us to the fact we are dealing here with archetypal symbols. A royal marriage is one of the perennially employed esoteric images for enlightenment or spiritual fulfillment. In its broader meaning, this story speaks to the intricate evolutionary design underlying each of our lives as we move towards our own royal marriage, the union of opposites implicit within spiritual self-realization. Seen in a larger context, the twists and turns of fortune that impact each of us make sense only when seen against the backdrop of our long-range spiritual development.

To be sure, this philosophical viewpoint opens itself to obvious questions and concerns, recalling Voltaire's broadside against naively providential thinking in *Candide:* "All is for the best in the best of all possible worlds." After all, where is the "design" behind the child dying of starvation in Africa or the divine purpose in the story of a good person turned to a life of crime? And what providential energy would be responsible for the loving father murdered by a terrorist? It is just as obvious that the notion of design in an individual's life may not always mean a specifically spiritual design; for even though all lives are in some sense appropriate to the characters of those experiencing them, often these do not display any obvious sense of evolutionary, spiritual direction. The events in Hitler's early life, including his failure as an artist and numerous close calls with death, may be said to exhibit a certain fatedness in their unfoldment; yet one could hardly call this an evolutionary or spiritual pattern.

For the esotericist, however, such problems are perhaps best understood when seen in the framework of reincarnation. That is, while the spiritual dimension of life-purposiveness may not always be obvious within the context of a single lifetime, over the course of many lives, the seeming detours and cul-de-sacs of destiny take on far different significance as integral stages in a much greater journey of evolution. As mystics have been careful to stress, the higher Self perceives with a very different sense of time than the surface ego, and evolves in terms of spiritual growth over eons of time rather than the seventy or eighty years of a single human lifetime. As one example of this, the famed authority on death and dying Elisabeth Kübler-Ross tells the story of a conversation she says she had with a nonphysical being she describes as one of her guides. The guide told Kübler-Ross: "When I'm born again to a human body, I want to die of starvation, as a child." Never one to believe in the ennobling effects of suffering, Kübler-Ross responded with brutal frankness: "You choose to be born to die of starvation! What kind of idiot are you?" To which her guide remarked, with great love: "Elisabeth, it would enhance my compassion."[10]

THE LIVING GURU

Of all the forms through which the principle of spiritual evolution can express itself, perhaps the most direct is through the figure of the living spiritual teacher or guru. For while the divine teachings which propel us toward spiritual unfoldment can assume any number of forms as we have seen, because of the vitally interactive process possible with another human being, a flesh-and-blood spiritual mentor offers a more concentrated vehicle through which divine guidance may be imparted.

On the most basic level, the spiritual teacher serves as a valuable source of advice and instruction, dispensing wisdom to the student on a need-to-know basis. Esoterically understood, however, the outer teacher is understood to be the embodiment of an individual seeker's own *inner* guru, or innate spiritual wisdom. In the words of the Tibetan Buddhist teacher Sogyal Rinpoche,

> *When we have prayed and aspired and hungered for the truth for a long time, for many, many lives, and when our karma has become sufficiently purified, a kind of miracle takes place. And this miracle, if we can understand and use it, can lead to the ending of ignorance forever: The inner teacher, who has been with us always, manifests in the form of the "outer teacher," whom, almost as if by magic, we actually encounter. This encounter is the most important for any lifetime. . . .Who is this outer teacher? None other than the embodiment and voice and representative of our inner teacher. The master whose human shape and human voice and wisdom we come to love with a love deeper than any other in our lives is none other than the external manifestation of the mystery of our own inner truth.[11]*

Through the mirror of the outer guru, or spiritual teacher, we are introduced to the truth of our own higher Self. Through his or her example, we see a mirror image of our highest nature in concrete form, and thereby may discern the direction we need to follow in terms of compassion, wisdom, and balance. In a form of practice broadly referred to as "guru yoga," every action or interaction with the guru may be contemplated for the important insight it offers into the lessons one is struggling to learn.

However, precisely because the teacher is the divine mirror through which we see ourselves, he or she may also serve to highlight all that is less than fully pure or spiritually refined in ourselves. Some would argue the chief value of a living master is his or her laser-like ability to highlight our least spiritual aspects, in a way not possible in interaction with a symbolic representation of spiritual wisdom, such as a book of scriptures. As the controversial Western guru Da Free John once summed it up, "Dead gurus don't kick ass. . ."

For this reason, even the most disillusioning encounter with a teacher or guru can hold great value in teaching us vital lessons about ourselves. For instance, consider the case of someone who studies under a teacher who demands unquestioning obedience and servitude, leaving no room for independent thought or decision-making. Later, this person discovers that the guru is selfishly using his students for personal ends. Even here, there may be important insights for the student, if only in dramatizing the dangers of being overly naive or of locating the source of divine guidance so completely outside himself. However painful such a tragic awakening, the teacher's flaws could still serve the ultimate end of bringing the student closer to divine truth. Indeed, it is sometimes said that we get exactly the teacher we deserve, each of us being brought to ultimate truth in the manner most fitting our personality and our spiritual needs.

INVOKING THE TEACHING OF LIFE

Among the more intriguing aspects of the teleological principle is that it can be invoked at will. Recall the well-known spiritual axiom, "When the student is ready, the teacher will appear"; so through the cultivation of a properly receptive and reverent attitude, we can accelerate the teaching process as it appears not only through living teachers, but though events, dreams, and symbols of

many types. In *Out Of Africa,* writer Karen Blixen (Isak Dinesen)
expressed a similar sentiment in these words:

> *Many people think it an unreasonable thing, to be looking for a
> sign. This is because of the fact that it takes a particular state of
> mind to be able to do so, and not many people have found them-
> selves in such a state. If, in this mood, you ask for a sign, the
> answer cannot fail you; it follows as the natural consequence of
> the demand.*

The process of asking for spiritual signs and teachings can be
facilitated through fervent prayer, fasting, and meditation, all of
which can help serve to align one more fully with the hidden intelligence guiding our lives. A dramatic example of this idea is seen in
the Native American "vision quest," in which the participant leaves
ordinary life behind and lives for a time in an isolated condition in
nature, in the hope of receiving a specific vision or life-teaching.
Though it is commonly believed the sought revelation must take
the form of an actual vision of some sort, it can just as easily take
the form of a dramatic natural event or synchronistic happening
involving an animal, object, or process of nature. And while prefer-
able, one does not necessarily need to go out into the wilderness to
undertake a vision quest. The cultivation of a spirit of receptivity
will produce results in almost any environment, sometimes in an
unexpected and unconventional symbolic form. Even a city dweller
can undertake a vision quest of sorts by engaging in several days of
mild fasting, periods of daily meditation, and an extra attentiveness
to dreams and other symbols that appear. During such a period,
every telephone message, remembered dream, encounter with a
stranger, invitation—and even the advertisements on the sides of
buses—can carry potent messages about one's life direction or spiritual choices.

In summary, the evolutionary principle which propels us toward spiritual unfoldment draws not only on the qualities of the

present moment, but on the influences of both past and future. If we liken our life-drama to a kind of script, ours is a story comprised of karmic factors from an earlier time along with the purposive influences of future potentialities. Like the acorn, which is both a product of past influences (genetic, environmental, and chemical conditions) and future influences or coded biological potentialities, our own lives and circumstances represent a meshing of both past and future influences, seen in the symbols arising within ordinary experience. These interact in a dialectic process to reweave the legacies of past karma with the possibilities of future imperatives, drawing us ever closer to the enlightened realization of Self.

CHAPTER 8

THE WAY OF RITUAL

You see, man is in need of a symbolic life ... But we have no symbolic life. Where do we live symbolically? Nowhere, except where we participate in the ritual of life. But, who, among the many, are really participating in the ritual of life? Very few.

—Carl Jung

n 1986, television viewers around the world witnessed the modern re-enactment of an ancient ritual, as the Summer Olympics commenced on American soil for the first time in history. In the weeks leading up to the opening ceremony, viewers watched as relay runners made their way across the continent, each carrying the ceremonial torch that would be used to ignite the Olympic flame atop the Los Angeles Coliseum.

Almost as fascinating as the ritual itself, however, was the reaction of men, women, and children lined up along the route taken by the runners. Panning through the crowd, television cameras revealed face after face streaming with tears in enthusiastic but reverent awe at this first-hand glimpse of history unfolding. People of all ages and races were profoundly moved by the occasion—but what were they really responding to?

As I pondered this question, I wondered not only about this

particular ritual but about the nature and power of symbols generally. How might this same ritual have affected people had the runner been holding a flashlight instead of a torch? Or, even more incongruously, a ceremonial briefcase? And suppose the runners had been dressed in business suits instead of running shorts, and instead of making their way on foot, rode in the back of open-air limousines? Somehow it seemed obvious, to some degree at least, that the power of this spectacle resulted from the specific choice of symbols, and that these symbols spoke to the psyches of viewers in a way other images might not. Perhaps the image of a lone runner traversing a vast distance to ignite a great fire draws its power from echoing the trek each of us is engaged in, as we journey alone toward the great light of spiritual illumination. Indeed, the succession of runners trading off the torch might be seen as symbolizing the series of reincarnated lifetimes esotericists say we all pass through—a spiritual journey which requires a series of bodies over time.

For many esotericists, *ritual* has been defined as the art of using symbols to transform reality or consciousness in accordance with the will. To understand this definition, recall the discussion in chapter one of the theory of correspondences. This theory holds that all objects and events are linked through a network of subtle affinities or sympathies. Ritual draws upon this natural interrelatedness. Through the manipulation of objects and events, a ritual is thought to effect corresponding phenomena in both outer and inner reality. Ritual which seeks to influence or transform outer, physical reality has traditionally been termed *thaumaturgical*, while ritual which seeks to affect inner, or spiritual reality has been called *theurgical*. Using magical techniques to attract wealth or to bring harm to an enemy are examples of thaumaturgical ritual; partaking in the sacrament at Mass in hopes of achieving higher states of spiritual attunement, or reciting mantras or using visualization techniques during meditation to induce changes in consciousness are examples of theurgical ritual.

Expressed in psychological terms, symbols such as the wine and bread of the Mass speak directly to the unconscious mind. Ritual thus attempts to bypass the surface consciousness and act directly upon the deeper psychic nature, subconsciously or superconsciously. Indeed, as some have argued, the reason that religion engages us so much more powerfully and passionately than either politics or philosophy is that it speaks to us in the language of symbols and images rather than in facts or ideas. Politicians have always known this, and often employ powerful secular rituals—saluting the flag, laying a wreath, bestowing a medal—to move constituents to support them and their views.

Taken to its logical extreme, this mystical understanding of ritual holds far-reaching consequences; for if everything is interrelated, and if all objects and events have correspondences with inner states, then theoretically there is no action which is *not* "ritual," which does not have resonances or effects on higher planes. As magicians and esoteric practitioners throughout history have known, all actions are "magical"; how one walks, sits, sleeps, arranges one's home, eats, works, even the thoughts one holds in mind have subtle effects, reverberating across the levels of reality. Said another way, lifestyle *is* religion.

THE SECRET POWER OF RITUAL

But if all actions are rituals, why do certain actions hold more power than others? And what determines a ritual's degree of effectiveness? And why does the same ritual or action lead to different results for different people? To answer such questions, we need to explore the important distinction between ritual *form* and ritual *intent*.

Consider two men who travel great distances to reach the river Ganges in India. One is a devout Hindu who has waited his entire life to bathe in the holy waters of the sacred river, while the other is a travel-weary tourist for whom the river represents another stop on a seemingly endless tour of India. The devout Hindu arrives at the banks of the river, ecstatic at finally achieving a lifelong goal, and while bathing in the river's waters, has a profound mystical experience. The tourist, by contrast, walks to the edge of the river, inadvertently gets his feet wet while walking near the banks, then returns to the tour bus, unfazed by his encounter with the "sacred" waters.

In both cases, the same essential action was performed: a long journey to the river, climaxed by physical contact with the waters— yet the results are different. Why? Whereas the Hindu invested the action with a lifetime's worth of devotion and expectation (with roots extending deep into the collective Indian psyche), for the tourist, the only feelings or thoughts brought to the action were boredom and inattention. Thus the attitude or intent of the person performing an action largely determines whether the action has symbolic or ritual content and what its results will be.

Thus while the external form is by itself an important part of a ritual process, its true power lies in the quality of attunement or imaginal "charge" brought to bear on the symbolic form. To say it another way, a true ritual is an internal rather than an external event. The outer ritual form serves as a kind of lens through which the participant focuses psychic energies and the energy of the universe toward a specific end. In turn, the transformative qualities of any action are in direct relationship to the state of awareness brought to bear upon it. Although the ritual form may itself possess a certain power due to the nature of the symbols being used, without the application of conscious intent or attunement, its effect will be limited.

Another example of this idea is music. A piece of sheet music, say, Beethoven's "Moonlight Sonata," can be seen as a kind of ritual form in the way it employs a set of abstract symbolic patterns (musical tones and their geometrical relationships) to transform the consciousness of the performer or listener. Yet the power that a musical score holds depends on the state of mind of the performer and the listener. Even a work of Beethoven will have little or no transformative power if played without emotion or if heard by an unresponsive listener. This does not mean that the score itself is not important or useful; rather, it serves the valuable function of helping one better "tune into" a desired state.

THE ORDINARY AS SACRED

While it may be tempting to think of ritual as something exotic and arcane, our everyday lives are filled with ritual forms or archetypal acts, each with symbolic properties and transformative possibilities. The *Flower Ornament Sutra* of Buddhism discusses the ritual potential of many mundane activities, such as climbing a stairway, entering a house, catching sight of flowers in bloom, or even putting on one's belt![1] Indeed, for a mystic, even eliminating bodily waste can be a spiritual activity. Tibetan master Dudjom Rinpoche has said, ". . . when you go to the toilet, consider all your obscurations and blockages are being cleansed and washed away."[2] This way of thinking is the essence of the Eastern spiritual practice known as *tantra*. Though commonly misunderstood as concerned chiefly with sexual practices, in its broadest outlines, tantra involves employing all worldly experiences toward spiritual ends. Through the application of imagination and conscious attunement, such simple activities as eating, lovemaking, breathing, or emotional states serve as channels for awakening the divine. Hence, an experience of anger during an argument might be transformed into a powerful encounter with the energies of a particular deity; or a simple meal become an opportunity for spiritual awakening when the food is viewed as an offering to deities imagined as residing within the body.

To some, or course, everyday activities may seem too simple to serve profound ritual ends; yet in some ways it is this very simplicity which invests them with power. Many seekers have journeyed far to find spiritual masters willing to teach them special meditation techniques or mantras which promise to awaken their deeper spiritual potentialities. Yet we need only recall that the nine-teenth-century English poet Alfred Lord Tennyson induced "a kind of waking trance" by repeating his own name to realize that spiritual experiences are ultimately the result of inner rather than outer dynamics. Tennyson described his meditative experiences as transcendental, including a dissolving of the limits of selfhood until the infinite alone seemed real.[3] Recall, by analogy, the Christian saying: "Short prayer pierces heaven!" As we look more closely at everyday actions, we begin to recognize in them the basis for many of the world's great spiritual or magical rituals. What follows is a brief look at some of these ordinary actions and their "magical" possibilities.

RITUALS OF THE HOME

As the center of our emotional lives, activities within the home exert a profound influence not only on the psyche but, some esotericists claim, on our overall life-destiny. Many spiritual teachings stress the importance of creating a sacred or ritual place within the home, such as a meditation space, an altar, or simply strategically placed symbols of divinity. Carl Jung underscored the importance of such sacred space when he wrote:

> Have you got a corner somewhere in your home where you per-form the rites, as you can see in India? Even the very simple houses there have at least a curtained corner where the members of the household can lead the symbolic life, where they can make their new vows or meditation. We don't have it; we have no such cor-ner. We have our own room, of course—but there is a telephone which can ring us up at any time, and we must always be ready. We have no time, no place. Where have we got these dogmatic or these mysterious images? Nowhere![4]

The establishment of a sacred place within the home serves as a subtle reminder of the transpersonal dimension of life, which acts upon both the conscious and unconscious mind, especially when reinforced through daily ritual work within the space. According to the ancient Chinese teachings of *feng shui* (a complex philosophic system detailing the proper arrangement of the environment to maximize the flow of positive energy), if constructed in the proper way and frame of mind, an altar or other sacred space within the home invokes a vibration that energizes the entire living space, influencing the subtle mind-field of the entire household and affecting the lives and destinies of those living there.

As in the construction of temples in ancient times, the reverent placement of the proper symbols within the altar-shrine serves as a focusing mechanism for drawing down subtle spiritual energies into manifestation. Thus after setting aside a sacred space, many teachings recommend placing in it a statue or photo of the deity or spiritual figure that most embodies the qualities one seeks to manifest in one's life. If one is hoping to invoke compassion, for instance, one might choose Kuan-Yin, Mary, or St. Francis. If it is enlightenment one desires, an image of the Buddha would be appropriate; or, should one want to generate wealth or abundance, either physical or emotional, the Hindu goddess Lakshmi would be a good choice.

For many traditional systems of environmental symbolism, commonly termed *geomancy*, the entire household can be viewed as a complex set of symbolic compartments, with each room or part of the home having unique significance in the overall domestic energy field. For practitioners of feng shui, for instance, the front doors and windows represent symbolic points of interaction with the outside world (much like the eyes, mouth, and ears on the body). Thus a jammed or squeaky front door might be seen as relating to problems with one's public image or reputation, since the doorway is an important access point to the energies of the universe. Likewise, windows that are broken or papered over might indicate problems of vision, literally or figuratively, for the inhabitants; while blockages in the plumbing might reflect emotional blockages for those living in the house or even financial difficulties, because of the traditional Chinese association of water with money.

Feng shui suggests a wide range of remedies for environmental imbalances, involving mirrors, wind chimes, water containers, or plants strategically placed around the home. For instance, the negative effects of a front door opening in toward a blank wall, which would be regarded as contributing to a blocked flow of energies throughout the household, might be counteracted by placing a mirror on the facing wall to open up the entrance space symbolically and reflect incoming energies in a muted and more harmonious way. Similarly, a cramped, dimly lit bedroom which could adversely affect the destinies and fortunes of a married couple might be remedied by the addition of lights, plants, or even an aquarium (because of the auspicious symbolism associated with bubbling water). A bed situated on an angle or away from walls is likewise considered problematic. Moving the bed to a wall so as to provide symbolic support for the couple sleeping in it can counteract the negative symbolism.[5]

One young man I knew who had been a student of both feng shui and astrology decided to paint a beautiful mural featuring symbols of prosperity and images of Tibetan deities on a prominent wall of his home exactly as a powerful planetary energy was culminating in his life. When it was finished, he claimed to feel a noticeable shift. In addition to some unexpected gifts, he was asked to play host to a group of Tibetan monks touring his city. To his mind, the ritual of painting these powerful symbols under an expansive celestial energy served to magnetize more harmonious energies into his home. Though these may be bizarre notions to our modern sensibility, they are less problematic for individuals who believe in the essential pervasiveness of mind and the corresponding notion that all things partake in a greater continuum of meaning.

Even without a working knowledge of geomancy or feng shui, however, the simplest actions in the home are capable of producing important psychological or spiritual effects. For instance, who has not experienced the tangible emotional shift that accompanies a thorough housecleaning? The act of moving through the rooms of one's home and cleaning out the dust and clutter can serve as a powerful—and readily noticed—ritual for changing consciousness, especially if performed in the appropriate spirit of *inner* housecleaning. For many, such activities take on even greater power when coupled with significant natural cycles (new moons, solstices, equinoxes, birthdays and, particularly, eclipses).

The potential ritual importance of everyday housecleaning activities is well illustrated by another traditional Buddhist teaching story. It tells of a monk who was too simple-minded to memorize lengthy meditation texts and prayers. Instead, his teacher gave him the task of sweeping out the temple every morning and every evening. After several years of this activity, the monk achieved profound spiritual illumination. Questioned about his practice, the monk explained, "As I sweep the floor, I say to myself, I am sweeping away my anger. I am sweeping away my attachment. I am sweeping away my ignorance." Thus through a simple activity, great spiritual work was accomplished.

Moving from one home or apartment into another also carries potential ritual significance. Viewed symbolically, changes in environment are reflections of corresponding inner shifts in one's karmic propensities, and thus provide important opportunities for closing off old patterns and initiating new phases of personal growth. In leaving an old home, one might perform a simple ritual to bless and release the former dwelling space and those inner lessons or challenges associated with the time one lived there. For instance, one might pack the pictures and other articles of the house altar as the last action before leaving the house, after meditating or praying there for a final time.

Ritualized in this way, each act of moving echoes the archetypal process of leaving the womb and entering into a new stage of growth and independence. This symbolism can be underscored by a ritual or house blessing for one's new home designed to banish negative energies lingering in the house from previous owners and to inaugurate a new phase of experience on an auspicious note. The Native American practice of smudging, burning sage, and wafting the fragrant smoke into corners and around doorways and windows is one possible house-blessing ritual. Inwardly, one might hold to the idea that this new environment offers the possibility of a clean start in one's psychological and spiritual development. As a subtle amplification of this principle, some traditions have suggested that the first item one carries into a new house be auspicious, such as a bouquet of flowers, a basket of fruit, an image or statue of spiritual significance, or even a container of money to ensure prosperity in one's new life! Jewish tradition holds that one should bring bread and salt into a new kitchen to symbolize that it will always contain the necessities of life.[6]

WORK AS RITUAL

A person's job or career may play a ritual role unfolding over many years. Most spiritual traditions support this view. One aspect of the Eightfold Path taught in Buddhism is Right Livelihood, which urges practitioners to pursue an occupation that contributes to spiritual development; while Hinduism speaks of *karma yoga*, a path in which action in the world, including work, is viewed as a form of spiritual practice. Jewish esoteric tradition likewise emphasizes the development of skills in a specific craft as a valuable adjunct to any spiritual discipline.

Why is work so highly regarded by mystics of various traditions? Obviously, work serves to ground us, as does any practical activity in which we routinely engage; more important, however, through focusing attention on the mastery of a particular task, we simultaneously focus our inner energies as well. Not only can the discipline we cultivate be transferred to other areas, but through attaining excellence in a single area, we gradually create a subtle opening or hub through which the higher energies of divine genius can flow into manifestation. Though this notion sounds esoteric, we can easily see it in operation when we observe a person who has attained mastery in any area—be it tennis, music, meditation, or carpentry—and glimpse the presence of spirit or genius in their actions.

Elisabeth Kübler-Ross tells of the time she had given a lecture to an audience which included several Tibetan lamas. During the course of her talk, she mentioned that she did not practice any formal meditation technique. Afterwards, the Tibetans spoke to her and objected to this statement, saying she was actually a very good meditator. In her work with dying children, Kübler-Ross described being so completely focused on the children that everything else fell away; it was as if she had become at one with them in soul, mind, and heart. This state, the Tibetans claimed, is a form of meditative attunement which is in its own way very powerful and spiritual.[7] In short, wherever we direct our devotion and creative attunement is the place the divine can enter into our life.

THE MAGIC OF RELATIONSHIPS

For the esotericist, our daily interactions with others provide a rich source of ritual possibilities for self-transformation. If each person in our life corresponds to an aspect of our inner world, then our way of relating to other people impacts on corresponding inner dimensions in untold ways. For instance, we often can identify people in our lives who mirror aspects of our internal nature which are undeveloped or out of balance. Through consciously cultivating our relationship with these individuals, we can also facilitate growth of those corresponding aspects of our personality. For instance, suppose a man who has difficulty earning money knows a skilled entrepreneur and self-promoter who has become quite wealthy. If the man feels jealousy or resentment toward his acquaintance's success, he may obscure, by symbolic association, the karmic propensity for success within himself. By genuinely affirming and rejoicing in the other's success, on the other hand, the man might enhance and encourage the ripening of energies of prosperity in his own life.

Expressed in astrological terms, the way we deal with the people in our external lives has profound effects upon our inner horoscope and its attendant energies. We saw in chapter five how the patterns of the astrological chart describe an elaborate web of symbolic correspondences which include the various people we interact with on a daily basis. Thus, the women around us reflect our inner Moon, authority figures and elderly people reflect the condition of our inner Saturn, teachers and communicators reflect our inner Mercury, and so forth. These associations can be worked with ritualistically to offset the negative influence of a difficult planetary placement. Thus, for example, Saturn in the twelfth house, which may indicate a tendency toward fear, isolation, and self-limitation, might be balanced by volunteering in an institution for the elderly.

The relationship most frequently described by esotericists as a potential area for transformation is one's romantic partner. As spiritual traditions around the world have taught, a lover or spouse offers a profound opportunity for the ritual balancing of inner polarities, which some mystics have termed the "marriage of the Sun and the Moon." As one Taoist master expressed it, "For the mature person, the Tao begins in the relation between man and woman, and ends in the infinite vastness of the universe."[8]

The royal marriage.

A wide variety of techniques have been employed as aids in this balancing process, though all of them rest fundamentally upon one essential principle: through drawing closer to the beloved, one attempts to merge with the partner so completely that all sense of separate ego-self dissolves in an ecstatic experience of unitive bliss. In some traditions this state may be enhanced by imagining the partner as the embodiment of a particular god or goddess, or more broadly as an expression of the archetypal masculine or feminine. Viewed in this manner, all unions can be transformed into "royal marriages," lifted to the plane of a divine union of opposites.

TRAVEL AS PILGRIMAGE

Mecca, Jerusalem, Benares, Lourdes, Medjugorge—all are focal points of pilgrimage for the devout. Exoterically, the idea of pilgrimage rests on belief in the sacredness of particular geographic locations, which have the capacity to impart blessings to all who approach in the proper state of mind. The actual destination of the sacred journey, however, is recognized by mystics to be a vehicle for an inner process of attunement, through which pilgrims align to their inner divinity as symbolized by the sacred site.

The underlying principle of pilgrimage can be applied ritually to destinations beyond the overtly spiritual. For anyone in any field of interest, journeying to a place aligned to one's aspirations can awaken inner potentials. For an actor, the destination of a pilgrimage might be Hollywood or Broadway; for an author, it might be the birthplace of a favorite writer; for a nature lover, Yellowstone or Yosemite. Early in his career, songwriter Bob Dylan made a pilgrimage to visit his ailing idol Woody Guthrie. Whatever the destination, the inner sense of attunement determines the power the pilgrimage holds for travelers approaching a place of veneration.

Pilgrimages are also significant for the dramatic way they seem to trigger meaningful symbols or synchronicities in the lives of travelers. These symbols can shed important light on the traveler's inner state. Say, for example, an aspiring art student plans a trip to a foreign city to view the work of his favorite artist in a museum there. On the flight overseas, he finds himself seated next to a young girl and her mother, who spends the entire trip scolding the child. The negativity of the mother reaches its peak when the child does a drawing with crayons, which the mother promptly criticizes for its imperfections. For the student, this scene may relate symbolically to a tendency for self-criticism or perfectionism which has blocked his ability to access the inner source of inspiration represented by the artist whose work he is journeying to see.

On the other hand, a person might experience coincidences or symbolic events of a more helpful nature, which likewise reveal important clues about his or her spiritual search. Consider, for example, the story of a woman in her twenties who embarked on a search for a mysterious teacher in the Himalayan foothills. After days of frantically inquiring about his whereabouts and getting nowhere, she resigned herself to the possibility that she would not locate the teacher on this trip. Absorbed until that point in her own spiritual drama, she was able to relax for the first time and see the sights around her. She then noticed an elderly man making his way with great difficulty down a nearby road—a man she had seen several times previously but to whom she had paid no attention. Approaching him with compassion for his apparent discomfort, she discovered that while he was not the sought-for teacher, the man did know the teacher's whereabouts. That she had stumbled onto perhaps the only person in the area who had the information she wanted, and did so only after having put aside her own preoccupations to reach out to another, seemed to her, in retrospect, a powerful message concerning her true path. The event indicated symbolically that she would find her inner guru not through seeking a spiritual goal for herself, but through kindness and compassion for others.

RITUALS OF THE BODY

The human body is also a significant arena for ritual practice. Historically, virtually every function of the body has served, at one time or another, as the basis for spiritually oriented ritual. Here are some of the more important of these rituals.

Bathing and Cleansing Symbolically perceived, washing the body represents inner purification and renewal, in which the sacred waters of spirit cleanse away obscurations of the body, emotions, and mind. This belief finds common expression in the ritual of baptism; yet for the mystic, every shower or bath can provide an opportunity for ritual purification and the transformation of consciousness.

This idea can be utilized in a number of ways. For instance, while taking a shower, we might hold the thought that the water cascading across our body is washing away any negativities or impurities and carrying them down the drain. We might also visualize the water as a stream of luminous light pouring over our body, or even imagine that the water is a fluid energy emanating, not from a shower head, but from the heart chakra or "third eye" of a deity or spiritual teacher of personal significance. When conceived of in this way, the water brings with it spiritual bliss or wisdom. Some yogic schools teach that sitting in bath water is an especially auspicious time for meditating on spiritual symbols or for chanting mantras. The power of such rituals is said to be amplified during important astrological events, such as an eclipse of the Sun or the Moon.

Body Position and Posture   The positions and gestures of the body are also viewed by esoteric thinkers to be mirrors of inner states and a means of influencing one's disposition. In many meditative traditions, teachers have emphasized the importance of maintaining an upright posture not only during meditation practice but throughout the course of waking life. Buddhist teachers hold that to sit in meditation in the lotus posture of the Buddha, and to move through life with his nobility, is to feel Buddhahood beginning to manifest through one.

While commonly viewed as a technique for exercising and stretching the body, hatha yoga and its classical postures are intended to work upon the mind as well. Yoga postures allow the serious student access to states of mind linked to the chakra energy centers. For example, exercises focusing on the neck area, such as neck rolls or shoulder stands, are thought by some teachers of hatha

yoga to activate the energies of the throat, or *Vishuddha* chakra. Elaborate hatha yoga exercises like the "Salutation to the Sun" are said
to activate all the chakras.[9] When performed with mindful attunement, yoga offers a subtle but tangible way of purifying one's physical vehicle and altering one's consciousness.

Hatha yoga practice also affects one's flexibility. Body and mind
are significantly linked; thus the increasing rigidity many of us experience as we grow older tends to accompany and reinforce a corresponding inflexibility of our mental processes. By keeping the body
supple through such exercises as yoga, we help maintain a fluidity
of our mental and emotional makeup as well.

Breathing   Mystics from many traditions have taught that patterns
of breathing are a means of transforming consciousness. On the
purely physical level, the breath is significant because of the link
between breathing and our mental and emotional states. When we
are upset, our breathing becomes constricted and more rapid, while
in states of repose or deep meditation, breathing slows and deepens.
Utilizing this connection in a deliberate way, mystics in India and
elsewhere devised many breathing techniques designed to act upon
the body-mind. For example, slowing the breath, whether during
meditation or in ordinary activity, gradually shifts the rhythm of
the mind to a more tranquil state; while deepening the breath effectively draws upon subtle energies (or *prana*) in the air. Expanding
lung capacity is also said to expand and deepen the mental and
emotional natures. One yogic saying sums this up as: "Deep breath,
deep mind."

From a slightly different perspective, the breath takes on ritual
possibilities because of its two stages of inhalation and exhalation.
A common visualization practice draws on these dual aspects. While
inhaling, one imagines that the entering breath carries with it the
healing energies of the cosmos, perhaps envisioned as white light;
while on the exhalation, one imaginatively releases the negativities
and toxins from one's physical, emotional, or mental body, visual-

ized, perhaps, as dark smoke. A variation on this practice is found in the Tibetan technique of *Tonglen*, in which one imagines on the inhalation that one is drawing the pain of all suffering beings into one's heart, where it serves to destroy selfishness and break open rigidity, leading to a luminous awakening of compassion; while on the exhalation, one projects a blessing outward to beings everywhere in the universe. However, it is recommended by many teachers that this technique be practiced only by experienced meditators under the guidance of a qualified master.

Food and Eating   Food and eating have been employed by most cultures as elements of ritual. The subject is vast; what follows are but a few aspects of this important subject.

On one level, the ritualistic dimension of eating is linked to the occult properties assigned to different foods or food types. In one sense, of course, every food is a kind of drug or "medicine," in that all substances affect the human body and mind in unique ways. In classical systems of occult philosophy, however, these effects extend to archetypal dimensions beyond the purely material level, and are linked to an elaborate network of subtle correspondences. Thus through selecting and combining certain foods, one can amplify or minimize symbolic influences in one's life. For example, if a woman's astrological chart indicates a weak Saturn, a condition associated with a lack of practicality or groundedness, she might try to include Saturnine foods, such as vegetables grown underground, like potatoes or beets, heavier dairy products, such as eggs or cheese, or meat in her diet. Similarly, some astrologers warn against eating fish under difficult Neptune aspects or dairy products under difficult Moon aspects. These foods might tend to amplify the negative energies in effect during such times. Importantly, for most astrologers and yogis, symbolic concerns of this sort are not intended to replace conventional nutritional or medicinal considerations in determining diet but are meant to supplement and enhance the effects of various foods.

A related approach is offered by the Hindu philosophy of Ayurveda, in which foods are grouped into three categories: *Tamasic, Rajasic,* and *Sattvic.* Tamasic foods dull the mind, and include such things as fatty or starchy foods, hard liquor, deep-fried foods, and all "dead" foods, such as processed, frozen, or canned foods. Rajasic foods make the mind restless or overly energized, and include spicy foods, meats, and all "stimulants" such as coffee, sugar, or chocolate. Sattvic foods are calming to the mind, and include vegetables, fresh fruits, and whole grains. Foods from these groups are prescribed for different individuals based on their needs.

An intriguing system of dietary classification proposed by some teachers concerns the "distance" between various foods and their source in the energy of the Sun. "Sun" here refers both to the star of our solar system and to the source of divinity within each of us. For example, vegetables and fruits are only one generation removed from the Sun's energy and vitality, since they draw on the Sun's energy directly through the process of photosynthesis. Meat products are one generation further removed, their energy coming from the animal's diet of plants or other animals. Thus meat products carry a decreased level of vitality and, symbolically, a diminished level of spiritual resonance. Vegetarians are, therefore, closer to the source of spiritual vitality than are meat-eaters, whose food is two generations removed from the Sun's light and "divine vitality."[10]

Earlier we distinguished between the form and the intent of ritual actions. In a similar way, we might draw a distinction between the properties intrinsic to foods and the properties they acquire because of the attitude we bring to eating them. A simple example of this principle is the placebo effect described by doctors, in which a patient who is given a pill with no medicinal properties becomes healthier because of the patient's expectations of the pill's curative powers. In the same way, mystics have long been aware of the role our attitudes play in modifying the effects of the foods we eat. Indeed, some teachers have claimed it is less harmful to eat

junk food in a loving state of mind than it is to eat natural, organi-
cally-cultivated food in an angry or disturbed state of mind.

Yet there are subtler ways of adding potency to food. For example, a simple food-based ritual might be to take symbolically
resonant foods like honey and milk (which relate to the esoteric
principles of masculine and feminine, or Sun and Moon and, by
correspondence, the Solar and Lunar spiritual principles of consciousness within us), and stir them together over heat, while imagining
that through merging these two substances, one is drawing together
the polarities of one's being. As an ancient hymn to Orpheus says,

> Mix honey with milk. Drink it before sunrise so you can have
>   something holy in your heart.
> Remember—many pretend; few know.[11]

Or consider the many rituals which involve accepting food from
a priest or other spiritual figure, as in the Catholic Mass, the Hindu
practice of eating blessed foods known as *prasad*, or the Buddhist
ritual feasts called *tsog* offerings. Eating sacred food is said to trans-
mit higher vibrations to the participant in such rituals, while also
sending a symbolic message to the higher mind that one is opening
to (or eating) the divine principle of life. Esoteric traditions also
suggest that this same principle can be applied to ordinary meals.
We can visualize that all food we eat is being given to us by a chosen spiritual mentor, whether it be Christ, the Buddha, or one's personal spiritual teacher, thus transforming each meal into a ritual
event.

Taking this process one step farther, we might imagine that our
food is actually the body or substance of a deity or spiritual figure.
This idea is actually not as far-fetched as it sounds, as Holy Communion seen esoterically is eating the body and blood of Christ.
Though some Protestant and other more liberal theologians have
argued that the wafer and wine are merely reminders or symbols of
Christ's sacrifice, the more literal interpretation is, perhaps, more

powerful symbolically and ritually. In eating divinity, we become more like that divinity ourselves, on both the conscious and unconscious levels of our being.

An even deeper message is implicit in these uses of everyday activities as ritual forms. Whatever else they help us achieve, rituals are *celebrations of the sacred in the ordinary*, transforming the simple actions of daily life into vehicles aimed at lifting consciousness. The Eucharist, for instance, is at base a celebration of the ordinary act of eating, while baptism celebrates washing the body, and chanting sacred verses or mantras celebrates speech as a sacred act. Thus ritual seen in this way is not designed so much to carry participants beyond mundane experience into a state of transcendence or otherness, but rather to channel awareness more fully into the here-and-now and unveil the intrinsic divinity inherent in ordinary action.

Thus seen in its most subtle sense, ritual is not goal oriented but process oriented. In other words, the ritual form itself contains the meaning. In the Japanese tea ceremony, for example, each aspect of the event, from preparing, to pouring, to drinking the tea and wiping the cup is seen as complete unto itself and is approached as both an art form and a sacred act. Entered into with complete attention, the patterns of the cup, the taste and texture of the tea, even the weight of the ladle, reveal worlds of beauty, bringing the participants more deeply in touch with the nuances of the moment.

In the ultimate sense, then, ritual can be seen not as an isolated or occasional activity, but as part of a general philosophy toward life, in which, as in the Japanese tea ceremony, every action serves as a vehicle toward awakening the divine. Though ritualistic work may begin with a simple practice performed once a day or once a week, it can ultimately include every form or action in our life. Imagine the transformative effect of approaching even the most mundane activity with reverence and attunement, as if one were partaking in a wedding ceremony or Holy Communion. The Zen master Dogen expressed this well when he wrote, "Those who regard mundane life as an obstacle to the sacred know only that there is no sacredness in mundane activities; they do not yet know that no mundane activities exist in the sacred."[12]

Although emphasized more overtly in Eastern traditions such as Zen, the inherent sacredness of every action is the deeper message of all great spiritual traditions. To the Sufi, every aspect of our lives holds potential as a form of spiritual communion; Orthodox Jews practice 613 ritual commandments, which transform every action, even the most trivial, into an act of worship. The Christian Church originally emphasized seven sacraments, a number which attests to the pervasiveness of Spirit in every aspect of our ordinary lives. In this all-pervasive quality lies the deepest mystery associated with ritual. For the esotericist, the human form is regarded not as the prison of spirit, but as the crucible in which spirit is transmuted into new possibilities. Even the act of incarnation itself may be seen as a profound ritual through which divine awareness is honed to a greater degree of focus and intensity. Indeed, the entire cosmos might be seen as a vast ritual through which aspects of the divine nature are renewed or reborn, from cosmic cycle to cosmic cycle. Seen in this manner, the way of ritual is the process of life itself.

CHAPTER 9

THE ASTROLOGICAL UNIVERSE

That the circuit of the stars indicates definite events to come but without being the cause direct [as the general opinion holds] of all that happens, [can be] . . . proved by some modicum of argument: but the subject demands more precise and detailed investigation, for to take the one view rather than the other is of no small consequence.

—**Plotinus,** *Ennead II.3*

f the many esoteric systems touched on in this book, perhaps none is as critical to a deeper understanding of the symbolist imagination as astrology. Commonly seen as an arcane method of fortune telling or simplistic sun-sign psychologizing, astrology is the quintessential science of symbols, which in its broader outlines constitutes an archetypal language which can help us revision our lives. This chapter explores a problem which has long occupied the minds of astrology's proponents and critics: how astrology works. If there is a link between the position of the celestial bodies and the lives of humans, what is the nature of that connection? The answer to this question can help us understand the mechanism that underlies all of symbolist philosophy.

ASTROLOGY: CAUSAL OR ACAUSAL?

Many theories have been proposed to explain the nature of astrological influence. In simplest terms, these fall into two groups: causal, or force explanations, and acausal or synchronistic explanations.

According to the causal school, human beings are influenced by the positions of the stars and planets at birth by means of an energy or force transmitted from celestial bodies to beings on Earth. Some link this energy to a force of nature already known, such as electromagnetism or gravity. For example, astrophysicist Percy Seymour writes of the complex way the Solar System interacts with the Earth's geomagnetic fields: "The whole Solar System is playing a symphony on the magnetic field of the Earth . . . we are all genetically 'tuned' to receiving a different set of melodies from the symphony."[1] Still others believe this force consists of an energy in nature which science has not yet discovered, perhaps of a paranormal or occult nature, as was believed by such Renaissance magical philosophers as Cornelius Agrippa. However, both scientific and magical theories of this type hold that celestial forces act upon humans at the moment of birth by means of a classical, cause-and-effect mechanism.

The acausal, or synchronistic explanation, on the other hand, suggests that the secret of astrological influence will never be found completely in mechanistic theories of cause-and-effect, but only in conjunction with a holistic worldview which sees all phenomena as embraced within a deeper network of interconnectedness. As esoteric writers like Dane Rudhyar and H. P. Blavatsky have argued, the appearance of a particular planetary pattern in the sky at the moment of an individual's birth may not *cause* particular traits within the individual so much as arise *in tandem* with them. Blavatsky, for example, draws an analogy to an ancient Egyptian who yearly noticed the relationship between the flooding of the Nile and the rising of a certain star in the eastern sky. To the sophisticated Egyptian, it would have been apparent that the appearence of the star was not responsible for the flood but merely coincided with it. In this same way, she argues, "the stars do not cause our good or bad luck, but simply indicate the same."[2] The simultaneity of earthly and heavenly events may be called, using Carl Jung's terminology, "a meaningful coincidence," with both the position of the planets and the life of the individual representing joint expressions of an underlying pattern of meaningfulness.

Since the advent of the "new physics," some esoteric writers have looked to Bell's Theorem as contemporary support for the acausal explanation. Bell's theory holds that subatomic particles once in contact, then separated, are able to communicate with one another instantaneously, in seeming defiance of both traditional physics and Einstein's postulate that nothing can travel faster than the speed of light. The instantaneous connection of entities regardless of distance implied by Bell's Theorem is known as the "principle of non-locality." To some minds, non-locality suggests a parallel with the astrological model, which also implies an instantaneous and noncausal relationship between entities—humans and celestial bodies.[3]

Despite considerable support from many in the astrological community, the acausal or synchronistic explanation for astrology can be shown to have serious limitations. To illustrate these, let us look at two arguments raised recently by critics of the synchronistic model of astrological influence.

Bell's Theorem has been used to support the argument that everything is instantaneously connected to everything else. But as Percy Seymour has pointed out, the theorem also states that the communication between particles is not weakened by distance; two subatomic particles linked in the manner described by Bell will remain connected no matter how many light years distant they are. Applying this theory to astrology, it follows that stars and planets located at the far reaches of the galaxy should be as influential in human destiny as local planetary bodies. Yet astrologers have traditionally considered only the closest planets and stars in their calculations. As a result, it might be argued, the synchronistic model cannot be used to explain the workings of astrology without accounting for the apparently localized, highly selective nature of the influences involved.[4]

Whereas Seymour's objection to the synchronistic explanation of astrology centers around distance, a second objection concerns the problem of time. Consider the following example: Astronomers tell us that in A.D. 1054, a massive supernova appeared in the constellation of Taurus, now commonly referred to as the Crab Nebula Nova. Over the years, astrologers have discussed the symbolic significance of this event in relation to events taking place during this period of history, such as the schism between the Roman and Byzantine empires in 1054, or the rise of Norman power in England beginning with the Battle of Hastings in 1066. Moreover, the early 1050s are viewed by many scholars as the beginning of a major cultural blossoming which unfolded in Europe at this time and continued through the twelfth century and included the building of the great cathedrals and the birth of modern individualism. The premise underlying such interpretations is that the Crab Nebula Nova corresponded to personal and collective events on Earth by means of a meaningful simultaneity rather than any mechanism of cause-and-effect.

The problem with this interpretation is that the supernova did not occur in 1054. Traveling at the speed of light from distant space, the image of this event became *visible* for Earth observers in 1054, though the actual explosion took place at least six thousand years earlier. Thus it hardly seems sensible to speak of effects related to this nova as synchronistic, or as due to a grand simultaneity or underlying wholeness; if this were the case, the effects would have been felt at the time of the explosion, not six millennia later. Rather, if the astrological influence of celestial events occurs primarily at the time of their visible appearances, as astrologers have almost universally contended, it suggests that the underlying process is delayed rather than simultaneous, the influence presumably traveling at the speed of light.

In slightly different form, this example parallels a critique leveled at the synchronistic explanation of astrology that utilizes the research of Michel Gauquelin, a controversial French statistician. Briefly summarized, Gauquelin was able to validate statistically one of the main principles of classical astrology: a connection between the births of prominent individuals and the appearance of certain planets at key positions in the sky at the moment of the births. Gauquelin showed that more notable scientists were born while the planet Saturn was rising on the eastern horizon or positioned directly overhead than would be expected through chance alone. Somehow, the position of Saturn seems related to certain character traits or career predispositions, though precisely how this is possible was not readily apparent from Gauquelin's statistical research.[5]

But as Peter Roberts[6] and Michael Harding[7] have pointed out, it can take light from Saturn well over an hour to reach the Earth. Thus the position of Saturn in the sky as viewed from Earth at any given moment is not where it actually is in space. Due to the rotation of the Earth, when we see Saturn on the horizon, it is some twenty degrees removed from that point. Or, to couch the paradox in even more dramatic terms, were it possible to vaporize Saturn, observers on Earth would not see it disappear for an hour, and its astrological influence would presumably linger for the same period, even though the planet no longer existed! For the Gauquelin findings to be so consistently accurate suggests that it is the planet's *perceived* position rather than its *actual* position that determines its effect. Thus, whatever the true nature of astrological influence, it seems to propagate at a specific velocity, presumably the speed of light, and is therefore not simultaneous nor synchronistic.

These arguments against a synchronistic explanation of astro-

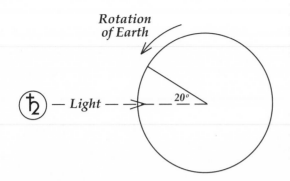

Rotation of Earth

♄ — *Light* — → — — 20° —

Because of the time delay associated with the speed of light, combined with the rapid rotation of the Earth, the visible location of a distant planet like Saturn is always dramatically different from its actual location in the sky. (Adapted from Michael Harding's Hymns to the Ancient Gods, *Arkana Books, 1992.)*

logical influence are initially compelling; however, there is a different way of interpreting the problems they address. Approached metaphorically and philosophically, the line of reasoning sketched above does not so much overturn the synchronistic model as force us to reframe it. As an illustration of this alternative, consider the following non-astrological example of symbolic connection between distant events: Imagine a man living on an island far from his native country, with little or no access to modern telecommunications. Back home, his beloved sister has given birth to her first child; but due to the great distance separating the siblings, it takes a full month for news of the birth to reach the man by mail. Curiously, during the period immediately before and after the man's receiving the news, many events take place on the island which seem linked to the birth, such as a spectacular rainbow and a rare and beautiful bird building a nest outside his window. Most significantly, only minutes before the letter arrived, the man had decided to buy a boat and begin a new business venture. Thus the news of his sister's giving birth seemed to the man an uncannily fitting symbol for the rebirth taking place in his own life at that time.

In the minds of most symbolists, this confluence of events would qualify as synchronistic, because the news of the birth did not *cause* the unusual circumstances in the man's life, but simply coincided with them. The problem, however, is the same we encountered with the example of the nova explosion: The sister's childbirth took place a month before the news arrived on the island and thus a month before the corresponding changes in the man's life. Does this delay disprove the synchronistic relationship between the childbirth and the events in the man's life? Not necessarily; it depends on what one is choosing to synchronize. In this case, a perfect symbolic synchronicity exists between the *news* of the childbirth and the events in the brother's life, rather than between the events and the birth itself.

The problem may thus lie in defining synchronicity strictly in terms of instantaneous connectedness. In fact, as theorists like Paul Kammerer have noted, and as even Jung himself was forced to admit, events which are not simultaneous may, at times, be linked in a significant fashion. This possibility suggests a distinction between what might be called "simultaneous" and "sequential" acausality. *Simultaneous acausality* is any meaningful, noncausal connection between events occurring at the same moment in time, such as a person coming across a photo of a childhood friend precisely at the moment the friend calls on the phone. By contrast, *sequential acausality* is any meaningful noncausal connection between events taking place consecutively, such as the number fifty-eight coming up several times during the same day.

Applying this distinction to astrology, the six-thousand-year delay between the Crab Nebula explosion and its "influence" on Earth in 1054 does not necessarily negate a synchronistic connection. The configuration of events in medieval Europe could be viewed as synchronistic with the *news* of the nova by means of simultaneous acausality, and synchronistic with the nova itself, despite the time delay, by means of sequential acausality.

LIGHT AND CONSCIOUSNESS

To take this argument a step further, let us consider the possibility that people are connected synchronistically with phenomena taking place around them in several ways at once. Most astrologers hold as meaningful the dates on which celestial events are seen from Earth rather than the dates on which the events actually occurred. This belief is borne out by the research of Michel Gauquelin, which demonstrates statistically that it is the position of celestial bodies as they *appear* in the sky rather than their *actual* position that correlates to their influence on Earthbound observers. However, it is possible that both positions are meaningful, and that an astronomical event influences beings on Earth both when it actually occurs *and* when it is perceived. In the case of the Crab Nebula Nova, for example, its effect could have been experienced both simultaneous to the nova as well as six thousand years later when its light and energy reached Earth, but on different levels of the collective consciousness.

Astrology itself suggests this interpretation. Most astrologers believe a celestial body's proximity to and degree of visibility on Earth correspond symbolically to its position in the minds of observers. Thus, more visible bodies like the Sun or Venus represent forces closer to the surface ego consciousness, while more distant planets, like Neptune or Pluto, both of which are invisible to the naked eye, represent relatively unconscious forces in the personal or collective psyche. The discovery of previously unknown planets is seen as corresponding to the surfacing of latent forces into active consciousness. In short, more visible celestial bodies represent psychic forces of which people are more aware, while more distant and less visible bodies correspond to forces more recessed in consciousness.

Thus the Crab Nebula explosion could have been experienced by beings on Earth instantaneously, but on a subliminal or unconscious level. The arrival of its light on Earth six thousand years later would correspond to the *emergence into consciousness* of previously latent effects.

It is ironic that from the standpoint of light itself, the distinc-

tion between these
dual perspectives
does not even exist.
According to Ein-
stein's theories, time
is relative; it slows
down as a body
moves closer to the
speed of light. Thus

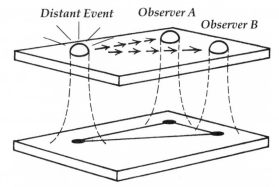

Distant Event *Observer A* *Observer B*

as seen from the per-
spective of a photon
traveling from the
Crab Nebula Nova to
Earth, there would be
no delay whatsoever
between the moment
of departure and that

Top level: The universe as perceived at the level of the conscious finite ego, characterized by separateness, causality, and time delay in information transfer.

Bottom level: The universe as perceived at the level of the deep unconscious, or Divine Mind, characterized by simultaneity, acausality, and absolute interconnectedness.

of arrival. From light's perspective, both events would take place in an eternal now—symbolically, the viewpoint of enlightened, transcendental awareness.

A RELATIVITY THEORY OF ASTROLOGICAL INFLUENCE

We can conclude from these examples that any model of astrological influence must take the subjective perspective of individual human beings into account. Given the way astrology has been practiced, this conclusion is not surprising. Even after Copernicus demonstrated that the Sun was the center of the solar system, astrologers have cast horoscopes using the Earth as the center of the universe, calculating the positions of the planets as they appear to an observer on Earth. Is this practice due to an error of thinking based in tradition? I would say no, for while the heliocentric view may be true objectively, from the experiential, or phenomenological perspective of earthbound observers, the Earth *is* the center of the visible universe. Thus, while it might be demonstrated scientifically that a given planet appearing on the horizon at the moment of a child's birth might not actually be in that position—or might have been vaporized into dust—the phenomenological reality of the planet is precisely where one perceives it to be.

The role of the relativity principle in astrology can be likened to the impact of Einstein's theory of relativity on conventional physics. In pre-twentieth-century science, it was thought that human beings might someday come to understand the laws of nature as they exist in an absolute sense, independent of individual observers and their subjective viewpoints. However, Einstein demonstrated that the vantage point of an observer radically affects the characteristics of the universe being perceived, so that a person traveling near the speed of light would perceive an essentially different universe from that perceived by a person at rest. Thus after Einstein, science was no longer just a matter of discovering objective universal laws, but of calculating the role perspective plays in determining how a profoundly relative universe acts or appears.

A similar problem has plagued esotericists, who have for centuries searched for objective laws of nature that might explain the workings of astrology and other systems of influence or interconnectedness. This presumption has traditionally led esoteric theorists to postulate subtle energies and correspondences in the outside world as if these principles might somehow operate independent of human observers. Yet all such searches for a universal and objective explanation for astrology have been at best incomplete. Astrology is a human art, and it is human participation in the play of objective cosmic forces that underlies its unique power. The phenomenology of human experience and the human perspective of observing the heavens with our feet firmly planted on the Earth underlies astrological thinking and analysis. Like the post-Einsteinian scientific universe, the universe of astrologers is profoundly relative.

SPIRIT AND SOUL: A TRANSPERSONAL PERSPECTIVE

It may be true, as esotericists have long believed, that at deeper levels, people are linked to each other and to the various phenomena of the world in an instantaneous and noncausal fashion. However, from the viewpoint of the individual, finite human ego, the world is characterized by separateness, time delay, and subjectivity, all of which combine to produce a distorted view of reality. Yet, such a subjective view, however mistaken, might in a deeper sense be exactly right. From a symbolist perspective, one could argue that the "distorted" worldview of a given individual is exactly appropriate symbolically to his or her level of consciousness.

Let us recall here the traditional distinction suggested in many esoteric systems between spirit and soul. Esotericists have described *spirit* as the essential ground of being for each individual, characterized by nonduality, timelessness, and absolute interrelatedness. *Soul*, by contrast, is the more personal aspect of an individual nature, closer to the ordinary ego and more associated with the emotions. The soul also contains the imprints of individual memories and thoughts. While people may share a certain commonality of nature at the level of spirit or Divine Mind, at the level of soul or personality, each individual enjoys a distinct admixture of personal and archetypal elements. These differences are reflected in the subjective vantage point represented by the horoscope, which charts the position of the planets and stars relative to the time and place of a specific person's birth. The cosmos and its various planets, stars, and galaxies may be objectively the same for all humans, but each human is at a particular and individual stage of soul development. Thus each individual's horoscope must be relative and subjective, and the astrological symbolism revealed by a person's chart is unique for that soul.

ASTROLOGY AND PARTICIPATORY MEANING

All this suggests that the dimension of meaning in any astrological interpretation is neither entirely subjective, as the modern scientific viewpoint would argue, nor entirely objective, as many classical astrologers have argued. Rather, astrological meaning is a symbiotic fusion of both dimensions. An example from my own experience may help illustrate this point.

One evening I drove to a community center to begin teaching a course. As I pulled into the parking lot, I noticed an unusual sight in the sky. The lights from jet planes at a nearby airport combined with the light from stars to form a perfectly shaped, five-pointed star. This seemed an auspicious symbol for what, in fact, turned out to be a very fruitful teaching experience.

Now, the question raised by my experience is this: Was this image of a five-pointed star actually out there in the night sky, or was it purely a subjective impression? Five-pointed stars are widely recognized as universal symbols. I actually saw such an image and could have photographed it if I had wanted to. Yet the appearance of this "star" was dependent on my location at a precise moment. Had I moved a city block in either direction, my perspective would have shifted sufficiently to eliminate the "star." Clearly, the image I saw could be characterized as both an objective *and* a subjective event, objective to the extent it was a genuinely perceived, external symbol, yet subjective in that it existed only from my vantage point at a particular moment.

This principle helps us to understand many key elements of astrological theory besides those already mentioned here. Take for example the role of the constellations in sidereal astrology. Purely objective explanations of astrological influence see the constellations as representing actual force fields or patterns of energy located out in space, which radiate their energies toward beings on Earth. However, if one were to travel by spaceship to the point in the night sky where an astrologically meaningful constellation such as Aquarius or Pisces "exists," one would not find the particular patterns we call by these names, since most constellations are made up of stars widely scattered in space, which only assume the appearance of being linked when seen from the vantage point of Earth. Even in cases where the stars of a constellation may be physically "close" to one another, the shape they form relative to each other is likely to be completely different when viewed from a point beyond our solar system.

Does this mean that constellations and star patterns do not really exist, or that they do not carry experientially verifiable meaning? By no means. Rather, the star patterns linked to astrological interpretations are both objective *and* subjective in nature; in other words, like the five-pointed star I saw, the constellations express genuine archetypal patterns which arise in conjunction with subjective frameworks of perspective and interpretation. Such substantial entities as the planet Jupiter or the Crab Nebula nova do, of course, possess an objective, external reality, but any meaning assigned to these cosmic influences will always in some way be modified and contextualized by the subjective perspectives of finite observers.

This discussion has important implications for understanding symbolist philosophy as a whole. The life events which we have been examining for their symbolic and synchronistic dimensions also have both objective and subjective (or relative) dimensions. For instance, for many people, a temperature of fifty degrees Fahrenheit might seem warm in spring yet chilly in fall. Similarly, a small apartment might be viewed quite differently by two individuals from dissimilar backgrounds. A woman who lived previously in a mansion might find a three-room apartment claustrophobically small, while a man who grew up sharing a small rural cabin with a family of eight might regard the same three rooms as the embodiment of spacious freedom. Likewise, someone witnessing a shooting star from one part of the country may perceive it as moving from right to left, whereas a person in a different state sees it moving from left to right.

Thus, the signs and symbols presented to us by the events of our daily lives may be thought of as objective events with a unique meaning of their own. As personal symbols, however, their meaning results from a combination of subjective and objective elements, as modified by the unique perspective of each individual. The reality of this world is therefore one in which universal, archetypal symbols express themselves through the transitory forms of ordinary experience, just as the eternal mathematical concept of "two-thirds" can find expression through a nine-gallon clay jug holding only six gallons of water.

From this we may further conclude that all meaning is a product of dualistic experience, requiring an observer and an observed, a subject and an object. Only in the transcendent state beyond duality, such as mystics postulate is experienced during enlightenment, does meaning, and by extension, symbols, archetypes, and synchronicities, cease to exist. In a state of pure Being, we move beyond all conceptual knowing or inflection.

ASTROLOGICAL INFLUENCE — A SYMBOLIST INTERPRETATION

In light of this discussion, we turn again to the question of the mechanism underlying astrology. We have seen that astrological influence is based neither on a purely mechanical model of cause and effect nor on any sort of universal instantaneous interconnectedness, such as Bell's Theorem seems to imply. However, we have also seen that astrological influence *is* synchronistic—but in a very sophisticated way. The "mechanism" of astrology, like the other esoteric systems we have been examining, is *symbolism*, through which intrinsically meaningful, objective events are invested with layers of additional, subjective meaning by means of their relationship to the perspectives of earthbound observers.

As we survey the techniques and theories of traditional astrology, we discover that the vast majority of these are purely symbolic in character, with little or no basis in empirical reality. As one example of this, let us consider the phenomenon described in astrological circles as "Mercury retrograde." Mercury is said to be "retrograde" when its skyward path relative to the Earth seems to reverse direction. In actuality, of course, Mercury is traveling in its orbit around the Sun, just as the Earth is. However, in the same way that a train overtaken by a faster one will appear to be moving backwards, when in fact it is still moving forward along its own path at a steady rate of speed, the "reversal" of Mercury is a perceptual illusion caused by the position of Mercury in its orbit relative to the Earth's longer and slower orbital path.

When Mercury's skyward path seems to reverse for several weeks at a time, business contracts run into complications, comunications break down, and technical difficulties abound. In all fairness, many astrologers allow for the possibility of more positive effects to accompany these same periods in the charts of individuals, though these are generally interpreted as occurring on more psychological and spiritual levels.

Though the effects of a Mercury retrograde are observable and are born out by personal experience, the cause-and-effect model cannot logically account for them. Clearly, it is nonsensical to postulate any "backing up" rays or emanations coming from the planet itself, since the retrograde phenomenon has nothing to do with the objective status of Mercury. Rather, the communications problems and other effects associated with the "reversal" of Mercury might more effectively be understood as a metaphor for conditions taking place for humans and existing only in relation to the phenomenological dynamics of observers on Earth.

Astrology, then, as Shelly Trimmer has suggested, might be defined as *astronomy, symbolically interpreted*. Astrology uses the same essential facts as astronomy, but infuses them with a symbolic or qualitative dimension absent for the conventional scientist. As seen by astronomers, Jupiter, for example, is a large gaseous planet traveling at a particular speed exhibiting certain magnetic and gravitational characteristics. For astrologers, however, Jupiter symbolizes a particular set of *qualities*: expansiveness, joviality, excess, spiritual learning. This interpretation cannot be apprehended through experimental, scientific means. If one were to travel to Jupiter and take samples of its gasses or measure its energy fields, one would still not be able to isolate the symbolic meaning associated with the planet by astrologers. Astrological interpretation requires a perceptual shift.

Moreover, the worldview underlying astrology sees not only the planets but *all* of reality as symbolic in nature. To the symbolist, the heavenly bodies are threads within a great tapestry of affinities and correspondences. Thus, when a child is born, the symbolist can find important clues pointing toward the child's character and destiny everywhere—in the flight of birds, the movement of clouds, and other natural signs and omens; in coincidences and events in the lives of the parents and their community; in political and social happenings; as well as in the position of the stars and planets in relation to the time and place of the birth.

The mystical Neoplatonic philosopher Plotinus, who is frequently cited as being critical of astrology, echoes this understanding. In Ennead II. 3, his primary essay on this subject, Plotinus criticizes the simplistic understanding of astrological mechanism which holds that the stars "cause" things to happen on Earth. Rather, Plotinus argues, astrological influence is based on a philosophy of cosmic unity. Since all things emanate from the One, the Divine Source, all things are intricately coordinated or "enchained" with one another and are therefore "signifiers" of each other within a supremely regulated design—the stars no less so than birds or any other phenomena. "The wise man is the man who in any one thing can read another," Plotinus wrote.[8] In other words, the stars and planets are meaningful just as every other object and event is meaningful, as all things are equally enchained and significant within the universal order. As Plotinus remarks elsewhere, one would have to be far removed from the awareness of Divine Unity to think that anything is truly accidental or the result of chance.[9]

Given this philosophical framework, questions of "mechanism" seem inappropriate. Does a Native shaman who names a child "Swift Eagle" because of the great bird which circled the village during the birth ask what manner of force emanated from the eagle towards the child that influenced its personality, biology, and destiny? Or by what means this force is transmitted, or its precise speed? Does it matter whether the "influence" of the eagle traveled at the speed of light or, in the case of a child born to the sound of thunder, the speed of sound? More useful than such inquiries is an appreciation of the wonder of a universe in which such synchronicities occur, and in which meaning expresses itself in such manifold and multi-dimensional ways—through not only planets and people, but animals, weather, colors, landscapes, in short, every perceivable thing, large and small. As Plotinus wrote, "All things must be enchained; and the sympathy and correspondence obtaining in any one . . . organism [is entwined with that of] the All." Thus asking what influence the planets have on human beings reflects a misconception, because the planets themselves are elements of a much larger picture, in which each part interlocks with the other in a mutually arising symphony of meaning.

One final analogy may make the point. Let us imagine a play in which the lead character comes near the end of the drama to understand a truth he has long hidden from himself. As the playwright has written the scene, at the moment of this breakthrough, the audience sees the Sun rising through a window at the back of the set, a dramatic device complementing the change of perception experienced by the character.

Now, how should we understand the relationship between the sunrise and the psychological change of character? Are there secret rays emanating from the mock Sun to the character such as a scientist could measure? Is there an energy field set up among the characters acting on stage, or among the objects and props which make up the stage setting? Clearly, there is not. Nonetheless, there *is* a connection between the character's psychological shift and the lighting change—a connection that is reflected in the emotions of the actors on stage and in those of the audience watching the scene. But the connection is symbolic rather than causal. Each element unfolds within a larger framework of meaning and is interpretable only in relation to a transcendent ground of reference—the dramatic design conceived in the mind of the playwright.

Here, as in astrology, meaning exists only through a particular perspective of symbolic interpretation. Each person's experience is a unique and highly personalized context of meaning. The seemingly unrelated events of a life, which include among other factors the positions of the constellations and planets in the sky, can be understood as mutually arising elements in a greater field of significance—the archetypal script of a life and consciousness, which is reflected in the natal horoscope.

Moreover, the personal context of meaning of any set of circumstances is unique to each individual perspective. As we have seen, the objective position of any heavenly body is less significant in some respects than its perceived position—or even whether the body exists at all. Yet for all of its subjectivity, each life drama is perfectly suited to the context of meaning for a specific individual at a specific moment, however inaccurate it may appear from a more objective vantage point.

Like solar systems in a stately procession of spiral rings around a vast galaxy, so all personal dreams are nested within greater dreams, broader contexts of meaning, each level providing a deeper and broader perspective on the meaning of the personal dream. Like Ezekial's "wheels within wheels," the symbolist universe is a vast web of ascending hierarchies, each increasingly objective vantage point yielding a more complex worldview, which is apt and true for that level. "A subtle chain of countless rings," wrote Emerson, "the next unto the farthest brings . . ."[10] In the end, mystics proclaim, all personal dramas converge on an ultimate hub of meaningfulness, called God, the Tao, the Cosmic Dreamer, Brahma, the Absolute, the Ground of Being. At this still center point, a great consciousness holds all in balance. As Schopenhauer wrote:

> *It is a vast dream, dreamed by a single being; but in such a way that all the dream characters dream too. Hence, everything interlocks and harmonizes with everything else.*[11]

Now that we have some notion of how astrology works, we turn to a closer look at its symbols and their interpretation. Astrology, we discover, is a veritable Rosetta stone of symbolic meanings, with rich and meaningful interconnections with other esoteric and symbolic systems.

CHAPTER 10

THE ARCHETYPES — WITHIN AND WITHOUT

Beneath the accidental surface effects of this world sit—as of yore—the gods.

—Joseph Campbell

entral to the symbolist worldview is the conviction that underlying the apparent complexity of the world is a deeper simplicity—a primary language of symbols which governs all experience. Just as all musical compositions are based on a scale of notes, and all paintings are variations on a spectrum of colors, so philosophers and mystics have taught that all forms or phenomena are reducible to a set of essential universal principles or *archetypes*.

To ancient Chinese mystics, for example, all phenomena were seen as expressions of the five cosmic elements and the sixty-four hexagrams of the *I Ching*. For ancient Pythagoreans, the archetypes were described in terms of divine Numbers or numerological principles thought to lie at the heart of all existence. Plato and his followers spoke of the transcendental Ideas, forms of which everything in this world is a shadow or reflection. In Jewish esoteric thought, the world was seen as comprised of patterns symbolized by the twenty-two letters of the Hebrew alphabet and the ten *sephiroth*, the mystical principles of existence which make up the Kabbalist Tree of Life. Students of Tarot look to the twenty-two cards of the major arcana for symbols of the dynamic processes of reality. Astrologers past and present describe these universals through the symbolism of the planets and the twelve signs of the zodiac. Even in societies where the archetypal hypothesis may not have been explicitly articulated, its presence can still be glimpsed in the view of a world governed by a pantheon of gods and goddesses, each of whom rules over an aspect of reality.

Different cultures have explained these universal principles in different ways. At the subtlest level of understanding, archetypes are not static symbols so much as living *processes*—in linguistic terms, akin more to verbs than to nouns, active principles rather than objects. Because of their essentially dynamic nature, an archetypal symbol cannot be limited to any particular form; rather it manifests in many ways, on every level of experience. The ancient Greeks described archetypes as a kind of "prime imprinter," an original text from which later copies could be derived. Like the letters of an alphabet, archetypes can be combined in a multitude of ways to produce the variety of familiar events and experiences.

For the mystic, knowledge of these archetypes is valuable on several levels. An understanding of these principles is a skeleton key to decode the patterns of everyday experience. If life is a sacred text, archetypes are its language, and a familiarity with their meaning, the key to reading its hidden messages. A knowledge of the archetypes reveals the hidden connections linking disparate phenomena, allowing us to discern the hidden shape underlying the unfoldment of our personal and collective lives. Philosophically, understanding archetypal qualities also permits us to recognize the commonalities uniting the symbolic systems of diverse cultures and to uncover the deeper truth informing them all.

Let us take a closer look at archetypes as they have been viewed

---

within two important systems of traditional symbolism, astrology and the yogic philosophy of the chakras. On the surface, these systems seem quite different, astrology largely concerned with the outer world or *macrocosm;* the chakras describing the inner, psychological realm or *microcosm.* In fact, these philosophic systems are connected in important ways, and blending them can help us understand more precisely how the outer world reflects the inner.

THE ARCHETYPES WITHOUT: THE PLANETS

As a philosophical system, astrology is best understood as an expression of *sacred cosmology.* Traditional societies saw the universe as a living presence; celestial bodies were ensouled, each with a unique meaning and set of qualities. The ancients clothed these associations in myth, viewing each celestial form as the embodiment of a god or goddess, and the movements of the heavenly bodies as the actions of divine beings. While the personifications associated with this mythic perspective have long since disappeared, except for the names still associated with many planets and stars, astrologers have kept alive their ancient meanings. Thus though the planet Mars is no longer an embodiment of the god of war, astrology still sees it as symbolic of dynamic, aggressive energies, just as Venus is symbolic of life's alluring, harmonizing, and tranquilizing energies. Understood esoterically, then, each planet represents an archetypal principle, a reflection within time and space of a type of transcendental energy.

Each planet governs a class of symbols, which despite differences in form are linked by a deeper resonance of meaning. These symbols intermesh to yield a complex language which informs our lives. Just as the ancient Greeks and Romans viewed personal fortune as reflecting the influence of one or more gods, astrologers view the unfoldment of personal destiny as linked to the movements of the planetary archetypes. To better understand this relationship, let us look at the meanings and correspondences associated with the seven visible planets of ancient astrology, beginning with the slowest of the "great wanderers."

♄
SATURN

Of all the planets in the solar system, Saturn exhibits the most visible and dramatic ring system. Symbolically understood, this feature reflects this planet's long-standing association with the archetypal principles of limitation, matter, structure, and time—in all their constructive and destructive aspects. Without its influence, nothing would have structure or shape, all growth would proceed unchecked; yet when overemphasized, structure becomes constriction and confinement, strangling life and preventing development. In our lives, Saturn thus governs all events which provide limits and structures or test us in any way, including governmental figures or law enforcement officials, parents, delays, or constricting conditions of any sort. In the body, Saturn is associated with the structural elements, such as the bones, back, and knees. Because of its concern with matter, it also governs scientific and economic professions. Note as well the similarity of this planet's name with the word *Satan*—a linguistic reflection, some have argued, of the darker aspects of this planet's limiting or selfish influence.

Metaphoric qualities associated with Saturn: Dry, Cool, Hard, Slow, Heavy, Old.

♃
JUPITER

The largest planet of the solar system, Jupiter is associated with the archetypal principle of expansion and the transcendence of limitations. When Jupiter is absent, things cannot grow; life lacks enthusiasm. If too much in evidence, however, expansion turns projects or experiences toward excess. In our lives, it is associated with all conditions or symbols of an expansive nature, including long journeys, religious figures and institutions, gifts, winnings, and schools of higher learning. Whereas Saturn is the scientist with a materialistic perspective, Jupiter is the priest or philosopher, with an eye to the higher principles underlying matter. For this reason, Jupiter is related to the notion of divine providence and good luck—and in its flip side with the abuse of luck through gambling. Because of its size, Jupiter also determines gravitationally the plane of the ecliptic for the entire solar system; hence, it is the quintessential lawgiver, symbolically governing all situations involving the law, judicial systems, moral or religious dogma.

Metaphoric qualities associated with Jupiter: Moist, Warm, Light, Expansive.

♂

MARS

The mythological god of war, Mars governs the archetypal principle of force or power. As applied toward constructive ends, Mars relates to the expression of strength and courage; but when destructively expressed, it produces violence and conflicts. In our lives, its influence is associated with all situations or symbols relating to dynamic energy and forcefulness, such as athletes, competitive encounters, fires, "heated" exchanges, assertive individuals, and crusades for constructive or destructive change. At its most extreme, it is associated with weapons, wars, battlefields, and criminals. Although the energy of Mars is predominantly masculine, it expresses itself in the lives of women as well, most clearly seen in the lives of women who champion causes, fight battles, or pioneer change, such as Hillary Clinton, Amelia Erhardt and, more traditionally, Joan of Arc.

Metaphoric qualities associated with Mars: Hot, Dry, Fast, Hard, Sharp, Rough.

♀

VENUS

The mythological goddess of love and desire, Venus embodies the archetypal principles of beauty, harmony, and allurement in all their forms. In contrast to the coarse and abrupt quality of Mars, Venus brings refinement and pleasure to all that she touches. In our lives, this archetype expresses itself through situations or symbols that involve beauty, love, or pleasure, including romantic encounters, art or art museums, luxurious or refined environments, money, and rich or expensive foods. On our bodies, Venus governs all beautiful features and adornments. And whereas Mars seeks to divide and create boundaries, reflecting its role as the symbol of ego, Venus attempts to unify and bring harmony to all things. Thus this archetypal energy governs social interactions, including parties and other entertainment and occasions of mediation and diplomacy. However, just as the beauty of this planet conceals an inferno of raging heat at its surface, so the hedonistic pleasures of Venus can incinerate the unwary in its fiery crucible—note, for instance, its association with the word *venereal*. Thus this archetype must be approached with greater caution than planets like Mars or Saturn, which exhibit their dangers up front for all to see.

Metaphoric qualities associated with Venus: Moist, Cool, Soft, Slow, Sweet.

☿

MERCURY

The planet closest to the Sun, Mercury is symbolic of the mind, which likewise serves as messenger between spirit and soul, consciousness and matter. Through the principle of Mercury (in Greek,

Hermes), we understand meaning in all its forms. For this reason, Mercury/Hermes governs all symbolic systems and their study. The word *hermeneutics*, the art of symbolic interpretation, is based on this association. The fastest of the planets, Mercury hints at the speed and changeability of the mind's operations. In our lives, Mercury expresses itself through situations involving communication and knowledge, including books, media, libraries, conversations, teachers, classrooms, as well as short journeys. On the body, Mercury is linked to those areas most associated with communication and thought, including the brain, hands, tongue, and vocal cords. This archetype is also associated with the mythological trickster, a figure who surprises or upsets us with clownish or unpredictable behavior.

Metaphoric qualities associated with Mercury: Like quicksilver, its corresponding metal, this archetype paradoxically merges the polarities of Moist and Dry, Cool and Warm, Fast and Slow.

☽

THE MOON

Radiant with the reflected light of the Sun, the Moon is associated with the principle of reflectivity and the archetypal feminine in all her aspects. In our lives the Moon governs water, mirrors, women, and the emotions. As the Sun rules over the daytime, the Moon archetypally governs the night side of existence, when we retreat from the glare of the marketplace into our own private world. Thus the Moon expresses itself symbolically through our emotional life, as well as all family and domestic situations. In contrast with the harsh clarity of the Sun, the Moon's light is soft and nurturing. This archetype is the great nourisher, caring for all who come into its sphere. Thus it governs all situations involving nourishment of any type, including providing or receiving food, restaurants, mental or health care figures, babies and, in particular, the mother. On the body, the Moon governs those parts that provide or receive nourishment, including the stomach, breasts, and mouth. In reflection of the constantly changing phases of the Moon, this archetype also governs the processes of cyclical change—the natural cycles of growth and decay, life and death.

Metaphoric qualities associated with the Moon: Moist, Cool, Soft, Fluid, Changeable.

⊙

THE SUN

Symbolized by a circle with a dot at its center, the Sun is the central force of our solar system, and thus is the archetype of eminence and rulership. In traditional systems, the Sun is associated with kings, lions, the heart, and gold, the incorruptible metal—all symbols holding a central place in their respective realms. As the orb which illuminates the daytime world, this archetype governs the outer world in general, and thus public self-expression. In our lives, the Sun is linked symbolically to fathers and other prominent individuals—those we might call "stars"—along with all creative or theatrical institutions and situations involving public exposure or recognition. Just as the Sun is the source for all life and energy in the solar system, so in our own life the archetypal Sun represents creative gestation, without which life cannot begin. Yet like the desert Sun at noon, in excess it can produce a lifeless heat which makes nourishment or even survival impossible. When overemphasized, the Sun's archetypal force encourages concern with outer values, such as career and achievement, without the counterbalance of reflectivity or inner cultivation of soul.

Metaphoric qualities associated with the Sun: Warm, Dry, Bright, Loud, Regal.

Together, the Sun and Moon express the fundamental masculine and feminine polarities inherent in all phenomena.[1] Of the two, however, the Sun assumes a certain preeminence as the unifying principle underlying all archetypes; for just as the planets shine by the reflected light of the Sun, so all other archetypal principles draw meaning from the reflected light of the unitary solar source, or pure consciousness. For the ancient Pythagoreans, the Sun was therefore associated with the number One, the root of all other numbers, and with the mythological god Apollo, supreme in his brilliance.

When viewed symbolically, our lives reveal themselves as reflecting the influence of all of these archetypal principles, in varying degrees of emphasis. For one person, Jupiter may be the most influential symbol, manifesting as an assortment of expansion-related symbols and experiences, such as long journeys, involvements with churches or colleges, or possibly excess appetites; while for another person, the primary archetype may be Mercury, leading to a life emphasizing communication, thinking, or teaching. Commonly, an individual life will reflect a blend of several archetypes, such as a mixture of Saturn (structure) and Mars (force), which might lead a person to a life centered around law enforcement or leadership in the military.

Once we are familiar with the symbolic meaning of the planets, we can begin to discern the influence of the archetypes in the transitory circumstances of everyday life as well. Over the course of several days, for instance, a woman might find herself surrounded by a series of notable Mercury symbols—her plans to publish a book are delayed by legal problems, several pens she is using coincidentally run out of ink, and a letter to an old friend is returned due to insufficient postage. Since Mercury is the planet of mind, this confluence of problematic symbols might suggest that her thinking is more prone to error or mistakes during this time, and that she might need to be more cautious than normal in communicating with others or signing contracts. Ideas or plans formulated during this time would benefit from close inspection. By recognizing the network of correspondences associated with the planetary archetypes, the hidden threads of meaning connecting events can be better understood and their hidden messages and implicit warnings decoded and used.

Moreover, perceiving the archetypal dimension of circumstances allows for a deeper insight into the lessons unfolding in one's life. For instance, a woman may have a series of dramatic losses or disappointments, such as the dissolution of a long-term business arrangement and the ending of a marriage or other relationship. Looking at these events through the lens of the planetary archetypes, she might discover that she is under the influence of a powerful Saturn energy. Although Saturn can build up new structures, it can also, like the Grim Reaper, act to break down or cut away old patterns or personal "dead wood" that may be obstructing one's growth and, by so doing, reveal what is valuable in one's life. Through recognizing the signature of Saturn, the woman may realize that the losses she has experienced are not meaningless or accidental but are facets of a larger—albeit difficult—restructuring process which is setting the stage for a new life direction.

THE PLANETS THROUGH THE SIGNS

Yet the planets represent only one of several layers of interpretation in an astrological analysis. Astrologers also speak of secondary celestial patterns called *signs* and *houses*. Simply explained, these factors derive from dividing the sky into twelve segments, each of which serves as a kind of "filter" for the planetary archetypes.

Let us briefly consider the first of these indicators. Most of us have heard the term "Sun sign." Traditional astrology holds that the Sun takes on a certain coloring or emphasis as it moves through each of the twelve segments of the zodiacal year. Thus a person born in May while the Sun is in the segment associated with the sign Taurus is said to have "Sun in Taurus," while a person born in October has the Sun in Libra, and so forth. In fact, at the time of a person's birth, all of the planets are moving through one or another of the twelve zodiacal signs. Thus, while a woman's Sun may be in Aries, leading to a public identity oriented toward assertive or impulsive self-expression, her Venus might be in Pisces, giving an artistic, sensitive, or imaginative cast to her social expressions. Together, the arrangement of planets throughout the various signs combine to create a complex picture of archetypal qualities in a person's life.

The energies of the twelve signs are complex and multifaceted, but a sense of their flavor can be expressed through a few key adjectives. Below is a brief list of key words for each sign. Among the associations listed for each planet is one of the four traditional elements: earth, water, fire, and air. These relate symbolically to the four primary modes of experience through which the planetary archetypes manifest in our lives: earth to practicality, water to emotionality, fire to dynamic expressiveness, and air to intellectuality.

♈ Aries (fire): assertive, impulsive, daring

♉ Taurus (earth): practical, comfortable, beautiful

♊ Gemini (air): communicative, variable, entertaining

♋ Cancer (water): maternal, sentimental, protective

♌ Leo (fire): creative, expressive, egotistical

♍ Virgo (earth): analytical, methodical, mental

♎ Libra (air): interpersonal, indecisive, harmonious

♏ Scorpio (water): passionate, secretive, transformative

♐ Sagittarius (fire): expansive, enthusiastic, adventurous

♑ Capricorn (earth): authoritative, public, ambitious

♒ Aquarius (air): innovative, independent, social

♓ Pisces (water): inspirational, vague, emotional

Importantly, the ancients saw each planet as closely aligned in quality with one or more zodiacal signs. A planet whose qualities matched those of a sign was assigned the "rulership" of that sign. Thus the seven visible planets of the traditional solar system were said to govern the twelve zodiacal signs: Saturn ruling both Capricorn and Aquarius; Jupiter ruling Sagittarius and Pisces; Mars ruling Aries and Scorpio; Venus ruling Taurus and Libra; Mercury ruling Gemini and Virgo; the Moon ruling Cancer; the Sun ruling Leo. In the accompanying chart, the signs are arranged in a wheel, with the traditional planetary rulers aligned with the signs they "govern."

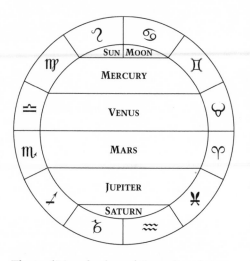

The traditional rulers of the zodiacal signs.

As we have seen, each planet in a person's horoscope is located within one of these signs. Sometimes, several planets will congregate in a single sign, while in other cases every planet will inhabit a different sign. The overall blending of the planets in the signs, along with other factors not explored here, determines the general character of the horoscope and the personality born under it. In short, the astrological chart could be described as a snapshot of the universe at the moment of a person's birth. Interpreted symbolically, the chart offers a glimpse into the archetypal patterns at play at the time of birth, which may manifest in such areas as career, money, health, family, romance, friendships, and journeys.

READING AN ASTROLOGICAL CHART

To illustrate how these various factors might come together in

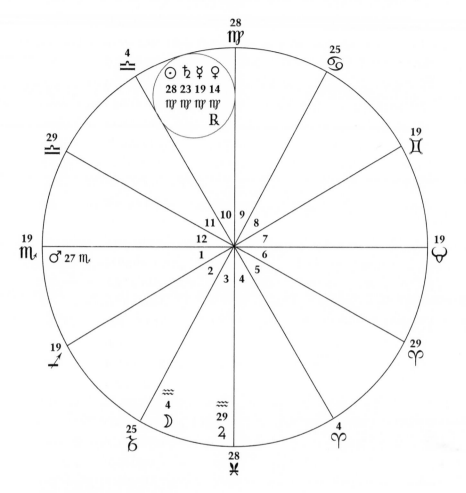

Astrological chart for John.

an astrological reading, let us consider the natal horoscope for a man I will call John. (For clarity, I have omitted the more recently discovered outer planets, Uranus, Neptune, and Pluto; in a more fully rendered reading, these would be taken into consideration as well.)

There are many things which an astrologer might consider in looking at a chart like this one; let us for now consider only the most prominent characteristics. First of all, notice the concentration of planets within the zodiacal sign of Virgo (circled here for emphasis). As we have noted above, Virgo, which is ruled by Mercury, is characterized by the key words *analytical, methodical,* and *mental.* Thus in broad terms, this configuration tends to indicate an individual whose life will be involved with mental development, analysis, and communication. Virgo is also associated with the constructive channeling of mental energies into such areas as public service and healing. Since both the Sun (public identity) and Saturn (authority figures) are included in the grouping of planets in Virgo, the configuration in this chart might indicate a person who would be regarded as an authority in these areas. Note also that the heavy concentration of planets is near the very top of the chart, indicating that they were literally positioned overhead in the sky when John was born. Because the upper and lower halves of the chart symbolize the public and the private aspects of a person's life, with the main horizontal line cutting across the chart representing the horizon of the Earth as seen from the birthplace, the position of the planets in Virgo directly overhead further emphasizes that John's talents or ambitions might express themselves in a public way, possibly thrusting him into a position of fame or recognition.

In fact, the man whose chart chart I am using as an example is a successful writer in the spiritual field, specializing in works of philosophy, astrology, and oriental healing. His writing is precise, conservative in flavor, and insightful in its analysis of philosophical concepts, with a bias toward traditional systems and values. He frequently lectures on these topics. Of course, a configuration such as the one in this chart could manifest in many other ways, including work as a doctor, public servant, or even a librarian.

In short, the horoscope is an archetypal diagram of our lives; within the symbols of the sky, we find a reflection of our own unfolding potentials. An astrological chart is not, I must emphasize, a blueprint for a rigid destiny. Rather, it is a map of the intricate and ultimately illuminating set of interconnections that exist between an individual life and the cosmic forces and archetypes of the universe. As such, astrology seems to illustrate well the traditional symbolist maxim, "As above, so below."

If astrology teaches us to find meaningful symbols in the larger universe or macrocosm, the yogic philosophy of the chakras teaches us to find symbolic meaning as well in the interior energies of our own body, a microcosmic universe. As we see below, the archetypal energies expressed by the planets and signs of the outer universe have inner, psychological correspondences in the chakra points of the body. To explore this concept more fully, we turn now to the yogic system of the chakras.

THE ARCHETYPES WITHIN: THE CHAKRAS

Just as external phenomena are linked symbolically with the planets, so psychological experiences can be associated with inner archetypes in a system of *sacred psychology* that holds that individual mental and emotional experiences are expressions of cosmic energies and universal principles. In many ancient societies, an emotion—desire, for example—was not simply a hormonal response to a stimulus; rather, it reflected the influence of a divine force, such as the classical goddess of love, Venus, or one of her cognate goddesses in other traditions, like the Egyptian Hathor or the Hindu Lakshmi. Thus the experiences of the psyche represented the interactions of divine principles in varying states of harmony or discord.

The inner archetypes are described in many traditional sources, but their most sophisticated expression is in the Hindu yogic system of the chakras. Literally translated from the Sanskrit as "wheels," the chakras are psycho-spiritual centers of consciousness located within the subtle body, along the length of the spine. There are thousands of chakric points in the body, though yogic philosophy chiefly emphasizes seven or, in some schools, eight. Each point corresponds to a particular area of psychological concern, ranging from the most basic drive for survival to the most elevated impetus towards self-realization and divinity. The interaction of the energies of these centers comprises the changing textures of human psychological experience.

According to a number of prominent teachers and mystics, each chakra can be linked with a planetary symbol; thus the chakra system comprises a solar system within in reflection of the planetary bodies without. The Christian Platonic philosopher Origen, writing in the third century after Christ, concurred with this correspondence: "Understand that thou art another world in little, and hast within thee the Sun and the Moon, and also the stars." An important key, then, to a whole system of symbolic analysis is the realization that *sacred psychology reflects sacred cosmology*. Thus, the qualities associated with each chakra can be aligned to the qualities of a particu-

Chakra Number	Sanskrit Name	Planetary Symbol	Element	Metal (Hermetic)	Keywords
8	Sahasrara	( )	( )	( )	Transpersonal Divine, Godhead
7	Ajna	Sun	( )	Gold	Personal Divine, Will, Consciousness
6	Chandra	Moon	( )	Silver	Reflective Awareness, Memory
5	Vishuddha	Mercury	Ether	Mercury (Quicksilver)	Rationality, Self-expression
4	Anahata	Venus	Air	Copper	Love, Harmony, Allurement
3	Manipura	Mars	Fire	Iron	Force, Energy
2	Svadisthana	Jupiter	Water	Tin	Enthusiasm, Emotionalism
1	Muladhara	Saturn	Earth	Lead	Practicality, Ambition, Discipline

Traditional astrological-chakric correspondences.

lar planet. On page 204 is a table illustrating the links between these systems, along with other important correspondences which will be important as the discussion develops.

To begin exploring some of the links between these systems, let us look in more detail at the symbolic meanings of the chakras, starting with the lowest energy center on the spinal tree. The associations cited here are drawn largely from the philosophic system of Kriya Yoga, but closely match those descriptions found in other schools of thought.

(1) MULADHARA CHAKRA ♄

Located at the base of the spinal column, this chakra governs a person's relationship with matter and all earthly concerns. Like its planetary counterpart Saturn, it concerns the awareness of structure and limitation in all situations. Psychologically, it relates to such psychological states as worldly ambition or status, as well as a person's capacity for inner structure, self-discipline, and perseverance. When overemphasized, it can cause a person to be depressed, greedy, or heavy. Underemphasized, it can lead to impracticality or spaciness. In general, this chakra is integrally related to an individual's sense of being grounded. Expressed in the imagery of subpersonalities, we might imaginatively think of this chakra as the Inner Architect or Inner Disciplinarian.

(2) SVADISTHANA CHAKRA ♃

Located at the small of the back, the second chakra constitutes a developmental leap beyond the material or survival concerns of the base chakra. It concerns an individual's awakening to the world of feelings and values. Just as Jupiter is the largest of all the planets, so this chakra relates to the expansion of consciousness beyond limitations, and thus to such states as devotion, religiosity, and enthusiasm. Whereas the first chakra is classically associated with the principle of earth, the second chakra is symbolized by the element of water, and thus with our emotions. As with Jupiter, when imbalanced this chakra produces a tendency toward indolence or excess in one's tastes and self-expression. Along with the third chakra, it is linked to the experience of passion and sexuality. In its healthy expression, we might describe the second chakra imaginatively as the Inner Optimist or Inner Cheerleader; in its unbalanced form, it can be the Inner Escapist or the Inner Evangelist, because of its potentially dogmatic energy.

(3) MANIPURA CHAKRA ♂

The third chakra, located at the level of the solar plexus, concerns the qualities of forcefulness and energy generally. Related to the planet Mars and the element of fire, it is associated with our dynamic emotions or passions. At this chakric level we awaken to the ego and our separate self-sense; thus it is strongly connected with such issues as power, competitiveness, and the forging of boundaries. When imbalanced, it produces anger or defensiveness; but when balanced, it confers strength and resolve. Personified, this chakra may be thought of as the Inner Warrior or Inner Athlete.

(4) ANAHATA CHAKRA ♀

At the level of the heart, consciousness turns from the animalistic drives of the ego and ascends toward the uplifting experiences of love and beauty. Like the planet Venus, the fourth chakra governs a person's basic sense of harmony, and thus the capacity for romantic or social interaction. Linked to the element of air, it represents the first movement beyond basic emotionality toward reason and intellect. Although potentially a source of great unselfishness, the energy of the heart chakra can, when imbalanced, lead to narcissism or, as in the case of the second, Jupiter chakra, excessive pleasure-seeking. When underemphasized, it can lead a person to be cold or distant toward others, whether romantically or socially. Imaginatively, the fourth chakra may be thought of as the Inner Lover, Inner Artist, or Inner Hedonist.

(5) VISHUDDHA CHAKRA ☿

The throat chakra is intimately bound up with the expression and development of the mind. Linked to the planet Mercury, this center is central in determining an individual's ability to formulate and articulate thoughts through verbal or written communication. An overly activate throat chakra can produce a hyperactive mind or tendency toward verbosity, while an underemphasized or blocked throat chakra can cause difficulty with creative thought or clear communications. Classically, the fifth chakra is associated with the element of ether, the symbol for pure mind. The throat chakra may be described as the Inner Communicator or Inner Thinker.

(6) CHANDRA CHAKRA ☽

Rarely mentioned in published writings, this center at the back of the head was described by Yogananda as the feminine counterpart of the solar, or third eye chakra at the front of the head.[2] Just as the Moon shines by the reflected light of the Sun, so this chakra relates to a person's capacity for reflectivity and responsiveness, and thus to such faculties as memory and psychic sensitivity. The energy of this chakra relates to a person's capacity to give or receive nurturing and is thus linked to such symbols as family, the mother, babies, cooking, home, and women generally. Personified, this chakra can be described as the Inner Mother, Inner Nurturer, or Inner Queen.

(7) AJNA CHAKRA ☉

Located at the center of the forehead, the solar chakra or "third eye" is the source of our spiritual awareness. Reflecting the dynamic properties of the Sun, this chakra represents the archetypal masculine, governing such factors as will, higher rationality, creativity, and one's sense of purpose or vision. As the fountainhead of personal consciousness, it concerns an individual's self-expression and essential personality. Mystics have claimed that at the heart of this chakra is a five-pointed star, the quintessential symbol of our personal divinity. In some respects, this chakra may be described as the only genuinely autonomous chakra of the entire chakric system; for in the same way that the planets in our solar system all shine by the reflected light of the Sun, so all the chakras below this point can be said to "shine" or draw consciousness from the reflected light of the Ajna chakra, the seat and source of personal awareness. This chakra can be symbolically expressed as the Inner Father or Inner King.

(8) SAHASRARA CHAKRA

Beyond the Sun and Moon chakras, yogic mysticism also describes a chakra at the top of the head. Sometimes referred to as the "thousand-petaled lotus" or the "crown chakra," this point can be viewed as the culmination and perfection of the solar and lunar principles immediately below it, analogous to the upper point of a triangle in relation to the two points of its base. Whereas the third eye, or solar chakra at the forehead relates to the realization of our personal selfhood, the Sahasrara chakra relates to the awakening of transpersonal divinity, or "God consciousness." Since the crown chakra lies beyond the archetypal framework of the lower seven chakras and their planetary correlates, it is sometimes referred to as the "Sun Beyond the Sun" or the "Sun Beyond Time." For most individuals, the crown chakra is essentially dormant; additionally, its energies are transpersonal rather than personal. Hence, its influence on chakric psychology and symbolism is indirect.

By understanding the symbols associated with each chakra, we can begin to understand other ideas discussed in traditional esoteric systems as well. According to some schools of thought, for example, each of the chakras and their corresponding planets can be associated with a metal: lead with the lowest or first chakra; tin with the second chakra; iron with the third; copper with the fourth; mercury (or quicksilver) with the fifth; silver with the sixth; and gold with the seventh. This set of correspondences gives insight into the ancient mystery of alchemy, the announced purpose of which was chemically transmuting lead into gold. Since lead represents the lowest, or Saturn chakra, and gold, the highest or Solar center, the transformation of lead into gold can be seen as a metaphor for drawing consciousness up from the gross material planes to its spiritual source. Incorruptible and immune to rust, gold is the perfect symbol for the timeless state of enlightenment. Expressed in esoteric terms, through the alchemical transformation of base lead into spiritual gold, the King regains his crown and throne and order is restored to the kingdom of one's personal universe.

Note that the Ajna chakra and the Chandra chakra represent dual expressions of the same basic level of being, namely, consciousness, in its active and reflective aspects. Thus the goal of the ascent of inner energies is not the Ajna chakra by itself, but rather the balanced merging of masculine and feminine energies, symbolically expressed as the "marriage of the Sun and the Moon." Viewed esoterically, the head is the "land of milk and honey"—milk being a symbol of the Moon, and honey, of the Sun. The state of consciousness associated with the head chakras is the promised land of enlightenment we seek to enter through spiritual awakening.

Just as our outer lives reflect the influence of the various planets of our astrological horoscope, so our psychological states reflect the combined influence of the various chakras of our subtle body. Leaving the transpersonal or crown chakra aside, varying degrees of emphasis among the seven personal chakras manifest as different

The Marriage of the Sun and Moon.

types of personalities. For example, an athlete or career soldier might have a highly activated third chakra as a life-long pattern, whereas an artist would be more likely to have an emphasized heart center. Considerably more complex combinations of energy among the chakric centers are possible as well. Both Plato and Aristotle, for example, could be characterized as fifth-chakra or intellectual personalities. However, in the more down-to-earth and scientifically-minded Aristotle, the energies of the fifth chakra would have been linked closely to the earthy first chakra, in contrast to the more purely rational Plato, who represented a relatively direct expression of the throat chakra.

THE TWELVE CHAKRIC SUBCOMPARTMENTS

Until now, we have considered the symbolism of the chakras only in its most general and simplified form. Yet as with astrology, a more comprehensive understanding is useful. The archetypes and symbols of chakric psychology are complex and multidimensional, with each chakra possessing three distinct modes of expression: *masculine, feminine,* and *balanced.* Thus, the energy of each chakra can be diverted to its right side, to its left side, or expressed in a balanced way within the center of the spine. In its masculine aspect, a chakra's energy will tend to be mental in nature and relate to events in the external world. In its feminine aspect, a chakra's energy will be largely internal or emotional in expression and relate to events in the astral or dream world. In its balanced or central expression, the energy of each chakra will be spiritual and may be expressed through subtle feeling states.

The states of consciousness associated with the peripheral energies of each chakra can be linked to the symbolism of the twelve signs of the zodiac. For example, the lowest or Saturn chakra is concerned with materiality and the principle of structure. In its feminine and internal expression, this energy often manifests in a sense of structure relative to one's personal status and position in the world, which in astrology relates to the sign Capricorn; while in its masculine and extroverted form, the Saturn chakra governs the awareness of structures or patterns within the collective, impersonal sphere, as in the study of scientific or social patterns, which in astrology is linked to the sign Aquarius.

A similar pattern of correspondences can be found for each of the other chakras. The second or Jupiter chakra concerns the awakening of enthusiasm and expansive perception. On the masculine side, this manifests as an outwardly directed spirit of exploration or evangelism, which is expressed in astrology by the sign Sagittarius. In its feminine and emotional expression, the second chakra concerns the movement toward inner exploration or possibly escapism, related astrologically to the sign Pisces. The third or Mars chakra concerns the vital force of one's personality. In its masculine mode, it manifests as outwardly directed aggression or forcefulness linked to the astrological sign Aries; while in its feminine or introverted expression, it governs the control or even repression of internal emotions and energies related to the sign Scorpio. The fourth or Venus chakra manifests on the masculine side as outer social or artistic harmony, or Libra; while in its feminine or introverted expression, as the awareness of inner peace or harmony, or Taurus. In its masculine, extroverted expression, the throat chakra expresses its intellectuality as communications or mental creativity in the outer world, linked astrologically to Gemini; while in its feminine expression, as the internal analysis and digestion of information symbolized astrologically by Virgo. The sixth and seventh chakras, feminine and masculine expressions of the energy of pure consciousness, are each related to a single sign. The sixth or Moon chakra is linked astrologically to Cancer, or reflective awareness of the inner world, and the seventh or Sun chakra, to Leo, or expressive awareness in the outer world.

The accompanying diagram shows the chakra centers and the astrological signs that correspond to the left-side and right-side expressions of their energy. The central expression of each chakra's energy is its most balanced or spiritual. Note that the masculine and feminine expressions of the energy of each chakra shift sides as one moves up the spinal tree. Thus the masculine expression of the Saturn chakra is on the left side, while the masculine expression of the Jupiter chakra is on the right.

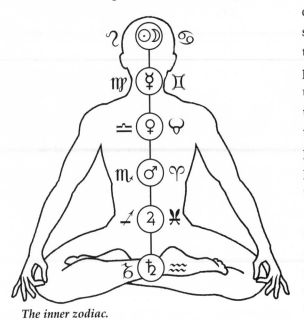

The inner zodiac.

This chart shows how the classical planetary rulerships for the twelve signs can be transposed onto the chakra system.

Thus, for example, the fourth or Venus chakra is lined up with its feminine expression, Taurus, and its masculine expression, Libra. Mystics such as Paramahansa Yogananda regarded this arrangement of the zodiacal signs as the "Cosmic Man."[3] Symbolically, it expresses the complex weave of interconnections between our inner, psychological universe and the outer cosmos. It illustrates that just as the planetary bodies of the solar system move through a twelve-stage zodiacal circuit, so the subtle energies of our consciousness travel through the pathway of an inner zodiac, in continual and restless unfoldment.

On one level, the right- and left-hand aspects of each chakra can be seen as repositories for an individual's karmic imprints and *samskaras,* the mental or emotional habit patterns acquired over many lifetimes. The inner zodiac can thus be regarded as an elaborate filing system for memories and karmic energies incurred over time. Karmic seeds related to the intellect, for example, are stored within the "compartments" of the throat center related to Gemini and Virgo; while karmic imprints related to material or Earth-plane energies are stored within the twin compartments of the base chakra symbolized by Capricorn and Aquarius. Over many lives, these patterns are built up and reinforced in our unconscious, predisposing us in a cumulative way toward specific sets of behaviors and modes of reaction.

Although yogic philosophy traditionally tends to discuss this subject in literal terms—karmic "seeds," and the like—it is more likely that karmic energies are not actually stored at specific points in the body, but simply find their greatest degree of resonance within particular chakric locations. By analogy, a diseased liver would be regarded by a holistic healer not as a problem only of the liver, but as a systemic condition that has its greatest focus in that organ of the body—indeed, since the liver is associated by astrologers with the planet Jupiter, we might even say symbolically that a person's liver condition extends out to encompass Jupiter itself! Similarly, it is perhaps more accurate to say that karma is a field phenomenon which extends through space and time on many different levels of consciousness, but which resonates to certain nodal points in the chakric system in particularly intense ways.

An individual's psychology represents a complex combination of chakric energies. For example, a woman might exhibit an especially powerful combination of energy at the fourth (heart) and first (base) chakras, the centers relating to aesthetic sensibility and to practicality and structure. This blend might manifest in a career as an artist, sculptor, or architect. A man might have a preponderance of karmic energies in the masculine side of the throat chakra (Gemini) and the masculine side of the navel chakra (Aries). This combination could manifest in an assertive communication style, as might be seen in the life of a public speaker, critic, or lawyer. A wide range of variations, many of them far more complex than those mentioned here, are possible among the twelve chakric states.

The essential point is this: an intimate correspondence exists between the archetypal patterns unfolding outside and inside of each person. Schopenhauer once asked, "Is a complete misadjustment possible, between the character and the fate of an individual? Or is every destiny on the whole appropriate to the character that bears it?" The symbolist tradition holds that misadjustment between character and fate is impossible; each person's destiny is—on the whole—appropriate.

THE HOROSCOPE AS CHAKRIC DIAGRAM

We have been exploring how the interlocking keys that symbolist tradition supplies allow us to decipher the destiny patterns of our inner and outer life. If we know how to interpret the symbolism of outer experience, we can read the energies of our inner universe and intuit which of our chakric energy centers are most active and psychologically influential. Thus if a person's outer experience reveals an abundance of Jupiter symbols—religious figures, gambling, long journeys—it suggests as well a dominant second or Jupiter chakra. Whether this energy will express itself in constructive or destructive ways can often be determined from examining the specific symbols involved. The wife of a minister whose life has been devoted to church work, for example, enjoys a very different relationship with the archetypal energies of Jupiter than, say, a man who spends every weekend gambling at the race track or casino. Thus the activities and events unfolding in our daily lives mirror our inner psychological and spiritual energies, and the obstacles and opportunities we encounter in life provide important clues to the archetypal forces unfolding in our inner being.

The same holds true for the patterns indicated in our horoscope as well. Chapter nine suggested that the relationship of the outer universe to the human psyche was essentially synchronistic. In other words, planetary configurations occur in tandem with psychological experiences, as joint expressions of an underlying pattern. The astrological chart can thus be used to give insight into inner energies and influences.[4] By examining the distribution of planets throughout the zodiac at the moment of someone's birth, we obtain important insights into the energy patterns of their chakras as well.

To illustrate this point, let us look again at the astrological chart analyzed earlier in this chapter and see what it reveals about John's chakric energies. If the circular astrological chart shown on page 201 is rotated so that the signs Leo and Cancer—corresponding to the Sun and the Moon chakras at the top of the spinal tree—are at the top of the chart, a fascinating set of parallels emerges between the astrological universe without and the chakric energies within.

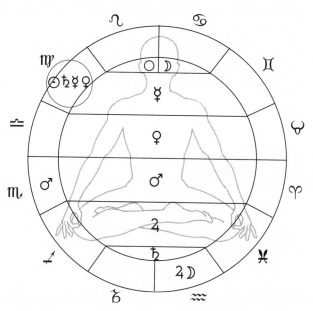

Astrological chart for John transposed onto chakra system.

Notice that the heavy concentration of planets in this diagram, which we earlier saw in the sign of Virgo, are located here at the level of the fifth or throat chakra. As in the astrological analysis, this placement indicates that John has generated considerable karmic mo-

mentum over many lifetimes toward developing the mind, perhaps in the areas of communication, writing, teaching, or even
healing—the constructive application of mind. As mentioned previously, such activities are indeed features of John's life. A clair-
voyant might actually "see" this concentration of energies at John's
throat, and John might perceive it himself in moments of heightened sensitivity.

Among other things, applying the horoscope to the chakric energies in this way allows us to step outside our subjective perspective and look at our psychic conditions from an objective vantage
point. Superimposing our astrological chart onto the body gives us
new insight into the archetypal forces which, in combination with
our karma, shape both personal behavior and external circumstances. If we choose to remain ignorant of these forces, we permit
them them to influence us unconsciously. Recognizing karmic patterns is thus an important first step toward the cultivation of free
will and the ability to direct our destiny by conscious choice rather
than through blind reactivity.

THE PATH OF BALANCE

Our discussion to this point has focused on the expression of
chakric energies through their masculine or feminine modes. However, the most balanced and spiritual expression of any chakra's
energy is within the center of the spine. For example, the throat
chakra, associated with Mercury, can express itself outwardly as
communication skills or inwardly as reflective analysis; but only
in its balanced state does it function in its highest form as the "messenger to the gods"—that aspect of intellect that communes with
spirit. To understand why this is so, we must look briefly at the
anatomy of the body's subtle energy system.

Weaving their way through the chakras are three energy channels, called *nadis* in Sanskrit. The masculine channel is called *pingala*;
the feminine channel *ida*; and the central, neutral channel *sushumna*.

Like highway systems, these channels connect the chakric centers, moving energy throughout the subtle body. Below is a simplified diagram of these channels. Note the similarity of the double spiral shape of the interweaving channels to the *caduceus,* the symbol of the Western medical profession. The shape is also reminiscent of the spiral double helix of the DNA molecule, the building block of all life.

In general terms, the "right-hand" or masculine channel relates to consciousness of the waking external realm and its symbols; the "left-hand" or feminine channel concerns consciousness of the astral or dream realm and its symbols. By contrast, the central channel or sushumna is the "crack between worlds," where consciousness exists in the form of balanced, blissful self-awareness. This channel is the one through which *kundalini,* the yogic energy of enlightened consciousness, travels.[5]

The peripheral channels, ida and pingali, are closely involved with karma and the mental and emotional imprints stored in the subcompartments on the right and left sides of the spine. Through most of our lives, our energies are diverted to one side or the other, as we operate under the influence of fear or desire, subject to karmic patterns which compel us to act in ways which have their roots in the past. Mystics refer to this state as "life on the wheel," an unsatisfactory existence character-

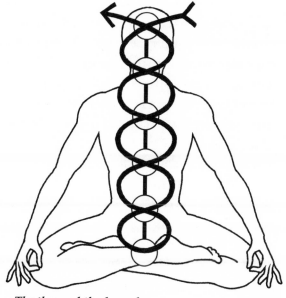

The three subtle channels.

ized by the suffering of living under the sway of the archetypal forces of the phenomenal realm.

As a diagram of karmic patterns, the astrological chart reveals the path of least resistance, the tendencies of destiny contained in the peripheral channels that will unfold if we surrender to the flow without exerting resistance. But the chart cannot show the degree to which a person will *resist* the compulsive forces of karma, by choosing instead to maintain a condition of balanced perception within the central channel. In its most profound form, spirituality can be thought of as a quality of freedom relative to all experiences, both subtle and gross. If ordinary life is characterized as one in which we act largely out of karmic compulsion, spiritual life is based upon free will. The spiritual adept may be aware of the archetypal cycles unfolding in his or her life, but has learned to maintain a balanced state of self-awareness which allows for greater latitude in responding to those patterns. The question at the root of spiritual consciousness is not whether the energies of the chakras and planets are good or bad, but whether an individual is aware of their influences and is striving consciously to overcome their compulsive aspects.

Towards this end, the mystic aims to cultivate a deepening sense of awareness within the central channel, what Yogananda referred to as the "highway to the Infinite." Within this middle pillar, awareness of our true spiritual nature dawns, and an individual becomes free of the influence of the archetypes—and of time itself. As expressed in the spiritual writings of ancient India,

> *Sun [ida] and Moon [pingala] establish time in the form of day and night. The sushumna is the consumer of time. This is said to be a [great] secret.*[6]

How does one enter this state of freedom? Yogic mysticism gives us several clues. As a result of natural cycles, we automatically move through this balanced state numerous times over the course of our lives, during the daily crossover points between waking and sleep, or at the threshold between life and death. At these natural balance points, when our energies shift from physical to astral, we momentarily glimpse this state of balance.[7] Yet amidst the noise and emotionality of everyday life, we remain largely unaware of this subtle and fleeting condition. A similar state of balance occurs within the collective psyche at those seasonal crossover points which occur during the spring and fall equinoxes, considered to be powerful times for personal or collective meditation.

However, yogic mysticism aims to bring a person's awareness *consciously* into the center channel rather than reaching this state of balance as a result of natural processes. Conscious control is achieved through such techniques as stilling the body, identifying and mastering the emotions associated with each chakra, and increasing attunement to the sushumnic state through meditation. The yogi works to balance the chakric energies one by one before ascending to the seat of spiritual awareness in the head. In Shelly Trimmer's words, "These seven [chakric centers] become the seven states of awareness balancing the maze [of Self] so that the spirit might climb back unto itself. But each center must grow stronger than the maze to maintain its balance; this can only be accomplished through self-discipline."[8] Having established him- or herself within a balanced condition, the mystic is free to utilize the energies of the horoscope and chakras by choice, rather than simply through blind reactivity.

The energies of our inner universe can manifest in uniquely different ways, simultaneously, in any of the three channels we have been discussing. For instance, a man may enjoy an enormous tide of good fortune in his career and worldly pursuits, corresponding to the ripening of positive karmic energies in the masculine side of his chakric fields. At the same time, his dreams may be full of troublesome symbols and his emotional state may be depressed, corresponding to difficult karmic energies ripening in the feminine side of his chakric fields. Sometimes, the symbols which appear in both the outer environment and the inner or dream life will be the same, either strongly pleasant or strongly unpleasant.

In essence, however, no matter what karmic energies are ripening at a particular time, the person observing these symbols has one recourse: Keep in mind the middle path of balance, in which the energies of each chakra manifest in their pure and spiritual form. Watch the symbols appearing in the outer and inner universe with as much interested detachment as possible, and with the sense that all patterns of manifestation—in the outer as well as the inner worlds—are, from a holistic perspective, cyclical and ever-changing. In the end, it is a certain comfort to know that we are each worlds in miniature and that, to quote Dante, "the love that moves the sun and the other stars" moves us as well.

CHAPTER 11

THE SONGS OF DISMEMBERED GODS

All meaning is an angle.

—**Ancient Greek saying**

s we have seen, the symbolist perspective regards all things as reflecting the interplay of a few essential archetypes or universal principles. Yet what gives the archetypes their meaning and power? And what is it we actually see when making that shift of perception necessary to detect the presence of Mars in a fire, or see the principle of potentiality in an egg, or discern the workings of Aphrodite beneath the surface forms of romantic love?

This chapter proposes that it is an underlying geometry at work in our lives, with each archetypal principle seen as an expression of a mathematical relationship or proportion. I am not referring, of course, to the obvious kind of geometry or math taught in high school or even to the kind of "sacred geometry" some esoteric writers see within the visible forms of nature, in the curves of seashells or the shapes of crystals. Rather, the kind of geometry I am describing here is visible only through a type of perception which links the symbolic language of form to the essence of meaning.

THE ANATOMY OF MEANING

To begin, let us consider a simple symbol: a circular patch of blue. For centuries, artists have used blue as a symbolic element in their paintings. From the color of the Madonna's cloak in the religious art of the early Renaissance to the old guitarist of Picasso's blue period, painters have ascribed a wide range of meanings to this color.

But is there an objective way of determining the nature or essence of blue? A scientist might answer by saying that blue is a particular wavelength of light. A Zen thinker might answer that blue is simply what it is. However, we might also say that blue is a proportion, or quality of relationship. To explain what this means, let us rephrase the question slightly, and answer by means of a simple word game we have probably all played.

Instead of asking what blue means, ask: *If the color blue were a fabric, what kind of fabric would it be?* Presumably, most of us would choose a fabric with a smooth and soft texture, like silk or satin, rather than something rough like burlap. By the same token, if we were to ask, if blue were a kind of *food,* what kind would it be? Most of us would select some food on the cooler and milder end of the taste spectrum, say a fruit sorbet, rather than something hot or spicy, like Mexican food.

Simple as they may seem, such exercises engage us in a highly sophisticated process of thinking about a thing's relative context and then comparing that thing and its context to equivalent patterns in other contexts. In other words, as the color blue is to the visual spectrum, so silk is to the spectrum of possible textures, and fruit sorbet is to the spectrum of possible tastes, and so forth. Such thinking is not comparing things as much as considering relationships or relative proportions.

This is to suggest that the meaning of any thing—a color, fabric, feeling, smell, or idea—is in essence a type of relationship, or ratio, not merely in a poetic or abstract sense but in a highly tangible way. Without relationship or context, no meaning exists. This is easily demonstrated by trying to imagine a particular shade of blue set against an entire world consisting *only* of that shade of blue. Not only would the patch of blue become invisible, but the very notion of blue would soon cease to hold meaning. Rather, what we know to be blue takes on its unique qualities only in relationship to other shades, other hues of the spectrum, possessing no intrinsic properties by itself. Moreover, the capacity for translating symbolic qualities across widely differing contexts involves a sophisticated metaphoric perception of the inner proportional qualities embodied by any thing or event.

A visually striking way of illustrating this principle of proportional equivalence may be found in the provocative work on sound and imagery undertaken by Swiss researcher Hans Jenny. Based on earlier research by seventeenth-century German physicist Ernest Chladni, Jenny showed how sounds could be translated into visual forms. Jenny's striking photographs show how, in response to a sound, metal filings on a metal plate reorganize into beautiful geometrical patterns that seem to correspond to the unique qualities of the sound.[1]

Over the years Jenny's research has captured the imagination of artists and philosophers, perhaps because it suggests something

of the mysterious process of transformation and proportionality encountered in life generally. In moving from the vibration of sound waves to geometrical patterns on a metal plate, something has crossed over—but what? I would argue that what has been translated is a set of relationships or inner proportions.

A similar transference can

Image produced by sound vibrations.

be seen in the mysterious psychological process known as *synesthesia*, in which sensory data taken in through one sense organ is interpreted by the brain through an entirely different sensory modality—as when an individual claims to hear the colors of a painting, or taste the sounds of a symphony, or see the smells emitted by a flower.[2] Each of us engages in a synesthesia-like process of thought when we employ metaphors in everyday speech, such as when we say a melody is "sweet," a person's retort is "sharp," or an obligation is "heavy." What we are doing when we use such phrases is translating relative qualities across divergent fields of experience, by drawing on the mind's ability to see through to the symbolic heart of phenomena, to what philosopher Gregory Bateson called "the pattern that connects."

In mathematical terms, this same understanding of proportional meanings and internal relationships, and their translation across different contexts of meaning, can be conveyed through the principle of the ratio, the root of our word *rationality*. As Aristotle knew more than two thousand years ago, the basic structure of meaning may be likened to a fraction and its inherent tension between elements held in proportion. Translating qualities of meaning across contexts (as in the Jenny images or in the metaphoric equivalence of the color blue with fabrics or foods) may thus be likened to a set of relationships, such as the following:

As six is to nine, so is twelve to eighteen

or

6/9ths = 12/18ths

or

6:9 = 12:18

Each equation is expressed in superficially different form, but each has the same qualitative essence or internal ratio, namely, two-thirds. The number six in the fraction 6/9 is not in itself similar to the number twelve in the fraction 12/18; yet in terms of relationship, as numerators in fractions of equal value, they are exactly equivalent. The same relationship exists between entities even more different in form than this, as between an auditorium with a seating capacity of three thousand in which two thousand people are sitting, and a water tank with the capacity for nine gallons which holds only six. Entirely different situations physically, yet each conveys the mathematical principle of two-thirds, or the ratio 2:3.

For thousands of years spiritually oriented mathematicians have perceived a deeper truth in the way variable and transitory forms express eternal truths by the inner relationships they embody. In ancient Egypt, enormous emphasis was placed upon the principle of the fraction, a fact frequently interpreted by scholars as evidence of the relatively low level of mathematical sophistication in Egyptian civilization. Considering the great subtlety of Egyptians in metaphysical and symbolist matters, however, it is more likely this emphasis on fractions indicates the tremendous importance they placed on the principle of proportionality. For the Egyptians, almost all relationships were expressed as fractions of one—as for example, one-third, one-seventh, one-fifteenth, or one-thirtieth. As independent Egyptologist John Anthony West has noted, the importance of fractions based on the number one in Egyptian thinking seems to illustrate their awareness that all forms of meaning derive from a relationship to the singular principle of divine unity, or spirit.[3]

PROPORTIONALITY AND CORRESPONDENCE THEORY

The idea of proportion sheds light on the correspondence theory which underlies the symbolist philosophy we have been discussing. When viewed in terms of their internal proportion, things which appear to have no obvious relation can be seen to be tied together by metaphoric relationships relative to their own contexts. Thus, for example, though gold, the heart, kings, lions, and the Sun are superficially different, they are linked vibrationally because each occupies a position of centrality or eminence in its respective framework. As gold is to metal, so the heart is to the body, the lion to other animals, and the king to other human beings.

Proportionality seems to crop up wherever we look in nature and in human affairs. In *Life Against Death,* Norman O. Brown mentions in the course of a discussion of the psychology of money the great value humans ascribe to the metals gold and silver—a value hardly explicable in terms of their practical usefulness, and more likely related, John Maynard Keynes suggests, to the traditional astrological connection of these metals with the Sun and the Moon. Throughout much of history, Brown points out, the value of gold has, for the most part, remained stable at 13.5 times the value of silver. This oddity has been difficult to explain simply in terms of conventional forces of supply and demand; yet a clue to this mystery may lie in the fact that this ratio matches precisely the relative orbital periods of the Sun and Moon: The solar year is 13.5 times longer than the lunar year. Whether we choose to view this correspondence between planetary and monetary patterns as reflecting how subliminal belief systems influence human behavior, or the hidden affinities by which all things hang together, this curious pattern illustrates the pervasiveness of proportionality in many spheres.

Proportionality also pervades everyday life and everyday thinking. The analogy game we played earlier is very revealing of our habitual ways of thinking about ourselves:

If your body were a make of car, would it be a Cadillac? A Volkswagen "beetle"? A Model-T Ford?

If your lifestyle were a kind of restaurant, would it be a fast-food joint? A family diner? An exotic oriental restaurant?

If your biography were a novel, would it be a tale of high adventure and intrigue? A philosophy book? A mathematics textbook? Or something else entirely?

We can use the same technique to reveal the proportional values that define our moods, ways of relating to others, and spiritual aspirations. The psychological and esoteric traditions abound with stories of skilled observers reading the character of individuals through such things as handwriting, facial structure, vocal inflections, and even the rhythm of a person's walk. In each of these instances, the inner personality has manifested through a particular set of forms—sound, image, or movement—with the same qualities of personality informing each modality of expression. Thus, the same traits indicated by a person's handwriting express themselves through the person's speech or body language.[4]

Underlying all of these instances is a subtle weave of correspondences which manifest in both external circumstances and inner states of mood or thought. Nineteenth-century poet and philosopher Ralph Waldo Emerson, among other symbolist writers, celebrated the web of relationship that links all phenomena: "Secret analogies tie together the remotest parts of Nature, as the atmosphere of a summer morning is filled with innumerable gossamer threads running in every direction, revealed by the beams of the rising sun!"[5]

THE ELEMENTAL QUALITIES

Proportion can also help us to understand the thinking behind Eastern medicine, astrology, and alchemy. When a doctor of traditional Chinese or Hindu Ayurvedic medicine speaks of excesses or deficiencies of heat or cold, dry or wet in a person's state of health, Western doctors may search in vain for objective corroboration of this seemingly arcane diagnosis. However, these terms actually refer to proportional balances within the body that can be sensed only through a metaphoric or relational mentality. Thus when a Chinese doctor prescribes a remedy with salamander skin as a key ingredient, a patient might wonder what chemicals underlie this strange choice, but the real motive may be the quality of heat (or *yang* energy) this ingredient can impart to the patient.

Likewise, when astrologers speak of an individual having a preponderance of air in the horoscope, the reference is not to any literal abundance of the element, but to a relative emphasis on signs linked to air in his or her chart, compared with those linked to earth, water, or fire. This proportional emphasis in turn reflects itself in certain qualities of personality. We use the same language when we say that a person is "earthy" or "spacey" or has a "fiery" personality. Such terms are metaphors which reflect a qualitative assessment of the inner essence of a personality in terms of subtle psychological states.

The ancient Greek philosophers further subdivided each of the four elements into finer shadings of meaning, or subproportions, with water seen as a combination of "moist" and "cool" qualities, fire viewed as a combination of "hot" and "dry" properties, and so on. The accompanying chart shows the traditional relationships, laid out in geometrical form.

Each of the elemental properties shown in this chart exist in our external life and inner personality in varying combinations.[6] Whether we recognize these dimensions consciously or not, we betray our intuition of them when we say that a person has a *hot* temper, is emotionally *cold*, or has a *dry* sense of humor. While such judgments

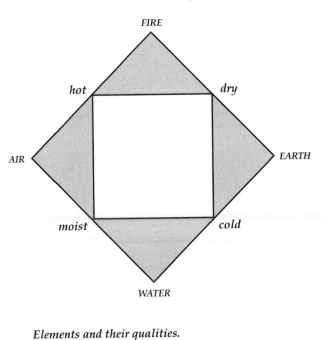

Elements and their qualities.

may not correspond to literal qualities, they convey real information and relate to a range of specific behaviors that could not be described by the opposite term. A dry person cannot be truthfully described as juicy, nor a person's fiery temperament as cold; these terms may be poetic, but they are accurate descriptions of real properties, not mere projections of the human imagination.

Each of the planets in a person's horoscope has a set of elemental or metaphoric qualities as well, which express themselves symbolically through the area of the person's life connected to that planet. Consequently, a man who has the planet Mars in the seventh house of his astrological chart (the area related to partnerships) will tend to experience heat, dryness, or fire in his interactions or relationships, manifesting in heated or passionate relations, or perhaps angry exchanges. Similarly, a woman with Saturn in the first house of her chart (the area governing the personality and body) may tend to be cool and dry in temperament, while another woman with the Moon in the same position may be more moist or emotional in her behavior. Any significant relationship between the planets in a chart likewise tempers each planet's qualities. Mars in relation to Mercury, for example, will bring qualities of heat and dryness to a person's mental or communicative nature, as well as to circumstances involving communication; while the Moon in relation to Venus will bring qualities of moisture and coolness to the person's romantic or social experiences.

The essentially proportional or "fractional" nature of planetary symbolism can be demonstrated dramatically by means of our earlier word game: If Venus were a musical composition, would it be hard rock, or a lush melody with sweet-sounding violins? If Mars were a kind of food, would it a mouth-searing chili, or an ice cream sundae? And if Jupiter were a kind of building, would it most likely be a functional office building, or an imposing cathedral?[7]

From an esoteric standpoint, it might be argued that the pervasiveness of such qualities as hot, dry, cold, and moist in many systems and ways of thinking arises from a common perception of the subtle astral dynamics underlying ordinary events. We might even say that physical reality is a surface reflection of deeper archetypal processes, around which the tangible circumstances of our lives congeal like iron filings in a magnetic field. We can only see and talk about these dynamics through metaphoric perception of the common qualities through which they manifest.

NUMBER AND MEANING

With this as a foundation, it becomes possible to see that the meaning of any symbol is an expression of relationship or proportion. Even the whole numbers described by classical mathematicians as the core principles of existence are not so much independent "things" as qualities of relationship. For example, we cannot speak of the number *seven* except in relationship to some unit of reference; *seven* specifically means *seven ones*. We could also depict *seven* in the form of a fraction or ratio, as 7/1, or 7:1. The number mystics of antiquity associated each number with elemental qualities as well, such that odd numbers were regarded as masculine and dry, while even numbers were feminine and moist.

We can extend this definition of meaning to many categories of symbolism that, on first glance, seem far removed from such considerations as ratio or proportion. For example, consider the word *mother*. The concept of motherhood is not meaningful in isolation; by definition, *mother* implies the complementary principle of children or, for that matter, of an inseminating father. As the progenitor of offspring, *mother* is therefore related to the number two, which signifies duality and the arising of forms. There is evidence some traditional cultures utilized this way of thinking in an explicit way. The pre-Columbian Mayans, for instance, associated specific gods with particular whole numbers, each of which had a certain set of qualities. Suppliants paid homage to the deity appropriate to the qualities they sought to invoke in their life.[8]

THE UNFOLDMENT OF COMPLEXITY

If all meaning is relationship, every symbol is at base a duality—a unity made up of two terms held in dynamic tension. The unfoldment of the meaning of such symbols on increasing levels of complexity is elegantly depicted by the Chinese philosophy underlying the *I Ching*. Chinese mystics believed that all phenomena reflected the relationship of archetypal principles. They symbolized this interplay by a set of sixty-four patterns of broken and unbroken lines, called *hexagrams*. The basic units of meaning contained within each hexagram are the primal feminine or *yin*, symbolized by a broken line, and the primal masculine or *yang*, symbolized by an unbroken line. The figure below shows one traditional progression of these patterns from their source into complex combinations.

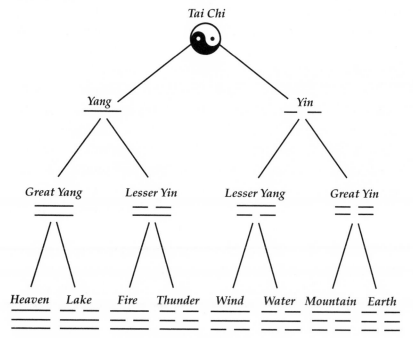

The **ba gua** *diagram of unfoldment.*

The Chinese believed that all things arise from a great unitive source of being, called the *Tai Chi,* represented here by a circle. Related to the idea of the *Tao,* the unconditional and unknowable source and guiding principle of reality, Tai Chi is consciousness beyond duality or differentiation. From this source emerges the primary principles of yang and yin, which in turn give rise to all other patterns of meaning. As the essential qualities underlying all phenomena, yang is associated with firmness, strength, warmth, and light, and yin with yielding, darkness, softness, and coolness. Every event or experience represents a combination of yang and yin, masculine and feminine energies in varying degrees of emphasis. This relative balance of opposites is in a continual state of organic transformation, as polarities shift to their opposites, and component parts undergo rearrangement. Through its symbolic images and their accompanying commentaries, the I Ching charts the subtle dynamics of these states of change—hence its alternate designation as the "Book of Changes."

The mystical Chinese reduction of all complexity to the basic principles of masculine and feminine reflects the fundamental polarity which underlies all phenomenal experience. Every perception of form is based on a duality, the interaction between the observer—the active, out-reaching aspect of consciousness—and the observed—the passive, receptive object of consciousness. On the cosmic level, it is through the interplay of the masculine and feminine aspects of the Divine nature that the universe and its "ten thousand things" arises.

In many cultures, this duality is portrayed mythologically as a god and goddess, such as the Hindu Shiva and Shakti. In their esoteric dimension, such constructs describe the process of Spirit reflecting upon its own nature, so that the divine One functions eternally as a Two. Through this process of self-reflection, a vibration is generated—the great "OM" shimmering beneath all creation. Since this process of self-reflection is continually shifting, the phenomenal world is in a state of continual change, resulting in the creation and dissolution of entire universes—what astrophysicists call "Big Bangs" and yogis know as the great breathings in and out of Brahma. On the individual level, this same basic polarity manifests as the principles of active and passive awareness, or observer and observed. In the Hindu scripture the Bhagavad Gita, this duality is known as the "field and its knower." Here, too, the act of self-reflection is continually shifting in resonance, bringing about the variations and secondary qualities which make up each person's symbolic drama.

THE PRIMARY ARCHETYPE

In mythological terms, the process by which the myriad forms of meaning unfold from their source in Spirit is poetically evoked through the image of the dismembered God who, like the Egyptian god Osiris, is torn to pieces. Like light dividing into colors as it passes through a prism or notes synthesized from shapeless white noise, so within the realm of time and space, Spirit fractures into many parts. Each embodies a facet of the divine nature, much like a particular color represents a single frequency of the entire spectrum. In a sense, the archetypes can be regarded as fragmented aspects of our own being.

While all archetypes are secondary and imperfect by nature, mystics have traditionally believed that one archetype comes closer to mirroring the divine Source than any other. This may be called the first or primary archetype and is expressed by such symbols as the Sun, the number One, the god Ra in Egyptian thought, or the Tai Chi principle in Chinese mysticism. All other archetypal principles draw their significance from their proportional relationship to this root symbol.

One way of explaining this idea is through a musical analogy. Western music is based on a scale of seven notes: *do-re-me-fa-so-la-ti*. Each note draws its meaning in reference to the primary note *do*. That is, if a soprano were asked to sing the note *fa* by itself, she could not do so. *Fa* can only be determined once a *do* has been established. Using the language of geometry, we might say that the notes of the scale represent angles of relationship to the primary point *do*. On the other hand, if a singer were asked to sing a *do*, any tone could serve. Unlike the other notes of the scale, *do* is the primary archetypal tone; completely independent and self-referential, it creates the context by which a musician establishes the entire scale.

The principle of complexity unfolding from a single source by means of proportion or relationship applies in many of the esoteric systems we have been discussing. For example, just as the planets of our solar system shine by the reflected light of the Sun, the planetary symbols of astrology can be said to derive their meaning from a proportional "angle" to the solar principle. A similar pattern is seen in sacred psychology, in which the chakras in our subtle body shine by the light of the Ajna chakra in the center of the forehead, which corresponds to the Sun and is the source of awareness of our Higher Self. The analogy holds in other symbol systems. In numerology, all numbers draw meaning from their relation to the number One, the first principle, or Unity. In geometry as well, all angles have meaning only in reference to a primary point. In a circle, for example, we must identify a primary or "home" point in order to measure the degrees to any other point on the circumference. That is, a 120-degree angle, a 30-degree angle, or a 180-degree angle can be located only in relation to a 0-degree point.

The pervasiveness of this pattern throughout various systems suggests that all symbols stand in relationship to the ground of Spirit, or Self-conscious awareness. We might say that any archetype expresses a particular trajectory relative to the Divine, like the angels (or shall we say *angles?*) mythologically constellated around God's throne. Hence, while the entire range of archetypes could be called "spiritual" because they are rooted in the divine Source, the central archetype represents spirit at its purest or most concentrated. Spirit in the mystical sense can be thought of as awareness in undilute form, in a state of complete and absolute attention upon an object or action or, in its undifferentiated state, on itself.

In religious terms, thus, the fountain from which all meaning flows is the fundamental I AM THAT I AM residing eternally radiant beneath all surface modifications of mind. With its roots deep in this luminous Source, consciousness is at its center eternally Self-aware, giving meaning to the world by forever reflecting upon itself. In mathematical terms, the process of Self-awareness in its perfected state is expressed by the fraction 1/1, as well as by the mathematical function of *power*, whereby a number is amplified by itself. In several esoteric traditions, the paradox of the Self reflecting upon its own nature was symbolized by the image of the serpent eating its own tail, called the *ouroboros*. The Self must forever eat of—meditate upon—the Self in order to sustain the Self. Through this act of Self-reflection, the Self not only regenerates its own existence, but all the existences of which it is aware. It has always done so and will always continue to do so, for were the Self to ever cease meditating upon itself,

> . . . it would cease to be; and if this could happen unto one's own spiritual being, it could happen to all. And in the infinities of existence, if it could happen to one, it would already have happened unto all, and you would not now be here [reading] this.[9]

THE ARCHETYPAL MUSIC OF EXPERIENCE

In the same way that archetypes draw meaning from their proportional relationship to the key archetype, so our experiences draw meaning by reflecting the illuminating consciousness at the heart of being. This is the great truth which the symbolist perspective imparts to us, when understood in its deepest sense. Each person's life expresses a particular arrangement or musical scoring of divine qualities expressed through the archetypes of being. Our lives are thus the songs of dismembered gods, the harmonies of divine energies in proportional relation to one another.

In the symbols of the horoscope we find an especially concise map of the archetypal qualities at work in our lives. With the sky seen as a vast canvas of the arenas of soul, the planets at the moment of our birth reveal symbolically where the archetypal principles are most intensely focused for us. As they manifest through the circumstances of our everyday lives, these universal principles appear to be relative or proportional, or rather, to express themselves in relation to particular contexts. For instance, the archetype or "note" of Jupiter (expansion, opportunities) might manifest in the life of a desert nomad as stumbling onto an oasis, while in the life of a native of the rain forest, as the discovery of a rare medicinal plant. To cite another example, a person born with a strongly emphasized Saturn will tend to be a late bloomer, in the sense of being slow to develop his or her personality or general potentials, in keeping with the archetypal quality of slowness associated with this planet. But this slowness is relative only to other humans, not as compared with a sequoia tree planted at that same moment!

Though the horoscope for any person or creature reveals a blueprint of archetypal or universal qualities, these qualities will express themselves through the transitory contexts of that life. As we have been discovering, all meaning is essentially contextual, resulting from the interaction of symbolic elements unique to a given observer. Thus, each person's life is a tapestry of archetypal meanings unique to that person, which in turn is enfolded within larger contexts of meaning.

In light of the proportional quality of astrological symbolism, we can begin to grasp other aspects of this discipline, some of which have been a source of heated debate for centuries. For instance, it is often asked, if a cow is born at the same instant as a great world leader, why wouldn't the cow likewise ascend to power? Precisely because astrology is a language of relative proportions, the individual chart offers a map of metaphoric possibilities which express themselves through whatever context in which they find themselves. Two destinies sharing the same horoscope are linked not through the specificities of each unfolding life story but rather through the proportional curves of each life, as played out within a particular framework. To continue the analogy somewhat facetiously, we might speculate that when the world leader experiences a great political victory, his bovine "astro-twin" might have a particularly good day at the feeding trough! In other words, a horoscope may not reveal the objective details of what events will transpire, but rather the proportional archetypal qualities which underlie them.

Yet as we have stressed, these proportional principles cannot be perceived through quantitative or literal means, but only through metaphoric knowing. Thus a surge of yang energy in a person's life might express itself through events or circumstances which express such qualities as hardness, heat, or dynamic forcefulness; for example, making an aggressive business decision. Similarly, when we use the language of subtle geometry to express our position relative to another person ("John and I are 180 degrees apart on this issue"), we do not mean that John is literally opposite us in space, but rather that his point of view is exactly opposite of our own. Note how often we use such geometrical metaphors to describe our situation: When we reconsider an earlier viewpoint, we say we have "come full circle"; when we reform our bad habits, we are "walking the straight and narrow"; when we change life direction, we are "veering off on a new trajectory." In none of these cases are we describing literal geometrical patterns, rather we are using geometrical imagery to convey the processes underlying these experiences. Such metaphoric embellishments of everyday language give intuitive glimpses into very real dynamics unfolding on deeper levels of our lives, subtle fractions or "angles" concealed from the literal eye. Such metaphoric knowing is needed to unfold the complexities of our horoscope as well.

RE-MEMBERING THE GODS

For most of us, the play of archetypes is experienced in unbalanced, even chaotic form. To continue the musical metaphor, in the symphonic unfoldment of our lives, the seven notes of the cosmic scale manifest largely as a cacophony of sharps and flats. In Kabbalistic terms, the kingdom of our spiritual nature is in disorder; the King—the observing consciousness—has lost his crown, and civil war is ravaging the country. In yogic symbolism, it would be said that our various planetary or chakric energies are not in their central or balanced modes. In particular, the Sun (symbol of Self-awareness) is not ruling the body from its proper place in Leo, at the point of the third eye.

The goal of mysticism is creating order out of this chaos—"stopping the war," as it has been expressed by some Buddhist teachers. For the yogi, this means first balancing the chaotic and uncontrolled energies at each chakric level and bringing the energies into the central channel. Thus Saturn is returned to its rightful place in the center of the base chakra, Jupiter to its place in the center of the second chakra, and so forth. Then, through a process of deepening reflection on the source of attention itself, aided in some traditions by mantras, breathing techniques, or visualizations, energy is lifted up through the spine into the head regions, thereby restoring order to the kingdom. When this takes place, the dismembered god is re-membered; observer and observed collapse into one; and all dualistic qualities, contrasts, proportions, and meanings are subsumed into pure awareness, having been reduced to ashes by the radiant light of the enthroned Self.

This state of balanced Self-awareness has been depicted in a variety of ways. In astrological symbolism, it can be expressed through the image of the Sun, or more accurately as the marriage of the Sun and Moon. In sacred geometry, it is sometimes expressed as a circle bisected by a line, an image associated with the mathematical formula for *pi,* the ratio of a circle's circumference to its diameter. Here, the diameter line connecting the two sides of the circle symbolizes the axis of balanced self-awareness by which consciousness observes its own nature, as if apart from itself. A similar idea is symbolized by a circle with a dot in its center, recalling the mystical statement that God is a "sphere whose center is everywhere and whose circumference is nowhere." Here, the polarities are reconciled

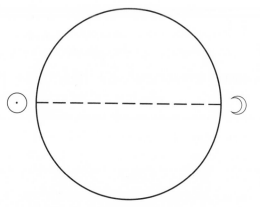

The two sides of the circle joined by a diameter line represents Self-conscious awareness, in which being is experienced as comprised of an "observer" and an "observed." However, since the line connects the circle with itself, the wave of Self-conscious awareness flows in both directions simultaneously, giving rise to the great OM underlying all creation. This image expresses the mystical paradox of the divine One which eternally functions as a Two.

within the center point, referred to in some kabbalistic sources as the "equilibrium of balance."

Another closely related expression of balanced self-awareness is conveyed by a triangle, specifically within the point at the top where the two angles of the base rise up to meet as one. We saw an example of this pattern in the diagram of the Chinese principle of Tai Chi, where the unitive source at the top branches down into the polarities of yin and yang below. The same trinity is found in many other traditions, such as the yogic chakras, where the Sahasrara (Crown) chakra branches down into the Ajna (Sun) chakra and the Chandra (Moon) chakra; and the kabbalistic Tree of Life, where the uppermost cosmic principle or sephira known as Kether branches down into Bina and Chochma. In all these systems, the two lower points of the triad represent the polarities of masculine and feminine, and the upper point signifies the balancing of these great opposites.

This triune symbol of balance is sometimes further expanded into the image of a four-sided pyramid, by means of which a more complex view of esoteric psychology is implied. Here, Self-conscious awareness is seen as consisting not only of an observer and an observed (a Sun and Moon), but also of the act of observing, along with a fourth factor, variously defined by esotericists as "memory," "the sum of all parts," or "the creation of Spirit." This four-fold depiction of consciousness finds expression in the Kabbalistic *tetragrammaton*, or four-letter name of God. Many interpretations have been given for this important linguistic symbol, yet at its most subtle, it can be seen as a formula for enlightened Self-consciousness itself, the potential of each sentient being. This interpretation is esoterically conveyed by the Old Testament story of God appearing to Moses in the Burning Bush. Moses asked God to divulge His name, so that he could tell the Israelites who had sent him. In response, Moses is told: I AM THAT I AM (IHVH or, in Latinized form, JHVH—generally pronounced "Jehovah"). In other words, in the process of coming face to face with God-consciousness, Moses discovers that "God" is awakened Self-awareness, the double "H" of IHVH corresponding to the dual aspect of perception, whereby consciousness doubles back upon itself, the observer viewing the observed and the reverse.

In astrological terms, this four-fold symbol has for millennia been associated with the four fixed signs of the zodiac, Leo (the lion), Taurus (the bull), Scorpio (the scorpion or eagle), and Aquarius (the human or angel). In the fire sign Leo, we see consciousness in its active, or observing aspect; in the water sign Scorpio, we find consciousness in its self-reflexive aspect, as the observed; in the air sign Aquarius, we see consciousness as the act of observing, thus the association of this element with the mediating principle of mind; while in the earth sign Taurus, we find the preserved memory of the soul's activity, hence the association of this zodiacal symbol with possessions and wealth. In both the Old and New Testaments, these same four creatures appear in a variety of passages, including the vision of Ezekial, the visions of Revelations, and the iconography associated with the apostles Matthew, Mark, Luke, and John, who prismatically reflect the supreme mystery of the Christ.

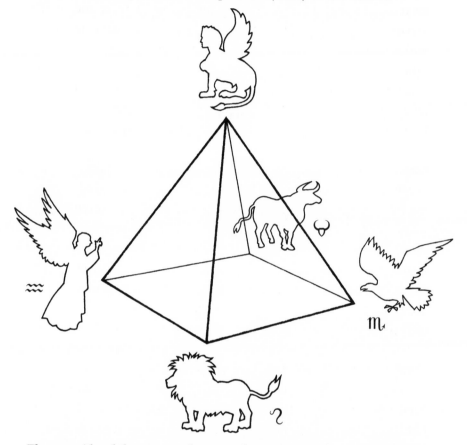

The pyramid and the tetramorph express the coming together of the four-fold aspects of consciousness. Although the Egyptian Sphinx does not have the four attributes found in the classic tetramorph, lacking the hooves of the bull and the wings of the eagle, it nonetheless conveys a similar insight: multiplicity within unity, the joining of the lion (animal nature), human (mental nature), and solar rays (divine nature).

In its most sophisticated esoteric form, the four are traditionally collapsed into a single composite creature, technically called a *tetramorph,* with the head of a human, the wings of an eagle, the body of a lion, and the hooves of a bull. In meditation, this image expresses the condition of perfectly balanced awareness, the four aspects of being—observer, observed, the act of observation, and the memory tract (or sum of all parts)—in unity.

Having awakened to this realization, the mystic is able to reenter the world without fear of becoming lost in the maze of Self or in the realm of the ten thousand things, for he or she realizes that there is nowhere in the maze where Self is not. Like many mirrors reflecting the Sun, the things of the world and the various states of consciousness that arise are no longer seen as symbols because they point to another reality, but because they mirror the consciousness which is perceiving them, all things now revealed to partake of the same essential nature. Established in the source of true awareness, all things shine forth with the radiant truth of Self, as the Bengali mystical poet Ramprasad expressed:

> *This realm of reflection we encounter*
> *consists of mind, earth, wind, water,*
> *arranging and rearranging with increasing complexity.*
> *The principle of subtle energy*
> *evolves naturally into tangibility,*
> *blossoming as billions of worlds.*
> *A single sun reflects in countless water bearing vessels.*
> *As these earthenware worlds are broken, one by one,*
> *the sunlight of primal awareness remains the same.*[10]

CHAPTER 12

SYMBOLISM AND SYNCHRONICITY IN THE NEW MILLENNIUM

Everything in this world has a hidden meaning. Men, animals, trees, stars, they are all hieroglyphics . . . . When you see them, you do not understand them. You think they are really men, animals, trees, stars. It is only later that you understand.

—Nikos Kazantzakis, *Zorba the Greek*

 n these chapters we have explored the symbolist perspective from a number of angles, using a variety of lenses. Now let us summarize the essential ideas, this time employing a slightly different framework of classification. In its fundamental sense, the symbolist worldview includes four interrelated ideas:

(1) Central to this perspective is a cosmology, or view of the universe. This view considers that the world possesses an innate symbolic dimension and that ordinary physical reality is part of a multileveled order, with all manifest forms reflecting subtle patterns of consciousness. From this core

belief arises a series of secondary principles, including correspondence, contagion, condensation, cyclicity, compensation, conception, polarity, karma, and telos (or purpose).

(2) The symbolist perspective also comprises the collected wisdom of humanity encoded within such disciplines as astrology, numerology, sacred geometry, the chakras, the I Ching, the Kabbalah, and the Tarot. Each of these systems is a language by which people have attempted to understand the world and the forces of destiny. For this reason, these methods can be studied not only for their divinatory insights but for the intuitive philosophical truths they contain.

(3) At its most practical, the symbolist perspective includes the theory and techniques of ritual. Through ritual, humankind has tried to manipulate nature's symbolic dynamics, whether toward external and material ends (thaumaturgy) or internal and spiritual ends (theurgy). Under this category is also included all traditional knowledge concerning the practice of divination and magic.

(4) At root, the symbolist perspective necessitates a unique mode of thinking, an epistemology, or way of knowing. Rather than reasoning in facts, the symbolist engages the language of the soul through symbols and metaphors. Without metaphoric thinking, all phenomena would be perceived as flat, literal forms.

We also saw how each of these four aspects of symbolist thought can be applied on the personal level, in the life of individuals; collectively, in the events and activities of societies; and universally, in the forms of nature and the laws of geometry and mathematics. In this book we have focused our attention largely on the symbolist view as applied to the personal level of experience.

With this foundation, we turn in conclusion to the relationship between the symbolist worldview and several contemporary models of reality. First we consider Carl Jung's theory of synchronicity, which shares both similarities and differences with the symbolist view presented here. Then we look at the ambivalent relationship between symbolist ideas and contemporary science. We close with a brief discussion of what the symbolist worldview has to offer us today.

SYMBOLIST THOUGHT AND JUNG'S SYNCHRONICITY

In 1952 Swiss psychologist Carl Jung published *Synchronicity: An Acausal Connecting Principle*, one of the most controversial works of his career. In this short volume, Jung summarized decades of research and reflection on the subject of coincidence, concluding that such phenomena hold important secrets about the deeper nature of reality and the human place within it.

Citing a widely known case from his files, Jung described the time he had been working in therapy with a female client who had become blocked in response to the work they were doing. Concerned over this standstill, Jung wondered what it would take to break through her resistance. One day the woman was describing an unusual dream involving a scarab beetle, when Jung noticed the sound of tapping coming from the room's window. Looking more closely, Jung discovered a beetle trying to get into the room. Jung caught the beetle, the closest equivalent to the scarab found in those latitudes, and handed it to the woman, saying, "Here is your scarab!" Surprised by the timing of this event in relation to her present discussion, the woman was able to break through her resistance to the therapy.[1]

The joining of these seemingly unconnected events occurred at a moment which proved to be of great significance in the woman's life, and therefore, Jung felt, could justifiably be called a meaningful coincidence, or synchronicity. The timing of such events seemed to Jung to provide important messages concerning the compensatory relationship between the outer world and the unconscious psyche. Jung also believed that such coincidences reflected an archetypal foundation, since they seemed to arise in conjunction with key transitions in people's lives, such as changes in career, falling in love, marriage, divorce, death, illness, or spiritual transformation. In the case of his blocked patient, Jung pointed out that in ancient Egypt, the scarab was associated with rebirth. Thus the beetle at the window suggested a potential rebirth in the life of the woman who was discussing beetles at the moment it appeared. In the same way, Jung said, synchronistic events often serve as vehicles through which meaningful archetypes express themselves in our lives.

More broadly, Jung felt that synchronistic events suggested the existence of a law of nature which differed markedly from conventional principles of causality. Whereas classical physics explained phenomena largely in terms of linear chains of cause-and-effect, synchronistic events seem connected without a physical, causal relationship. The appearance of the beetle at the window and the woman's dream were in no way caused by one another, but appeared to arise simultaneously out of an underlying pattern of meaning of which the events were mutual expressions. This conviction led Jung and many theorists in his wake to suggest the presence of an all-encompassing acausality which exists at right angles to ordinary cause-and-effect, and which serves not only to connect external phenomena, but to unite the outer and inner worlds of experience, giving rise to the *unus mundus,* or "one world" described in antiquity.

In many respects, Jung's theory represents a modern resurrection of traditional symbolist principles—a fact Jung himself acknowledged in his primary essay on the subject. In discussing the roots of synchronistic thought, Jung offered a brief survey of the historical precedents for his theory, ranging from the medieval theory of correspondences to the ancient Greek notion of *sympatheia.* As Jung noted, although the notion of acausally connected events may seem strange to us now, it would have seemed commonplace in pre-scientific times.

Despite obvious similarities, how do Jung's theory of synchronicity and the symbolist view really compare? As explanatory models of reality, I would suggest that there are several important differences. Let us look at three of these.

The first concerns what Jung and his followers considered to be the relative infrequency of synchronistic phenomena. While there is reason to suspect that Jung may have privately entertained a more comprehensive view, he formally professed the opinion that synchronistic events were "relatively rare." Jung took great pains to distinguish meaningful coincidences from more conventional ones, which could be dismissed as chance groupings without deeper significance. To Jung, the truly synchronistic event is frequently characterized by a confluence of events so startling that "their 'chance' concurrence would represent a degree of improbability that would have to be expressed by an astronomical number."[2]

In the symbolist perspective, by contrast, coincidence is the visible aspect of a more pervasive framework of design which undergirds all experiences. Taking the broader view, the circumstances of an entire life comprise a rich tapestry of meaningful connections, both outer and inner. The events in our lives are connected by an intricate chain of linked analogies, involving the body, events, actions, dreams, and even the contents of our daily imagination. The occasional and dramatic coincidence in an individual's life—what was called in chapter one a literal correspondence—is simply a particularly obvious cross-connection between separate events or states of mind. "The whole world is an omen and a sign. Why look so wistfully in a corner?" Emerson asked. "The voice of divination resounds everywhere and runs to waste unheard, unregarded, as the mountains echo with the bleatings of cattle."[3] The esoteric perspective further holds that symbolism and synchronistic connections extend far beyond personal experience to include the collective and universal levels of reality. On any one of these three levels, one can find important symbolic messages which are not necessarily entwined within readily obvious coincidences.

A second and equally important distinction between symbolist philosophy and Jung's synchronicity theory lies in their understanding of *timing*. Jung saw synchronistic phenomena as essentially unpredictable; in a sense, one could no more predict when a synchronicity might occur than foretell what a person might dream on a given night. Indeed, Jung believed that if one could somehow predict coincidences, they would reflect the operation of causal processes and would thus no longer be synchronistic or acausal. Psychologist Ira Progoff, a former student of Jung's, echoes this view decisively: ". . . archetypes cannot be predicted in advance with respect to the spontaneous events of life."[4] Symbolist systems like astrology, however, offer a model in which the events and phenomena in our lives are recognized to be unfolding according to a regular set of cycles and rhythms. Even Jung's rare meaningful coincidences can be said to occur in accordance with these cycles, so that even though it may not be possible to predict the exact form an impending coincidence will take, one can loosely forecast the times a coincidence is likely to occur and what general archetypal qualities will accompany it. It is ironic that Jung held astrology in high regard, yet did not appropriate these implications for his own model.

The traditional symbolist perspective offers a further modification to synchronicity theory, specifically with regards to its emphasis upon the element of simultaneity. Whereas Jung's predecessor in this field, Paul Kammerer, placed a greater emphasis on sequential coincidences—hence his term "seriality"—Jung focused his attention primarily on acausal connections involving a simultaneous link between events or states taking place in the same moment of time. Jung wrote: "The synchronicity principle asserts that the terms of a meaningful coincidence are connected by *simultaneity* and *meaning*."[5] At the same time, Jung was aware that his time-based model could not adequately account for the full range of events which might be termed synchronistic, as in the case of a person who sees an omen pointing toward an event which occurs in the future or who dreams of an event which occurs shortly afterwards. Jung himself summed up this problem: "Synchronicity, a term for which I am to blame, is an unsatisfactory expression in so far as it only takes account of time phenomena."[6] In the final analysis, Jung concluded that synchronicities could sometimes involve events that weren't exactly synchronous, but which were still related by meaning.[7]

Jung's attempts at clarification did not prevent students of his theory from identifying it almost exclusively with the idea of simultaneity. The complications this posed were most apparent in the field of astrology, since many astrologers had come to believe that Jung's theory represented the most likely explanation for astrology's mechanism. However, as we have seen, researchers like Michel Gauquelin demonstrated that astrological connections are not based on a "grand simultaneity," since his statistics suggest a correlation between the moment of a scientist's birth and the perceived location of Saturn, rather than the planet's actual location in space.

Yet once we jettison simultaneity as the defining mark of synchronicity and adopt instead a broader approach which incorporates both simultaneous and sequential acausal connections, such as is implied by the symbolist perspective, such paradoxes and problems disappear. Moreover, the symbolist viewpoint allows for the phenomenological possibility that each person may be connected to the universe on several levels at once. Recall our earlier example of the Crab Nebula nova, which occurred six thousand years ago, yet didn't appear to human observers until A.D. 1054, because of the time needed for the light from the image to travel across space to earth. I suggested that humans might be connected to events of this sort at both stages of the process: subliminally at the moment the event occurred and, more consciously, when it became visible millennia later. In short, the dynamics of meaning in each person's life are complex ones, involving several different types of relationship operating simultaneously.

Without in any way diminishing the pivotal role Jung's theory of synchronicity has played in calling attention to the study of coincidence, which he felt to be "philosophically of the greatest importance,"[8] a closer examination of his theory reveals limitations that can be helpful to bear in mind in developing a more comprehensive understanding. For one thing, since Jung's theory focused on isolated coincidences, it lacks the wide scope necessary to appreciate the pervasiveness of symbol patterns in our lives. Imagine, by way of analogy, an oceanographer who sets out to study the Pacific by analyzing the properties of only the visible waves on its surface. After decades of collecting data, the oceanographer would be no closer to comprehending the richness of the vast world below, with its multilayered currents, its countless life forms living in intricate symbiosis, the varied landscape of the ocean floor, not to mention the properties and composition of sea water itself. In a comparable way, trying to understand synchronicity by focusing on isolated coincidences, or even on the idea of acausality, limits one to comprehending only the most obvious features of the greater ocean of meaning that encompasses the archetypal structures and dynamics of consciousness itself.

And the mode of consciousness used to perceive events may itself be the key to this broader conception. As we have seen, symbolist epistemology requires and encourages a shift of perception which makes it possible to perceive the metaphoric levels of phenomena. Thinking in terms of concrete facts or literal qualities allows one to see only the most obvious coincidences in daily life, such as the uncanny recurrence of an obscure name several times over the course of a day, or a book falling from a store shelf and opening to the page containing the answer to a problem with which one has been struggling. Such connections are indeed unusual. But once the shift toward recognizing metaphoric nuances takes place,

suddenly, like donning night-vision glasses in a darkened coun-
tryside, a new world of subtleties, cross-connections, and archetypal subtexts reveals itself to consciousness. In this new world,
all events of everyday life are meaningful, not just its remarkable
coincidences.

ANCIENT WISDOM, MODERN SCIENCE

We turn now to another contemporary model of reality with
possible connections to symbolist thinking. As we saw earlier, the
decline of the symbolist worldview occurred in tandem with the
advent of modern science in the seventeenth century. In recent decades, however, a series of important scientific theories have
emerged which bear striking resemblance to key symbolist principles. Some writers have even gone as far as to suggest that science
may be on the verge of explaining traditional symbolist notions, as
well as Jung's theory of synchronicity. We looked in chapter nine at
the problems inherent in applying Bell's Theorem to the workings
of astrology. Here I focus on three other contemporary scientific
theories which are often employed in discussions of the mechanism underlying symbolic connections: the holographic principle,
fractal geometry, and Rupert Sheldrake's theory of morphic resonance. Each of these, in its own way, invites provocative compari-
son with aspects of symbolist thought.

THE HOLOGRAPHIC PRINCIPLE

Among the many developments that resulted from the discovery of laser technology was the advent of holography, or three-di-
mensional photography. Perhaps the most compelling feature of this
new medium was the unique way that a fragment of a holographic
image appeared to "contain" the whole image. If one tears off a
piece of a conventional photographic print, the piece contains only
a portion of the complete image. However, an entire holograph can

be reconstructed from a portion of a holographic image, although in diminished resolution. Since its discovery, researchers in many fields have used this principle to model or explain a wide range of phenomena, from the deeper workings of the brain (Karl Pribam) to the characteristics of space itself (David Bohm).[9]

The holographic principle can be likened to the symbolist notion of condensation, which holds that a part can reflect a larger whole. We have seen numerous examples of this principle, as in the traditional belief that the ruler of a society (such as emperor or pharaoh) embodies the entire society, or the notion that a single event can encapsulate larger trends in a person's life. In essence, every act of divination invokes this principle, in holding that the moment of inquiry can capture the image of a broader field of concerns and life choices.

FRACTAL GEOMETRY

Closely related in principle to the holograph, a fractal is a form which displays qualities of self-similarity in that the shape of the whole is repeated in octave fashion throughout all of its details. This principle can be seen, for instance, in the patterns of snowflakes, where the design of the whole repeats itself in decreasing size within the patterns along its edges. In fact, it is increasingly apparent that fractal-like features permeate all of nature, such as in the shorelines of large rivers, where the smaller inlets and tributaries branching off the main waterways mirror the meandering pattern of the entire river.[10]

The underlying principle of the fractal has been correlated with the traditional notions of condensation and vertical correspondence, as most succinctly expressed in the axiom, "as above, so below." In the same way that a small detail of a fractal reflects the larger design, so esotericists have described the way that patterns in our lives repeat themselves at increasingly higher levels or "octaves." This principle is found in the ancient idea of the microcosm, which holds that each person is a reflection in miniature of a larger universal order. Indeed, all symbols express this principle in their ability to imply subtler processes or meanings across higher levels of experience.

MORPHIC RESONANCE

For centuries scientists have puzzled over the way organisms acquire and develop their specific forms. To cite one aspect of this problem, if each cell in our body contains the same genetic instructions, how does one set of developing cells know it should become a leg, and another set, an arm, and another, an eyeball?

Rupert Sheldrake's answer to such problems can be summarized in simple terms as follows: At root, every form in nature is linked to other forms of its kind by means of a subtle web of relatedness, which Sheldrake calls a morphogenetic field. This field operates not according to ordinary laws of causation, but through a process of similarity or resonance, extending through both space and time. Every new form thus derives guidance in its development from the accumulated experiences of its predecessors throughout history, as embedded within the archetypal field of that form. Thus a specific species of bird will, in its growth and development, be influenced by the morphic field of that species, while at the same time contributing to that pool of stored patterns which will continue to influence all future members of that species. The same principle also holds true, Sheldrake theorizes, with modes of behavior and ideas. This view helps explain why scientists working independently often come up with identical theories or discoveries, or why today's children have an easier time learning to use computers than their parents did.[11]

For some, Sheldrake's model bears obvious resemblance to the esoteric theory of correspondences, which likewise holds that hidden connections unite similar forms or ideas across time and space. For the symbolist, all things are linked by secret chains of affinity on all levels of experience, across both time and space. It should be noted, however, that despite widespread interest and even enthusiasm, the scientific evidence for Sheldrake's theory remains a matter of heated debate within the scientific community itself.

As we have noted, each of these scientific models recalls key elements of symbolist philosophy. Yet as with Jung's synchronicity theory, there are limitations to such comparisons. First of all, it is important to note that, in and of themselves, these ideas do not constitute *proof* of the symbolist worldview, which implies a multileveled cosmology that cannot be proved or disproved in concrete terms. Nor do these theories verify the existence of the esoteric laws they most closely resemble. For example, a scientist might fully accept the role of fractal geometry within nature, as seen in the branching patterns of trees, rivers, or snowflakes, without accepting the varied ways this principle might operate on psychological or spiritual levels of experience.

Indeed, to the extent that these modern models resemble their esoteric counterparts, they tend to do so in an essentially one-dimensional way. Recall our discussion in chapter one of the distinction between the literal and metaphoric forms of symbolist laws, which illustrated the subtle and gross expressions of correspondence, contagion, and condensation. Generally speaking, modern scientific parallels resemble symbolist principles only in their gross or obvious form. For instance, Sheldrake's theory of morphogenetic fields describes the way forms or ideas can be linked to related patterns by merit of formal or functional similarity. It is quite different from the esoteric claim that apparently *dissimilar* objects such as fire, sex, the color red, passion, and rams are related in that each is governed by the astrological principle Mars. Thus these objects or qualities share a connection less of surface form than of archetypal or metaphoric resonance. Sheldrake's theory does not exclude the possibility of such connections; it simply is not designed to address them, since they belong to an entirely different order of relatedness. Of the scientific theories mentioned, perhaps the most purely symbolic in nature is the fractal, with its geometric depiction of self-similarity upon increasing or decreasing levels of magnitude—a simple yet clear echo of condensation or vertical correspondence. Yet as with our other examples, extending this idea to other levels of consciousness is beyond the scope of scientific verification or even concern.

To summarize, while each of the scientific theories offers an intriguing parallel to higher esoteric ideas, they are not identical in every respect, nor do they constitute conclusive evidence for them— indeed, it is only in conjunction with the philosophical framework of symbolist philosophy that such physical models reveal their deepest implications as esoteric laws resonating across all levels of experience, from the gross physical plane to the level of pure mind. What can be said about them without hesitation is that these emerging scientific models represent developments *more compatible* with classic symbolist principles, and to that extent represent an important shift from the mechanistic models of pre-twentieth-century science.

SCIENCE AND MYSTICISM— ALLIES OR ENEMIES?

This discussion draws attention to a problem in the philosophical study of modern physics: whether science can support or confirm mystical truth. In recent years this point has become a source of increasing debate, with one side claiming that modern science has in some sense vindicated ancient wisdom, and the other arguing that science and mysticism cannot be integrated without injustice to the aims and integrity of each. This question is worth exploring, as it sheds light on our ability as moderns steeped in the scientific worldview to adopt and use aspects of the ancient wisdom as set forth in this book.

As we have noted, in recent years, a wide range of writers have looked to the New Physics because it seems to offer helpful insights into the ideas of mystical thought. According to this perspective, the laws or forms of nature are seen as mirroring the experiences of higher states; so that, for example, holography images the mystical relationship between the part and whole. Critics of this view, however, have argued that this line of thinking mixes apples and oranges; whereas science concerns itself with the truths and facts of the physical world, mysticism concerns a level of experience utterly beyond the realm of transitory forms and manifestation. For this reason, science cannot reveal anything important about higher truths. As this position is sometimes expressed, we cannot hope to understand reality in its spiritual richness from the bottom up—by examining the properties of atoms or the laws of matter. While the higher levels of reality enfold and contain the lower levels, the lower levels do not enfold and contain the higher.

But while it may be true that lower levels of reality do not contain the higher, there is ample precedent in the perennial traditions for the fact that they can in certain respects *reflect* them, by means of symbolism—*as above, so below.* By way of analogy, the printed symbols on a piece of sheet music for Bach's *Mass in B Minor* do not "contain" the music or the higher aesthetic or spiritual experiences it evokes; yet in some sense these written notations accurately reflect the intricacies of Bach's musical statements and serve as useful guides toward evoking them. Moreover, even if we accept that the highest levels of spiritual experience lie beyond all forms and symbolic representation, this doesn't mean that physical-plane forms cannot tell us a great deal about those levels of reality just short of the Absolute and thus about the architecture and dynamics of the Divine Mind.

Another point which critics have cited is the fact that scientific knowledge is in a state of constant flux, and thus unreliable as a tool for understanding eternal spiritual truths. From age to age, humanity's knowledge of nature and her laws has given way to newer and seemingly more accurate theories, such that the solid and indestructible atom of one era gave way to the energetic and spacious atom of another and to the uncertain quantum realities of the current model. If we base a spiritual philosophy on current-day scientific knowledge, these critics argue, what happens to that spiritual truth when our scientific knowledge is modified or discarded? As particle physicist Jeremy Bernstein has remarked, "If I were an Eastern mystic the last thing in the world I would want would be a reconciliation with modern science, [because] to hitch a religious philosophy to a contemporary science is a sure route to its obsolescence."[12]

However, I believe there is a more moderate approach to this issue. While scientific truth is in general subject to change, certain aspects of empirical knowledge are demonstrably more timeless and "fixed" than others. Thus although Aristotle's natural laws have not weathered the centuries well, the symbolically potent discovery in our own century of the relative nature of time is unlikely ever to be proven wholly wrong. Similarly, in the field of astronomy, theories concerning the evolution and origins of the universe are continually being updated, yet the discovery in 1846 of the planet Neptune will presumably never be revoked as a mistake. In geometry and mathematics, such fundamental ideas as the relationship of a circle's diameter to its circumference (or *pi*), or the mathematical properties of whole numbers, are probably eternal and universal in their application, and thus useful mirrors of higher principles. I believe the same will probably prove to hold true for the contemporary theories mentioned earlier; each of these may indeed be modified in the years to come, yet will likely remain fixtures of our conceptual understanding of the way nature works. As Nick Herbert wrote concerning Bell's revolutionary contribution to physics:

> *Physics theories are not eternal. When quantum theory joins the ranks of phlogiston, caloric, and the luminiferous ether in the physics junkyard, Bell's theorem will still be valid. Because it's based on facts, Bell's theorem is here to stay.*[13]

In some cases, too, scientific models are not actually overturned as much as reframed. For instance, Newtonian physics has in many ways been superseded by quantum physics; yet it is not entirely accurate to say that Newton's ideas have been proven wrong—indeed, we would not have been able to fly to the Moon without them. It would be more precise to say that Newton's laws were found to exist within a broader context which now includes relativity theory, quantum physics and non-locality, and chaos dynamics. The same reframing is constantly occurring within spiritual thought. Astrology itself provides an excellent example. The relatively recent discoveries of Neptune, Pluto, and Uranus, for example, have not overturned traditional models of planetary archetypal rulership so much as complexified them, giving contemporary astrologers new influences to work with in creating and interpreting charts. Finally, humanity's changing models of the world, even when shown to be "wrong" by subsequent generations, arguably retain a certain symbolic meaning relative to their own level of reference. As creative products of the collective imagination, overturned theories may still merit study as synchronistic keys to the collective mind, just as would any work of art, historic event, or sociological trend.

Another, and potentially more serious problem in the effort to merge science and mysticism centers around the inability of science to directly address matters of *meaning*. Science is a quantitative process, confined to the study of measurable properties in phenomena. By contrast, the symbolist perspective is almost entirely qualitative or metaphoric in nature. To illustrate this distinction, consider the way each of these methods might approach a rose. The scientist might begin by examining the flower and noting its characteristics—the number and arrangement of petals, their relative size and color, the branching of leaves, thorns, and roots. Other relevant data might include the rose's genetic heritage; its internal cellular structure; its ideal soil conditions, temperature, and water needs. Now contrast this with the way an esotericist or symbolist might examine the same rose. His or her first consideration might be aesthetic—the play of color between petals and stem, the design and proportion of each element, as well as the flower's size and placement relevant to other aspects of its environment. As a symbol, a rose's most commanding feature is its beauty; thus the rose evokes the energies of the heart and of the goddess Venus, or Aphrodite, manifest in plant form. At the subtlest archetypal level, plants in bloom express the principle of unfoldment, thus resonating with such ideas as growth, awakening, and the realization of latent potentials—corresponding to the yogic theory of the chakras, for which petaled flowers are frequently used as symbols.

The symbolic approach of the esotericist can be termed *hermeneutic,* a term which refers to the art of symbolic interpretation. To the scientist, on the other hand, the symbolic properties of an entity tend to be ignored as irrelevant. Because of its emphasis on such factors as measurement and quantification, science seldom ventures into the dimension of meaning. Yet the level of meaning is the most important one in symbolist thinking, for it is upon this level that one encounters such vital factors as subtle correspondences, archetypal symbolism, elemental properties, proportionalities, and the other qualitative elements which comprise the symbolist intellectual universe. As important as these are, no scientific method or model is capable of capturing, in any definitive way, such elusive dimensions.

This same problem underlies any argument that science might someday provide a full explanation for Jung's synchronistic phenomenon. Over the last several decades, a number of theorists (including Jung himself) have expressed optimism that the new physics may eventually unlock the deeper mechanism by which meaningful coincidences occur in our lives. As Robert Anton Wilson, a prominent writer in this field, expressed it:

> *Jung was on the right track. He kept insisting that somehow, somewhere in quantum theory, the actual mechanism of synchronicity would be found and defined. In the late 1980s it begins to look as if we have started to understand it.*[14]

Yet to the degree that we fail to see the true heart, or "mechanism," of synchronicity to be one of meaning rather than acausality, any such hope is misdirected. No strictly physical method can explain the subtle significance of a synchronistic event any more than it can measure the beauty of a flower or the meaning of a dream. Hence, even though scientists may be able to verify the way distant objects are linked across time and space (as does Bell's Theorem, for instance), it cannot show us how this linkage occurs on subtler levels of meaning; nor can it ever provide us with a physical method of examining directly the archetypal qualities unfolding throughout our lives. For that, what is required is not another scientific model, but an entirely different worldview—a multileveled cosmology, with an understanding of reality beyond physical facts.

Taken to its farthest extreme, however, the hermeneutic argument has led some to charge that since meaning doesn't easily lend itself to scientific examination, meaning is not only irrelevant, but nonexistent. For the most skeptical, any suggestion of inherent meaningfulness is regarded as the fanciful projection of human values onto an essentially neutral world. From this extreme vantage point, scientific models cannot be vehicles of higher meanings, for the simple reason that there are no higher meanings in the first place!

However, on closer examination, this position does not hold up. First, the fact that science cannot directly examine meaning does not prove that meaning doesn't exist; as Carl Sagan has noted, absence of evidence is not evidence of absence. More important, neither does it mean that the presence of meaning in the world is not subject to verification of *any* sort. As Ken Wilber has argued, if we dismiss mystical or hermeneutic concerns for lack of concrete evidence, then we must summarily dismiss all nonempirical endeavors, from

> . . . *mathematics to literature to linguistics to psychoanalysis to historical interpretation. Nobody has ever seen, "out there" in*

the sensory world, the square root of a negative one. That is a mathematical symbol seen only inwardly, "privately," with the mind's eye. Yet a community of trained mathematicians know exactly what that symbol means, and they can share that symbol easily in intersubjective awareness, and they can confirm or reject the proper and consistent uses of that symbol.[15]

In the same way, one might argue that while the "private" and "subjective" models of reality entertained by symbolists may not lend themselves to verification along concrete scientific lines, they are nonetheless open to relative confirmation or rebuttal by experts conversant with the ideas and experiences of this philosophical perspective. On the personal level, yogis have long stressed that an individual's process of investigation should play a vital role in a student's acceptance or rejection of any important philosophical viewpoint. No externally derived model of reality—whether taught by a scientist, preacher, or astrologer—should be blindly accepted as true without first carefully examining it in a genuine "scientific" spirit to see whether it squares with one's own experience.

In this spirit, we each might observe the patterns of events in our own lives, putting aside all preconceived notions, and decide for ourselves if outer events do indeed reflect inner ones, or if subtle connections between separate events suggest themselves. Astrology offers an especially useful tool in this regard, by providing a systematic way to monitor the symbolic patterns and interconnections arising throughout one's life. For example, one might compare the cycles and symbols predicted in one's horoscope with the events that actually transpire during a particular period of time. As one who has experimented with this discipline for over twenty years, I find it hard to imagine that anyone approaching such a study with an open mind would not be impressed by astrology's accuracy in mapping the archetypal and synchronistic patterns of personal life or the culture at large.

Yet it may be possible to take this verification process one crucial step further. For even if science cannot directly confirm the presence of meaning in our lives, it may be capable of *indirectly* validating its presence. To explain the distinction between direct and indirect validation, consider the following analogy: Imagine an astronomer discovering and photographing a new planet, which is then confirmed by other astronomers; this is an example of direct evidence. On the other hand, suppose the same astronomer notices subtle perturbations in the orbit of an already known planet, apparently caused by another planet beyond it which is tugging on it gravitationally each time it passes by. This would be an example of indirect evidence, in which a claim is strongly suggested by the available facts, yet isn't proven conclusively.

In this spirit, I would argue that the ground-breaking research of French statistician Michel Gauquelin provides us with compelling evidence for the existence of meaning in our world. As noted in chapter nine, Gauquelin's work demonstrated statistically the correlations between certain planetary positions and the professional inclinations of men and women born under those placements. This aspect of his work proves, in a direct way, a relationship between the positions of planets and the lives of humans on earth; but what it indirectly proves is something potentially more momentous— the rulerships and correspondences traditionally associated with the planets by astrologers. Based upon years of research on the effects of planetary influence on thousands of individuals, Gauquelin's work suggests that Saturn is indeed related to a predisposition for the physical sciences (Saturn showed up prominently, for example, in the charts of eminent professors of medicine at a rate that exceeded odds of 10,000,000 to 1); Mars to martial and athletic involvements (Mars was prominent in the charts of athletes against odds of 500,000 to 1); and Jupiter to politicians—just as would have been expected based on traditional astrological theory.[16]

Why is this so important? Because Gauquelin's research clearly suggests that the planets hold qualities of *meaning*. After all, what physical force might conceivably connect Mars with a human predisposition for sports instead of, say, the arts? While it isn't inconceivable that researchers might eventually uncover a mechanical explanation for these correlations, this would seem unlikely. In their implications for the prevailing scientific worldview, Gauquelin's conclusions are nothing short of revolutionary in that they strongly suggest an organizing principle beyond physical causality. Once we validate the essentially symbolic character of astrological correspondences—whether through personal experimentation or controlled tests like those of Gauquelin—the materialistic worldview comes "crashing down like a house of cards," to use John Anthony West's apt metaphor.

TOWARD RECONCILIATION: SCIENCE IN A SYMBOLIST KEY

Seen as a whole, these ideas provide us with a foundation for revisioning the relationship between symbolist principles and scientific inquiry. In this context, the question of whether science "proves" the truths of esotericism becomes less important than understanding the ways science and symbolic thinking can usefully illumine one another. To use a simple analogy, a book containing the mystic verses of Rumi does not by itself constitute "proof" for the poet's higher spiritual realizations, yet this hardly means it cannot provide useful insights into spiritual matters—once one accepts the premise that there are spiritual levels of awareness in the first place. Presuming a meaningful universe, the theories of science—Newton's, Bell's, Einstein's—likewise provide information concerning the higher truths of consciousness, when seen anew in the light of symbolist perception.

The scientific and symbolist approaches lead to complementary types of knowledge. In the same way that adjusting a polarizing filter on a camera reveals different ranges of colors and contrasts in the scene being viewed, so the quantitative method of science and the qualitative method of esotericism extract different orders of information from the world.[17] Scientific inquiry may shed new light on matters of great interest to mystics and philosophers. In turn, the comprehensive vision of reality implied by the symbolist might be employed to infuse scientific inquiry with a dimension of meaning that evokes a richer and more complete understanding of the world. The end result of such cross-fertilization might be a more philosophically resonant science and more objectively grounded spirituality.

Ironically, in historical times, this fusion of science and meaning was a common one, as scientists were generally philosophers, and philosophy was considered a branch of science. Pivotal figures in these disciplines, from ancient Greeks like Pythagoras and Plato, through the Renaissance theorists Galileo, Johannes Kepler, and Sir Isaac Newton, to the great German thinkers Goethe and Hegel, saw in nature's patterns a source of important insights into spiritual and psychological principles. As Galileo commented, "Philosophy is written in the book which is ever before our eyes—I mean the universe—but we cannot understand it if we do not learn the language to grasp the symbols in which it is written."[18] The modern Islamic scholar Seyyed Hossein Nasr echoes the important contribution symbolist thinking can make to science:

> *The traditional sciences of all traditional civilizations . . . are based on a hierarchic vision of the universe, one which sees the physical world as the lowest domain of reality which nevertheless reflects the highest states by means of symbols which have remained an ever open gate toward the Invisible. . . . The psycho-physical world, which preoccupies modern science, is seen in the traditional perspective as a reflection of the luminous archetypes.*[19]

Even some contemporary scientists have begun to realize the potentially important role meaning might play in understanding our world. The late physicist David Bohm theorized that meaning might represent the subtle organizing principle for both matter and energy. Meaning, he wrote, is "a key factor of being, not only for human beings individually and socially, but perhaps also for nature and for the whole universe."[20] He speculates that there may be "cosmic meanings, beyond any human individual, or even the totality of humanity. . . ."[21] Nobel Prize winner Richard Feynman, too, sees a new era coming for scientific inquiry:

> *The next great era of awakening of human intellect may well produce a method of understanding the qualitative content of equations. . . . Today we cannot see whether Schrödinger's equation contains frogs, musical composers, or morality—or whether it does not. And so we can all hold strong opinions either way.*[22]

The reintroduction of meaning would have revolutionary implications for all scientific disciplines, from chemistry, astronomy, physics, and mathematics, to "soft" sciences like psychology, anthropology, and medicine. With this reconciliation in mind, let us consider a specific example of the symbolist contribution within the field of astronomical exploration. As I hope to show, the symbolist view offers the possibility of new levels of meaning and information concerning the cosmos.

ASTRONOMICAL EXPLORATION— A SYMBOLIST APPROACH

Humanity's exploration of the Moon is a powerful landmark in the history of science and technology. As noted, the Moon has traditionally been associated by mystics and astrologers with the feminine principle and with the quality of divine reflectivity. In modern times, however, symbolic thinking about celestial bodies has been replaced by a quantitative approach concerned strictly with measurable properties. In his philosophical study of space exploration *Approaching Earth*, Daniel Noel contrasts the clinical way scientists viewed samples of lunar rock brought back by astronauts with the reactions of poets and writers to the same rocks. As an example of the poetic approach, Noel cites Norman Mailer's *Fire on the Moon,* in which Mailer says that Moon rocks he saw on display in Houston possessed feminine qualities unacknowledged by the scientists on hand. Looking at the universe with the soul of a poet, Noel suggests, offers a way to unlock the deeper mysteries of the cosmos. Quoting Mailer, he underscores the importance of exploring the universe scientifically without losing sight of symbolist vision:

> . . . *yes, we might have to go out into space until the mystery of new discovery would force us to regard the world once again as poets, behold it as savages who knew that if the universe was a lock, its key was metaphor rather than measure.*[23]

In many ways, the merging of astronomy with symbolist values is not so much a new development as a contemporary revitalization of an approach that used to be standard. Even Galileo, the father of modern science, suggested that Mars and Jupiter had decidedly masculine qualities, exactly as Chinese astrologers had declared millennia earlier. In studying any newly discovered planet or celestial body, we must broaden our scope. Instead of concerning ourselves only with such quantifiable factors as topography, chemical composition, or magnetic fields, the symbolist perspective would oblige us to ask: What does this planet or celestial body *mean*?

I suggest, in fact, that we consider astronomical or scientific discoveries on three levels of significance: universal, collective, and personal. On the universal level, we might ask: What is the archetypal meaning of this discovery in itself, as a reflection of higher truth? At the collective level, the question becomes: What is the symbolic or synchronistic importance of this discovery for society at this time? Finally, on the personal level, each person might ask: What is the significance of this discovery for my life at this time?

To illustrate, imagine the discovery or exploration of a new planet. We might first consider the significance of this body in terms of its universal symbolism or meaning. This could be determined through a variety of methods. On one level, the archetypal significance of a planet might be glimpsed through reflection on the name assigned to it by astronomers, a method based on the belief among astrologers that the names chosen for newly discovered celestial bodies are synchronistically appropriate to their meaning—whether recognized consciously by scientists or not.[24] The most recently discovered planet in our solar system serves as a useful illustration of this idea. In ancient mythology the god Pluto was ruler of the Underworld; by correspondence, the planet Pluto has come to be associated with the psychological "underworld" and the dynamic forces of the subconscious mind. These include deep-seated emotions, the will to power, emotional transformation, and the processes of death and rebirth.

Another aspect of the meaning of a new planet is revealed by examining the historical events taking place at the time of its discovery, to see what synchronistic insights these provide into this planet's archetypal energy. For example, the period surrounding the discovery of Pluto in 1930 witnessed a number of important historical developments, such as the rise of Fascism, the discovery of atomic power, as well as the spread of the criminal "underworld" in America—all displaying features of the Plutonian archetype, as it has come to be understood by astrologers.

Next, on the collective level, the discovery or exploration of a new planet often holds profound meaning for society during that time. As shown above, planetary discoveries have been accompanied by dramatic cultural changes corresponding in marked ways with the symbolic meanings associated with the planet or its mythological namesake. Many astrologers take this to mean that the timing of such discoveries is not accidental but synchronistically connected to changes taking place in the collective psyche. We find examples of this not only in the area of planetary discovery but in all aspects of space exploration. Consider the period surrounding the first Moonwalk in 1969. The late 1960s

saw the rise not only of the women's movement, but of other elements of the collective feminine as well, as reflected in the exploration of the human unconscious via psychedelic drugs and the
rise of a Dionysian or emotionally unrestrained expressiveness in
the arts. Within hours of the lunar landing itself, two other stories
occurred with possible synchronistic links: Ted Kennedy's infamous Chappaquiddick incident, resulting in the drowning death
of a young woman (water, women, and alcohol, or liquid "spirits,"
all having lunar or feminine associations); and the discovery of
Aphrodite's most important ancient temple by archaeologist Iris
Love in present-day Turkey (the Moon having been associated by
the ancient Greeks with the worship of Aphrodite). If we read the
Moon mission as mirroring an opening to the feminine principle
taking place within society at the time, then synchronicities like
this may provide important insights into the specific state of our
collective relationship with the archetypal feminine—Kennedy's
scandal illuminating the darker underside of that connection, and
the discovery of Aphrodite's temple accentuating its more aesthetic
aspect and underscoring the Moon's symbolic association with
memory and the past.

Finally, on the personal level, the synchronistic effects of any
important discovery can be expected to manifest in different ways
for individuals across the planet. An astrologer might determine
this by examining the zodiacal degree inhabited by the celestial body
at the moment of its discovery, then looking to see what part of an
individual's personal horoscope this corresponds to. It may be further assumed that any significant correlations would be amplified
many times over for those individuals actually involved in the discovery. It is curious, for example, that the name of the figure most
responsible for Pluto's discovery, Percival Lowell, had initials closely
matching those of the planet itself, and that the woman who un-
covered Aphrodite's temple had the last name *Love!* In a similar
vein, astrologers have often pointed out the important role of the
Moon in Neil Armstrong's horoscope, as if to suggest a vital con-

nection between this energy in his personal life and the fact that he was the first human to set foot on this body in space.

This symbolist-inspired approach can be applied to any area of scientific inquiry. Loosely appropriating the terminology of their traditional counterparts, we might envision the following set of conversions: Geology and geography, understood symbolically, would evoke the ancient art of *geomancy*, the study of the symbolic dynamics of environmental forms and energies. Infused with symbolic meaning, chemistry would revitalize *alchemy*, the study of matter's subtle energetic properties and qualities, and their psychic equivalents. Geometry, seen qualitatively, would feed into *sacred geometry*, the study of pure forms and their higher significance. Read symbolically, mathematics would enhance our understanding of *numerology*, the study of spiritual qualities of numerical patterns. Approaching the human mind symbolically and archetypally gives rise to *sacred psychology*, the understanding of human motivation in its cosmic dimension, as exemplified by yoga's chakra psychology, the Kabbalistic tree of life, and modern-day archetypal psychology associated with theorists like James Hillman. Meaning-based health and diagnostic systems would give rise to *sacred medicine,* the study of the metaphoric and energetic dimensions of the body and mind and the deeper significance of illnesses. And astronomy interpreted symbolically yields new insights into *astrology*, the study of the meanings and dynamics of celestial phenomena. In this same vein, the application of symbolist principles would permit modern researchers to gain a deeper insight into each of these traditional systems and their ideas, such as the Chinese medical belief that physical health requires a balance between female (yin) and male (yang) properties in the body; astrology's belief in the symbolic dimension of celestial bodies; alchemy's emphasis on the elemental properties of moist, dry, cool, and hot; or sacred geometry's speculations on the higher meaning of visible shapes.

More broadly, the symbolist perspective raises the philosophical question as to whether any purely scientific method can ever wholly explain nature's workings. In recent years, prominent scientists like astrophysicist Stephen Hawking have suggested that science may eventually answer all the great questions concerning nature's laws and functions—a sentiment strangely reminiscent of nineteenth-century claims that only minor problems remained for scientists to solve before our knowledge of nature would be complete. The symbolist perspective suggests the inherent vanity of such claims; one can no more hope to obtain a complete understanding of the world without considering its qualitative dimension than to unlock the full importance of a rose using only scientific instruments or methods. Through the lens of metaphor and symbolism, scientists and, indeed, all human beings, have access to a more complete picture of our world than is possible through a purely quantitative approach.

THE RITUAL DIMENSION OF SCIENCE

In addition to revealing a new horizon of knowledge in our understanding of the world, the infusion of science with symbolist perspectives may have important practical ramifications. Earlier we reflected on the possibility that our actions may have synchronistic or "magical" effects on the world, since all forms of activity engage subtle dynamics within the larger network of correspondences around and within us. Applying this idea to science, we might ask, what subtle influences do our collective actions relative to the natural world have beyond what is readily apparent?

For instance, when human beings landed on the Moon, we necessarily affected its environment in subtle and gross ways, changing its atmosphere, scattering assorted debris, and even planting a flag into its surface. What symbolic or geomantic effects might this have set into motion in connection with the lunar field of meaning? And how do those effects extend synchronistically to our own inner universe, the domain of our "inner Moon"? Since the Moon corresponds with our collective feminine nature, is it possible that our intrusions upon the lunar surface have subtly colored the quality of our emotional life in ways we can't yet comprehend? Likewise, when we eventually capture and analyze an orbiting asteroid for its minerals, what subtle strands of the universal fabric are we affecting? If the asteroid holds an objective meaning and is entwined with the life streams of all beings, what chords within the great symphony would be altered by our investigations?

It is worth noting that since the earliest days of space exploration, elders from various indigenous cultures have cautioned scientists against insensitive or thoughtless tampering with the celestial environment, as exemplified by our careless littering of Earth's surroundings with defunct satellites and other hardware. Such concerns arise from an awareness not only of the sacredness of nature, but a sensitivity to the unforeseen side-effects these activities might set into motion. For instance, Hopi spokesperson Thomas Banyaca warned an audience in Los Angeles as a NASA mission returned from the Moon that human tampering with the Moon and stars could create an earthquake or a tidal wave. After delivering this prophecy, Banyaca left the area, saying that the dire consequences he predicted "might come tomorrow." At six o'clock the next morning, the San Fernando earthquake rocked Los Angeles.[25]

Understandably, coincidences like this may not convince the hardened skeptic, but they should at least give us reason to reflect on the deeper significance of our actions, not only in space exploration but everywhere in nature. When a forest of old-growth trees is leveled, or a species of animal hunted to extinction, what is the synchronistic impact of our carelessness on humankind's inner ecology? When we detonate nuclear devices beneath the Earth's surface, what repercussions are triggered in the subtle web of relatedness, beyond what can be measured on scientific instruments?

Taking symbolist ideas seriously would compel us to adopt new protocols regarding future scientific undertakings. This methodology would consider not only the sacredness of all life and environments, but the role of each species and locale in the greater field of interconnectedness. Scientists could benefit from a careful examination of the beliefs of Native Americans and other indigenous peoples, who approach all undertakings in the spirit of humility and sacramental reverence. Rather than setting foot on a new planet in a spirit of dominance and exploitation, one might envision a time when explorers first seek to establish a spiritual communion with the new environment, through ritual attunement and consecration. Ritual actions would additionally serve to seed the initial moments of new endeavors with auspicious symbols, since the symbolist view holds that a harmonious beginning influences a successful outcome.

To think in this way is to move beyond conventional ecological notions toward the perception that everything has a unique quality of meaning and subtle interconnection with all other things. As the mystical poet Frances Thompson wrote,

> *All things by immortal power near or far,*
> *Hiddenly to each other linked are*
> *That thou canst not stir a flower*
> *Without the troubling of a star.*[26]

THE PROMISE OF SYMBOLIST THOUGHT

The symbolist perspective represents a radical shift in the way we think about the world. In this book we have touched on a few of its implications. On the personal level, these include the discovery of new dimensions of meaning in the events of our lives and the suggestion that life is a sacred text, to be unlocked through the key of metaphoric knowing. Thus understood, life events yield information about our personality, our karma, and even our future potentials, pointing the way toward greater levels of awakening.

Extended to the collective sphere, the symbolist perspective holds the promise of a new understanding of the universe, through a science informed by qualities and values rather than concrete facts. It promises the fulfillment of a dream long held by esotericists— forging a grand science of correspondences by which to interpret and correlate phenomena. More fundamentally, symbolist thought suggests a radical revision of how we view knowledge itself. This expanded vision further asks us to question the ramifications of all actions relative to the world, both by individuals and by engineers and scientists.

Yet the most far-reaching consequence of the symbolist legacy is also the simplest—the realization that the cosmos is suffused with meaning. Why is this so important? The prevailing scientific worldview tells us that life is a dynamic, yet essentially meaningless affair. It holds that whatever symbolic significance it holds has been projected onto it by the human mind. To the symbolist, the world is a realm of magic and mystery which the mindset of science cannot fully explain. The symbolist vision shakes the materialist conception of reality to its core and shows the manifest phenomena of this world to possess a ground of meaning beyond purely physical explanations.

The holistic worldview which some contemporary theorists have related to the New Science and to Jung's synchronicity theory moves in this direction, but does not succeed in overthrowing materialism. Jung himself backed off from the metaphysical implications of his theory. In his original work on this subject, he emphasized meaning as the defining mark of synchronistic events; if meaning is inherent in coincidences, a transcendental dimension beyond the material world seems unavoidable. Yet as Aniela Jaffé points out in *The Myth of Meaning,* in his later writings, Jung shifted his emphasis from the idea of meaning as the dominant characteristic of synchronistic phenomena to the more objective concept of acausal connectedness—a decidedly less radical position, from the academic perspective. This shift of emphasis ultimately led Jung to conclude that the explanation for synchronicity lay not in philosophy or mysticism but in empirical science.[27]

In the final analysis, the deeper message of symbolist thought is that the world is a rich and multidimensional place in which, as Plotinus said many centuries ago, "All teems with symbol." Until we acknowledge life's qualitative dimensions, we are like flies crawling across the ceiling of the Sistine Chapel, ignorant of the archetypal drama unfolding around us. Like proponents of an old-time religion who insist on reading biblical stories as literal truth, ignoring their metaphoric and mystical possibilities, we are too often experiential fundamentalists, blind to the depths of meaning presented to us everyday. The symbolist perspective offers the possibility of a transformed vision, restoring lost dimensions of significance to our lives. Having regained this insight, we can revision our personal dramas in an archetypal context.

Towards this end, this book has suggested the value of re-examining the philosophical and symbolic systems of antiquity, in which we glimpse a deeper truth about the universe and our place in it. This is not simply to champion a return to a golden age of the past, in which esoteric knowledge supposedly flourished in pristine form. On the contrary, we today find ourselves at an especially privileged vantage point in the study of symbolist ideas, because of our unprecedented access to the esoteric systems and teachings of many historical cultures. In this spirit, what has been presented here is intended not as a scholarly survey so much as a tapestry of the themes of the symbolist legacy, modified for our own time and sensibilities.

Perhaps the deeper study of symbolism and synchronicity in our lives is best seen as part of an emerging Sacred Science, incorporating insights from both ancient and contemporary sources. This integrative approach would draw upon knowledge from such traditional disciplines as sacred geometry, astrology, mathematics, yogic chakra psychology, mythology, geomancy, and ritual theory, as well as the findings of modern science and psychology. These approaches would, in turn, be framed by the insights into consciousness presented by the world's great mystical and meditative traditions. Seen in this way, the message of meaningful coincidence would assume its rightful place as a facet of a greater framework of perennial philosophical and spiritual thought. It is my hope that this book has contributed towards this end.

ENDNOTES

INTRODUCTION

[1] Michael Grosso, *The Millennium Myth* (Wheaton, IL: Quest Books, 1995), 9.

CHAPTER 1

[1] Ralph Waldo Emerson, "Nature," from *The Writings of Ralph Waldo Emerson* (New York: Modern Library, 1940), 15.

[2] Arthur Schopenhauer, quoted by Joseph Campbell in *The Masks of God, vol. IV: Creative Mythology* (New York: Viking Press, 1968), 193-194.

[3] For a concise summary of Leibniz's theory of "pre-established harmony," see Ira Progoff, *Jung, Synchronicity, and Human Destiny* (New York: Dell Books, 1973), 67-76.

[4] John Maynard Keynes, "Newton the Man," in *Newton Tercentenary Celebrations* (Cambridge, England: Cambridge University Press, 1947), 27-29.

[5] Carl Jung, "Synchronicity: An Acausal Connecting Principle," in *Collected Works*, vol. 8 (Princeton, NJ: Princeton University Press, 1969).

[6] Quoted by Arthur Koestler in *The Roots of Coincidence* (New York: Random House, 1972), 87.

[7] Concerning omens, the Dalai Lama has remarked: "We [all the Buddhist schools] believe in oracles, omens, interpretations of dreams, reincarnation. But these beliefs, which for us are certainties, are not something we try to impose on others in any way." "The Dalai Lama in conversation with Jean-Claude Carriere," in *Violence and Compassion: Dialogues on the World Today* (New York: Doubleday, 1996), 20.

[8] "Ringing Down the Curtain on Joyce's 100th Year," Book World, *Chicago Tribune*, Dec. 26, 1982.

[9] Robert Anton Wilson, *Coincidance* (Phoenix, AZ: New Falcon Press, 1991).

[10] Aniela Jaffé, *The Myth of Meaning* (New York: Putnam, 1971), 153.

[11] Mircea Eliade, *Images and Symbols* (New York: Search Book, 1969), 177-178.

[12] Lin Yun, as cited by Sarah Rossbach, *Feng Shui: The Chinese Art of Placement* (New York: E.P. Dutton, Inc.,1983), 101.

CHAPTER 2

[1] Mircea Eliade, *The Sacred and the Profane: The Nature of Religion* (New York: Harper and Row, 1961), 165.

[2] Another way of understanding the historical context of symbolist thought is in terms of the distinction between mysticism and occultism. Strictly speaking, *mysticism* represents the path of direct union with God. By contrast, *occultism* is the effort to understand creation and its inner workings, with an eye toward the practical application of that knowledge. One way to illustrate the distinction between these two paths is as follows: If reality were a skyscraper, with the different floors representing various levels from gross to subtle, then the mystic is the individual whose sole concern is finding the elevator and riding directly to the uppermost floors. The occultist, by contrast, is interested in finding out what is on each of the floors, and might therefore study the architectural, plumbing, and electrical diagrams of the building to understand the layout and energy-grid patterns characterizing its operations. According to this basic distinction, symbolist philosophy theoretically falls under the heading of occultism rather than mysticism, its focus being understanding how the cosmos operates, rather than its ultimate transcendence or integration. In reality, of course, one rarely finds either of these paths in their pure and unadulterated state, with many mystics through history possessing considerable occult knowledge, and many occultists having a deep mystical sensitivity. In mythological imagery, the ideal merging of these dual paths can be seen in the Arthurian figure of Merlin, who embodies both spiritual insight and mystical knowledge.

[3] O.R. Gurney, "The Babylonians and Hittites," from *Oracles and Divination*. Michael Loewe and Carmen Blacker, eds. (Boulder, CO: Shambhala, 1981),142-173.

[4] W. Y. Evans-Wentz, *Tibetan Yoga and Secret Doctrines* (London: Oxford University Press, 1967), 165.

[5] Cited by Wendy Doniger in *Dreams, Illusions, and Other Realities* (Chicago: University of Chicago Press, 1984), 18.

[6] For an in-depth discussion of the multileveled character of Egyptian hieroglyphics, see Serge Sauneron's *The Priests of Ancient Egypt* (New York: Evergreen Profile Books, Grove Press, 1960), 132-135.

[7] A summation of both Schwaller de Lubicz and John Anthony West's ideas can be found in West's *Serpent in the Sky: The High Wisdom of Ancient Egypt* (Wheaton: Quest Books, 1993).

[8] Paraphrased from *Mythologies*, vol. I, compiled by Yves Bonnefoy, translated by Gerald Honigsblum, under the direction of Wendy Doniger (Chicago: University of Chicago Press, 1991), 591.

[9] Seyyed Hossein Nasr, *The Need for a Sacred Science* (Albany: SUNY Press, 1993), 100, 132-133.

[10] Cited by Anthony Aveni in *Conversing with the Planets* (New York: Kodansha International, Inc.,1994), 170-171.

---

[11] Edward Hoffman, *The Heavenly Ladder: A Jewish Guide to Inner Growth* (San Francisco: Harper & Row, 1985), 98-99.

[12] It would be an exaggeration to suggest that the symbolist perspective ever completely disappeared. Apart from its vestigial survival through popular superstition, it is possible as well to trace a variety of historical streams through which its more subtle expressions have come down to us. In the philosophical world, a short list of its most influential proponents would include Emmanuel Swedenborg, Ralph Waldo Emerson, H. P. Blavatsky, Manly Palmer Hall, and Carl Jung. As it concerns the level of cosmic, or nature symbolism, we must also note the historical role played by European Romanticism in general, and the *Naturphilosophie* movement in particular, as represented by Novalis, Goethe, Schelling, H. Steffens, and G. H. von Schubert. In the literary field, seminal influences include Herman Melville, James Joyce, August Strindberg (*Inferno, Occult Diary*), Thornton Wilder (*The Bridge at San Luis Rey*), and the movement of symbolist art and poetry as epitomized by the French poet Baudelaire. Heavily influenced by both Swedenborg and the earlier American symbolists such as Emerson and Poe, Baudelaire's poem "Correspondences" arguably represents the centerpiece of nineteenth-century literary symbolism: "Nature is a temple whose living columns sometimes yield confusing messages; man passes there across a forest of symbols which cast their familiar glances at him." Finally, on the popular level, perhaps the most influential channel through which symbolist notions have persisted into modern times has been the divinatory arts, including such disciplines as astrology, tarot and the I Ching.

[13] Carl Jung, "The Symbolic Life" in *Collected Works*, vol. 18 (Princeton: Princeton University Press, 1980), 255.

[14] Colin Wilson, *The Occult* (New York: Random House, 1971), 46.

[15] Mircea Eliade, *Images and Symbols: Studies in Comparative Symbolism* (New York: Search Book), 12.

CHAPTER 3

[1] Several books provide a useful introduction to a psychological approach to body symbolism. These include Ken Dychtwald, *Bodymind* (Los Angeles: J. P. Tarcher, 1986); A. Lowen, *Language of the Body* (New York: Collier Books, 1971); and Debbie Shapiro, *Bodymind Workbook: Exploring How the Mind and the Body Work Together* (London: Element, 1990).

[2] Until fairly recently, the primary source for English-speaking readers on Paul Kammerer's work on coincidence has been Arthur Koestler's *The Roots of Coincidence* (New York: Random House, 1972) and *The Case of the Midwife Toad* (New York: Random House, 1972). Recently, however, an intriguing new interpretation of Kammerer's work has been undertaken by Rob Schmidt and John Townley (as of this writing unpublished), based on Schmidt's translation from the original German. They argue that Kammerer's theory of synchronicity (termed "seriality") differs from Jung's conception in its disavowal of both non-causality and metaphysical notions of "meaning" as explanatory principles for this phenomenon.

3 Gretel Erlich, *A Match to the Heart* (New York: Pantheon 1994), 28.

4 Arthur Schopenhauer, cited by Joseph Campbell in *The Masks of God, Vol. IV: Creative Mythology* (New York: Viking, 1968), 193-194.

5 Georg Feuerstein, *The Mystery of Light* (Salt Lake City, UT: Passage Press, 1994), 28-29.

CHAPTER 4

1 Cornelius Agrippa, *Three Books of Occult Philosophy* (St. Paul, MN: Llewellyn, 1993), 160.

2 Plutarch, *The Lives of the Noble Grecians and Romans*, translated by John Dryden, revised by Arthur Hugh Clough (New York: *The Modern Library*), 802-803.

CHAPTER 5

1 Paul Reps, quoted by William Segal, *Tricycle*, vol. 1, no. 1, 53.

2 Arthur Schopenhauer, quoted by Joseph Campbell in *The Masks of God, vol. IV: Creative Mythology*, 344.

3 Cornelius Agrippa, *The Three Books of Occult Philosophy*, 163.

4 Cited in *True Remarkable Occurrences*, compiled and annotated by John Train (New York: Clarkson N. Potter, Inc., 1978), 36.

5 Gerhard Adler, "Reflections on 'Chance,' 'Fate,' and Synchronicity," *Psychological Perspectives*, vol. 20, no. 1, Spring-Summer 1989, 18.

6 Ibid., 30.

7 A good discussion of Jung's view of "compensation" in relation to his theory of synchronicity can be found in Robert Aziz, *C.G. Jung's Psychology of Religion and Synchronicity* (Albany, NY: SUNY Press, 1990), 16-18, 160-166, 207. Though somewhat academic in style, Aziz offers many useful observations and places synchronicity in the larger context of Jung's psychological and religious philosophy.

8 Arthur Schopenhauer, quoted by Joseph Campbell in *The Masks of God, vol. IV: Creative Mythology*, 344.

9 Carlos Castaneda, *The Fire From Within* (New York: Simon & Schuster, 1984), 25-43.

CHAPTER 6

1 C. G. Jung, "Mysterium Coniunctionis," *Collected Works, vol. 14* (Princeton. NJ: Princeton University Press, 1970), 419-420.

2 Quoted by Paul Reps in *Zen Flesh, Zen Bones: A Collection of Zen and Pre-Zen Writing* (Garden City, NY: Anchor, Doubleday, 1961), 106.

3 Transcribed from a lecture by Goswami Kriyananda at the Temple of Kriya Yoga, Chicago, 1982.

4 *I Ching*, translated by Richard Wilhelm, rendered into English by Cary F. Baynes (Princeton, NJ: Princeton University Press, 1950), 190.

CHAPTER 7

1 Sir Edwin Arnold, *The Light of Asia* (New York: Dodd, Mead & Co., 1926), 110.

2 Although the image of an acorn-as-potential-oak-tree is useful in describing the principle of teleology, it should not be taken too literally. We speak of the acorn as being "drawn forward" toward its potential as an oak tree, as if that future state already existed and was exerting its influence backward through time. However, as Rupert Sheldrake has pointed out, one can easily destroy a given acorn, thereby preventing it from reaching its end goal, thus effectively refuting the argument that the acorn's "destiny" as an oak tree exists in any metaphysical sense. Thus whatever destiny an acorn holds appears to be a set of genetic possibilities, which may—or may not—ever reach fruition.

3 Cited by Glenn Mullin, "Personal Glimpses," *The Quest*, Winter 1993, 96.

4 Paraphrased from Heinrich Zimmer, *Myths and Symbols in Indian Art and Civilization* (Princeton, NJ: Princeton University Press, 1962),159.

5 Medicine Grizzlybear Lake, *Native Healer* (Wheaton, IL: Quest Books, 1991), 27.

6 Cited by James Hillman in *Re-Visioning Psychology* (New York: Harper and Row, 1975), 195-196.

7 Arthur Schopenhauer, quoted by Joseph Campbell in *The Masks of God, vol. IV: Creative Mythology*, 193-4.

8 Edward Whitmont, "The Destiny Concept in Psychotherapy," *Spring*, James Hillman, ed., Analytical Psychology Club of New York, 1969, 73-92.

9 I have paraphrased and condensed this tale from *Tales of the Dervishes*, Idries Shah (New York: E.P. Dutton & Co., 1969), 72-74.

10 Elisabeth Kübler-Ross, interviewed by William Elliott, *Tying Rocks to Clouds* (Wheaton, IL: Quest Books, 1995), 39.

11 Sogyal Rinpoche, *The Tibetan Book of Living and Dying* (San Francisco: HarperSanFrancisco, 1992), 134.

CHAPTER 8

1 *Flower Ornament Sutra*, translated by Thomas Cleary (Boston: Shambhala,1985), 317.

2 Dudjom Rinpoche, cited by Sogyal Rinpoche in *The Tibetan Book of Living and Dying* (San Francisco: HarperSanFrancisco, 1994), 82.

3 Cited by Jerome Buckley in *Tennyson: The Growth of a Poet* (Cambridge, MA: Harvard University Press, 1967), 15.

4 Carl Jung, *The Symbolic Life* (Princeton, NJ: Princeton University Press, 1980), 273-274.

5 These examples are drawn from Sarah Rossbach, *Feng Shui: The Chinese Art of Placement* (New York, E. P. Dutton, Inc., 1983).

6 For a highly readable introduction to the ritualistic potentials of the home environment, see Scott Cunningham, *The Magical Household* (St. Paul, MN: Llewellyn, 1993).

7 Elisabeth Kübler-Ross, in William Elliott, *Tying Rocks to Clouds*, 33.

8 Quoted by Stephen Mitchell in *The Gospel According to Jesus* (New York: Harper Perennial, 1991), 46.

9 For a more detailed discussion of the relationship of hatha yoga postures to the chakras, see *The Spiritual Science of Kriya Yoga*, by Goswami Kriyananda (Chicago: The Temple of Kriya Yoga, 1988).

10 Goswami Kriyananda, in conversation with the author.

11 *The Hymns of Orpheus*, translated by R. C. Hogart (Grand Rapids, MI: Phanes, 1993), 39.

12 Cited by John Daido Loori during a talk at Zen Mountain Monastery, 1987. Also cited in slightly different form in Loori's *The Eight Gates of Zen* (Mt. Tremper, NY: Dharma Communications, 1992), 179.

CHAPTER 9

1 Percy Seymour, *Astrology: The Evidence of Science* (Luton Beds, England: Lennard Publishing, 1988), 13.

2 H. P. Blavatsky, *Collected Writings*, vol. III (Wheaton, IL: Theosophical Publishing House, 1968), 192.

3 For an excellent work on the details and implications of non-locality as derived from the work of Bell, see Tim Maudlin, *Quantum Non-Locality and Relativity: Metaphysical Intimations of Modern Physics* (Cambridge, MA: Blackwell, 1994).

4 Percy Seymour, *Astrology: The Evidence of Science*, 79-80. In fact, the use of Bell's Theorem to explain astrological influence is problematic on several levels. In addition to Seymour's objection, Bell's version of nonlocality extends only to particles which have previously been in contact with each other; in astrology, by contrast, an interconnectedness is postulated between distant bodies (human and celestial) for which no previous relationship truly exists.

5 See Michel Gauquelin, *Cosmic Influences on Human Behavior* (Sante Fe, NM: Aurora Press, 1985) and *Neo-Astrology: A Copernican Revolution* (New York: Arkana, 1991).

6   Peter Roberts, *The Message of Astrology* (Northamptonshire, England: Aquarian Press, 1990), 72-73.

7   Michael Harding, *Hymns to the Ancient Gods* (London: Arkana, 1992), 23-41.

8   Plotinus, *The Enneads*, translated by Thomas MacKenna (Burdett, NY: Larson Publications, 1992) Ennead II. 3. 7, 108-109.

9   Plotinus, Ennead VI.9.

10 Ralph Waldo Emerson, "Nature," *The Complete Writings* (New York: William H. Wise, 1929), 913.

11 Arthur Schopenhauer, *The Masks of God, vol. IV*, 344.

CHAPTER 10

1   While the Sun and the Moon embody the primary polarities of archetypal masculine and feminine, we should never regard the Sun as purely male or the Moon as purely female. Just as all women contain an inner masculine and all men an inner feminine, so these two archetypes contain their opposite qualities as well. In traditional Chinese thought, this point is conveyed by the symbol of yin and yang, in which each half of the circle contains a small dot bearing the shading of the opposite half—thereby illustrating the spiritual truth that everything contains the seed of its opposite.

2   According to Vedic scholar David Frawley, while there is no direct source in Yogic literature for the Chandra chakra as described by Yogananda, it could be related to the classical idea that the Ajna chakra ("third eye") has two "petals," which relate to the right and left eyes, governed by the Sun and the Moon.

3   See Paramahansa Yogananda, *Autobiography of a Yogi* (Nevada City, CA: Crystal Clarity Publishers, 1994), 234.

4   For a more detailed discussion of the art of chakrically interpreted horoscopes, see my article "Astrology and the Chakras: Toward a Sacred Psychology of the Horoscope," *The Mountain Astrologer* (April 1996).

5   In traditional Yogic thought, Kundalini energy, which in its latent state is described as a coiled serpent at the base of the spine, when awakened by spiritual practice, is said to rise up the spine to the chakra centers in the head. Many warnings are given about the dangers of activating Kundalini by the unprepared novice. Most of the difficulties arise when the awakened energies veer off into the right or left channels, rather than being contained within the balanced or central channel. The best advice is to consult a qualified teacher before engaging in meditative practices designed to activate this energy.

6   The "Hatha Yoga Pradipika," stanza IV.7, cited by Georg Feuerstein in *Wholeness or Transcendence* (Burdett, NY: Larson, 1992), 273.

7   For more information on the relation of the sushumnic channel to the symbols experienced in the near-death experience, see my article "A Yogic Perspective on the Near-Death Experience" in *The Quest*, Summer 1994, 35.

[8] Shelly Trimmer, *Esoteric Astrology* (unpublished manuscript).

CHAPTER 11

[1] See Hans Jenny, *Cymatics I & II* (Basil, Switzerland: Basileus Press, 1972).

[2] See *The Man Who Tasted Shapes*, Richard Cytowic (New York: Tarcher/Putnam, 1993). Cytowic argues that, in its physiological form, synesthesia is different from the metaphoric synesthesia described by poets and mystics. Tests performed on biologically synesthetic individuals suggest that this process takes place largely in the lower levels of the brain, the limbic or reptile brain. By contrast, tests run on individuals in a state of poetic/metaphoric thought indicate an involvement of the higher, rational levels of the brain's neocortex. This suggests that as a purely medical condition, synesthesia is not truly a "proportional" cross-referencing of sensory data so much as a genuine misinterpretation by the brain of information received through the senses. If true, this means that clinical synesthesia may not have anything metaphoric or mystical about it at all.

[3] John Anthony West, *Serpent In The Sky* (Wheaton, IL: Quest Books, 1993), 113-114.

[4] The notion that psychological states may possess a proportional, or geometric dimension finds support in Prof. Manfred Clynes' theory of "essentic forms." Clynes devised tests which asked laboratory subjects to link emotional states with various audial or visual forms. A consistent set of relationships emerged: anger corresponded to sharper forms, sensuality with undulating forms, etc. While the ramifications of Clynes' research are still debated, they illustrate how something as intangible as mood can translate into proportional patterns. For a more detailed explanation of Clynes' work, see Don Campbell, *Music: Physician for Times to Come* (Wheaton, IL: Quest Books, 1991), 121-145, 337-355.

[5] Ralph Waldo Emerson, *The Complete Writings,* vol. II (New York: William H. Wise, 1929), 949.

[6] French philosopher Gaston Bachelard has explored the relationship of elemental qualities to psychological states, demonstrating how the outward phenomena of nature share similarities with states of the soul. For a general introduction to Bachelard's thought, see Richard Leviton, "The Barefoot Philosopher: Gaston Bachelard's Reverie of the Elements" in *The Quest,* Spring 1995, 58-63, 78-81.

[7] My thanks here to Eric Klein for introducing me to the metaphoric method of understanding planetary qualities.

[8] Cited by Anthony Aveni, *Conversing with the Planets* (New York: Kodansha International, Inc., 1994), 46.

[9] Shelly Trimmer, *Esoteric Astrology* (unpublished manuscript).

[10] Ramprasad, as quoted in Lex Hixon, *Mother of the Universe: Visions of the Goddess and Tantric Hymns of Enlightenment* (Wheaton, IL: Quest Books, 1993), 77.

CHAPTER 12

[1] Carl Jung, "Synchronicity: An Acausal Connecting Principle," in *The Structure and Dynamics of the Psyche*, Vol. 8, *Collected Works* (Princeton, NJ: Bollingen Series, Princeton University Press), par. 843-845.

[2] Carl Jung, par. 843. The question as to the true frequency of synchronistic phenomena became a matter of considerable debate between Jung and his colleague, Swiss analyst C. A. Meier. Meier pointed out to Jung that if synchronicity is a phenomenon at "right angles" to causality, then by definition it must manifest as commonly in our lives as causality, not simply as an occasional feature. Conceding this point, Jung added a footnote to this effect in the book's next edition—failing, however, to cite Meier's role in clarifying this point for him. On being angrily confronted by Meier for this oversight, Jung modified the footnote (number 70) to credit Meier's contribution, which in subsequent editions has read as follows: "I must again stress the possibility that the relation between body and soul may yet be understood as a synchronistic one. Should this conjecture ever be proved, my present view that synchronicity is a relatively rare phenomenon would have to be corrected."

[3] Ralph Waldo Emerson, *The Complete Writings*, vol. II (New York: William H. Wise, 1929), 955.

[4] Ira Progoff, *Jung, Synchronicity, and Human Destiny: Noncausal Dimensions of Human Experience* (New York: Dialog House, 1985), 134.

[5] Jung, par. 916.

[6] Carl Jung, cited by Ira Progoff, in *Jung, Synchronicity, and Human Destiny*, 159.

[7] Jung, par. 849.

[8] Jung, par. 816.

[9] A good overview of the holographic principle and its implications for different disciplines is presented in Michael Talbot's *The Holographic Universe* (New York: Harper Collins, 1991).

[10] See Benoit B. Mandelbrot, *The Fractal Geometry of Nature* (New York: W. H. Freeman and Company, 1983).

[11] See Rupert Sheldrake, *A New Science of Life* (Rochester, VT: One Park Press, 1995).

[12] Jeremy Bernstein, quoted by Ken Wilber in *Quantum Questions* (Boulder, CO: Shambhala, 1984), 27.

[13] Nick Herbert, *Quantum Reality: Beyond the New Physics* (Garden City, NY: Anchor Press/Doubleday, 1985), 227.

[14] Robert Anton Wilson, "Synchronicity, Isomorphism, and the Implicate Order," *Gnosis* (Winter 1989), 50.

[15] Ken Wilber, *Sex, Ecology, Spirituality* (Boulder, CO: Shambala, 1995), 266.

[16] See Michel Gauquelin, *Neo-Astrology: A Copernican Revolution* (New York: Penguin, 1991).

[17] In fact, there are several other modes of interpreting reality besides the scientific (collective-rational) and symbolist (archetypal), which extract different kinds of information from the world. They include: the aesthetic (events as they might be seen by an artist); the subjective-emotional (events as filtered through personal memories and associations); the concrete-sensory (events as seen in terms of raw data, much as a camera or insect might perceive them); and the "luminous suchness" (where the event is seen divested of all conceptual overlays, as in the concrete-sensory mode, but enhanced by awakened self-awareness). Though it is tempting to rank these modes hierarchically, from lesser to greater importance, the truth is that different modes are appropriate to different contexts. Even a Zen master will employ different cognitive modes depending on whether he is bidding farewell to his mother on her deathbed, interpreting a dream, staring at the wall in meditation, or trying to decipher an owner's manual for a VCR!

[18] Quoted by John Robinson in *An Introduction to Early Greek Philosophy* (New York: Houghton-Mifflin, 1968), 69.

[19] Seyyed Hossein Nasr, *The Need for a Sacred Science* (Albany, NY: SUNY Press, 1993) 97.

[20] David Bohm, from *The Search for Meaning*, ed. Paavo Pylkkänen (Wellingborough, GB: Crucible, 1989), 43.

[21] Bohm, *The Search for Meaning*, 60.

[22] Richard Feynman, *The Feynman Lectures on Physics*, vol. II (Palo Alto, CA: Addison Wesley, 1964), 41-42.

[23] Norman Mailer, quoted in Daniel Noel, *Approaching Earth: A Search for the Mythic Significance of the Space Age* (Amity, NY: Amity House, 1986), 23-24.

[24] Some astrologers feel there are exceptions to this rule; for example, see Richard Tarnas' discussion of the naming of the planet Uranus in *Prometheus the Awakener* (Woodstock, CT: Spring Publications, 1995), 11-16.

[25] See "An Interview with Richard Kastl," in *East-West Journal* (December 1977), 40.

[26] From "The Mistress of Vision," by Frances Thompson, in *Columbia Granger's World of Poetry*, CD-ROM (New York: Columbia University Press, 1991-2).

[27] Aniela Jaffé, *The Myth of Meaning* (New York: Putnam, 1971).

BIBLIOGRAPHY

Adler, Gerhard. "Reflections on 'Chance,' 'Fate,' and Synchronicity." *Psychological Perspectives*, vol. 20, no. 1 (Spring-Summer 1989).

Agrippa, Cornelius. *The Three Books of Occult Philosophy*. St. Paul, MN: Llewellyn, 1993.

Aivanhov, Omraam Mikhael. *The Living Book of Nature*. Los Angeles: Prosveta, 1987.

Aveni, Anthony. *Conversing with the Planets*. New York: Kodansha International, Inc., 1994.

Aziz, Robert. *C. G. Jung's Psychology of Religion and Synchronicity*. Albany, NY: SUNY, 1990.

Baigent, Michael. *From the Omens of Babylon: Astrology and Ancient Mesopotamia*. London: Arkana, 1994.

Bamford, Christopher, ed. *Homage to Pythagoras: Rediscovering Sacred Science*. Hudson, NY: Lindisfarne Press, 1994.

Bateson, Gregory. *Mind and Nature: A Necessary Unity*. New York: E. P. Dutton, 1979.

Bell, John Stewart. "Nonlocality in Physics and Psychology: An Interview with John Stewart Bell." *Psychological Perspectives*, vol. 19, no. 2 (Fall-Winter, 1988).

Berman, Morris. *The Reenchantment of the World*. Ithaca, NY: Cornell University Press, 1981.

Blair, Lawrence. *Rhythms of Vision*. Rochester, NY: Destiny Books, 1991.

Blavatsky, H. P. *The Secret Doctrine*. Wheaton, IL: Theosophical Publishing House, Quest Books, 1993.

Boehme, Jacob. *The Signature of All Things*. New York: Dent and Sons, 1926.

Bohm, David. *Wholeness and the Implicate Order*. Boston: Routledge & Kegan Paul, 1980.

_____. *Unfolding Meaning: A Weekend of Dialogue with David Bohm*. New York: Routledge & Kegan Paul, 1985.

Bolen, Jean Shinoda. *The Tao of Psychology: Synchronicity and the Self*. San Francisco: Harper & Row, 1979.

Bonnefoy, Yves. *Mythologies,* vols. I & II. Translated by Gerald Honigsblum. Chicago: University of Chicago Press, 1991.

Briggs, John. *Fractals, The Patterns of Chaos: Discovering a New Aesthetic of Art and Nature.* New York: Simon & Schuster, 1992.

Brown, Norman O. *Life Against Death.* Middletown, NH: Wesleyan University Press, 1959.

Burckhardt, Titus. *Alchemy: Science of the Cosmos, Science of the Soul.* Translated by William Stoddart. London: John M. Watkins, 1967.

Campbell, Joseph. *The Masks of God.* New York: Viking. Vol. 1, *Primitive Mythology* (1959). Vol. 2, *Oriental Mythology* (1962). Vol. 3, *Occidental Mythology* (1964). Vol. 4, *Creative Mythology* (1968).

Capra, Fritjof. *The Tao of Physics.* London: Fontana, 1977.

Cicero. *On the Nature of the Gods. On Divination. On Fate.* London: G. Bell & Sons, 1902.

Cirlot, J. E. *A Dictionary of Symbols.* Translated by Jack Sage. New York: Philosophical Library, 1962.

Clark, R.T. Rundle. *Myth and Symbol in Ancient Egypt.* London: Thames & Hudson, 1959.

Combs, Allan, and Mark Holland. *Synchronicity: Science, Myth, and the Trickster.* New York: Paragon House, 1990.

Cunningham, Scott. *The Magical Household.* St. Paul, MN: Llewellyn, 1993.

Cytowic, Richard. *The Man Who Tasted Shapes.* New York: Tarcher/Putnam, 1993.

Da Avabhasa. *The Transmission of Doubt.* Clearlake, CA: Dawn Horse Press, 1984.

Davies, Paul. *The Mind of God: The Scientific Basis for a Rational World.* New York: Touchstone, 1992.

Davies, Paul. "Synchronicity in the Cosmic Blueprint." *Psychological Perspectives,* vol. 20, no. 1 (Spring-Summer, 1989).

Dickenson, C. Lowes. *The Greek View of Life.* Ann Arbor, MI: University of Michigan Press, 1958.

Doniger, Wendy. *Dreams, Illusions, and Other Realities.* Chicago: University of Chicago Press, 1984.

_____. *Other Peoples' Myths.* New York: Macmillan, 1988.

Dossey, Larry. *Meaning and Medicine: A Doctor's Tales of Breakthroughs and Healing.* New York: Bantam, 1991.

Durkheim, Emile, and Marcel Mauss. *Primitive Classification*. Chicago: University of Chicago Press, 1967.

Edinger, E. F. *Ego and Archetype: Individuation and the Religious Function of the Psyche*. Baltimore, MD: Penguin, 1973.

_____. *Melville's Moby-Dick: A Jungian Commentary*. New York: New Directions Books, 1978.

Eliade, Mircea. *The Sacred and the Profane*. New York: Harcourt, Brace, and World, 1959.

_____. *Cosmos and History: The Myth of the Eternal Return*. New York: Harper & Row, 1959.

_____. *The Two and the One*. New York: Harper & Row, 1965.

_____. *Images and Symbols*. New York: Search Books, 1969.

Emerson, Ralph Waldo. *The Writings of Ralph Waldo Emerson*. New York: Modern Library, 1940.

Evans-Wentz, W. Y., ed. *Tibetan Yoga and Secret Doctrines*. Oxford: Oxford University Press, 1967.

Faivre, Antoine. *Access to Western Esotericism*. Albany, NY: SUNY Press, 1994.

Feuerstein, Georg. *The Mystery of Light*. Salt Lake City: Passage Press, 1994.

_____. *The Yoga-Sutra of Pantanjali: A New Translation and Commentary*. Rochester, NY: Inner Traditions, 1989.

Fortune, Reo. "Divination." *Encyclopedia of the Social Sciences*. New York: Macmillan, 1931.

Ficino, Marselio. *The Book of Life*. Translated by Charles Boer. Dallas: Spring, 1994.

Fideler, David. *Jesus Christ, Sun of God: Ancient Cosmology and Early Christian Symbolism*. Wheaton, IL: Quest Books, 1993.

Fiedelson, Charles N. *Symbolism and American Literature*. Chicago: University of Chicago Press, 1981.

Franz, Marie-Louise von. *Number and Time: Reflections Leading Towards a Unification of Psychology and Physics*. Evanston, IL: Northwestern University Press, 1974.

_____. *On Divination and Synchronicity: The Psychology of Meaningful Chance*. Toronto: Inner City Books, 1980.

_____. *Projection and Re-Collection in Jungian Psychology*. Translated by William H. Kennedy. Lasalle, IL: Open Court, 1980.

Frazer, James G. *The Golden Bough: A Study in Magic and Religion.* London: Macmillan, 1911-1915.

Frawley, David. *The Astrology of the Seers: A Guide to Vedic (Hindu) Astrology.* Salt Lake City: Passage Press, 1990.

Gauquelin, Michel. *Cosmic Influences on Human Behavior.* Sante Fe, NM: Aurora Press, 1985.

_____. *Neo-Astrology: A Copernican Revolution.* London: Arkana, 1991.

Grasse, Ray. "Karma, the Chakras, and Esoteric Yoga." *Karma: Rhythmic Return to Harmony.* V. Hanson, R. Stewart, and S. Nicholson, eds. Wheaton, IL: Quest Books, 1990.

_____. "Myth in the Modern World: An Interview with Wendy Doniger." *The Quest* (Winter 1990).

_____. "The Crowd Within: Multiple Personality Disorder and Traditional Esoteric Psychologies." *The Quest* (Fall 1992).

_____. "A Yogic Perspective on Near-Death Experiences." *The Quest* (Summer 1994).

_____. "Astrology and the Chakras: Toward a Sacred Psychology of the Horoscope." *The Mountain Astrologer* (April 1996).

Greene, Liz. *The Astrology of Fate.* York Beach, ME: Samuel Weiser, Inc., 1984.

Gilson, Etienne. *The Spirit of Medieval Philosophy.* New York: Scribner's Sons, 1940.

Godwin, Joscelyn. *Robert Fludd: Hermetic Philosopher and Surveyor of Two Worlds.* London: Thames & Hudson, 1979. Reprint: Grand Rapids, MI: Phanes Press, 1991.

Gribbin, John, and Martin Rees. *Cosmic Coincidences: Dark Matter, Mankind, and Anthropic Cosmology.* New York: Bantam, 1989.

Hall, Manly Palmer. *The Secret Teachings of All Ages.* Los Angeles: Philosophical Research Society, 1959.

Harding, Michael. *Hymns to the Ancient Gods.* London: Arkana, 1992.

Hesse, Herman. *The Glass Bead Game.* New York: Holt, Rinehart & Winston, 1969.

Hoeller, Stephan A. *The Royal Road: A Manual of Kabbalistic Meditations on the Tarot.* Wheaton, IL: Quest Books, 1975.

Homer. *Odyssey.* Translated by G. M. Priest. New York: Knopf, 1963.

Howell, Alice O. *The Web in the Sea: Jung, Sophia, and the Geometry of the*

Soul. Wheaton, IL: Quest Books, 1993.

Hillman, James. *Re-Visioning Psychology*. New York: Harper & Row, 1975.

Hoffman, Edward. *The Heavenly Ladder: A Jewish Guide to Inner Growth*. San Francisco: Harper & Row, 1985.

I Ching (Book of Changes). Translated by Richard Wilhelm. Rendered into English by Cary F. Baynes. Princeton, NJ: Princeton University Press, 1977.

Jacobi, Jolan. *Complex/Archetype/Symbol*. New York: Pantheon Books, 1959.

_____. *Paracelsus: Selected Writings*. Princeton, NJ: Princeton University Press, 1979.

Jaffé, Aniela. *The Myth of Meaning*. New York: Putnam, 1971.

Jenny, Hans. *Cymatics*. New York: Schocken Books, 1975.

Joyce, James. *Ulysses*. New York: Random House, 1967.

Jung, C. G. *Collected Works. The Structure and Dynamics of the Psyche* (vol. 8, 1969). *The Archetypes and the Collective Unconscious* (vol. 9, part 1, 1968). *Mysterium Coniuntionis* (vol. 14, 1970). *The Symbolic Life* (vol. 18, 1976). Princeton, NJ: Princeton University Press.

Keynes, John Maynard. "Newton the Man," *Newton Tercentenary Celebrations*. Cambridge: Cambridge University Press, 1947.

Koestler, Arthur. *The Roots of Coincidence*. New York: Random House, 1972.

_____. *The Case of the Midwife Toad*. New York: Random House, 1972.

Keutzer, Carolin S. "The Power of Meaning: From Quantum Physics to Synchronicity." *Journal of Humanistic Psychology*, vol. 24, no. 1 (Winter 1984).

_____. "Archetypes, Synchronicity and the Theory of Formative Causation." *Journal of Analytical Psychology*, vol. 27 (1982).

Kriyananda, Goswami. *The Spiritual Science of Kriya Yoga*. Chicago: Temple of Kriya Yoga Press, 1988.

Lake, Medicine Grizzlybear. *Native Healer*. Wheaton, IL: Quest Books, 1991.

Lehner, Ernst. *Symbols, Signs, and Signets*. New York: Dover, 1950.

Lawlor, Robert. *Sacred Geometry: Philosophy and Practice*. London: Thames & Hudson, 1982.

Levi-Strauss, Claude. *The Savage Mind*. Chicago: University of Chicago Press, 1967.

Levy-Bruhl, Lucien. *Primitive Mentality*. Boston: Beacon Press, 1966.

Loewe, Michael, and Carmen Blacker, eds. *Oracles and Divination*. Boulder, CO: Shambhala, 1981.

Luck, Georg. *Arcana Mundi*. Baltimore, MD: Johns Hopkins University Press, 1985.

Mathers, S. L. MacGregor. *The Kabbalah Unveiled*. New York: Arkana, 1991.

Maudlin, Tim. *Quantum Non-Locality and Relativity: Metaphysical Intimations of Modern Physics*. Cambridge, MA: Blackwell Publishers, 1994.

Meier, C. A. "Science and Synchronicity: A Conversation with C. A. Meier." *Psychological Perspectives*, vol. 19, no. 2 (Fall-Winter 1988).

Melville, Herman. *Moby Dick*. New York: Hendricks House, 1962.

Michell, John. *City of Revelation: On the Proportions and Symbolic Numbers of the Cosmic Temple*. London: Garnstone, 1972.

Moore, Omar Khayyam. "Divination—A New Perspective." *Reader in Comparative Religion*. 4th edition. William A. Lessa and Evon Z. Vogt, eds. New York: Harper & Row, 1979.

Moore, Thomas. *The Planets Within: The Astrological Psychology of Marsilio Ficino*. Lewisburg, PA: Bucknell University Press, 1982. Reprint: Hudson, NY: Lindisfarne Press, 1990.

Nasr, Seyyed Hossein. *The Need for a Sacred Science*. Albany, NY: SUNY, 1993.

Needham, Joseph. *Science and Civilization in China*, vol. 2. Cambridge: Cambridge University Press, 1956.

Needleman, Jacob. *A Sense of the Cosmos: The Encounter of Modern Science and Ancient Truth*. Garden City, NY: Doubleday, 1975.

Noel, Daniel. *Approaching Earth: A Search for the Mythic Significance of the Space Age*. Amity, NY: Amity House, 1986.

Novalis. *Pollen and Fragments*. Translated by Arthur Versluis. Grand Rapids, MI: Phanes Press, 1989.

Otto, Rudolf C. *The Idea of the Holy*. London: Oxford University Press, 1950.

Peat, F. David. *Synchronicity: The Bridge Between Mind and Matter*. New York: Bantam, 1987.

_____. "Divine Contenders: Wolgang Pauli and the Symmetry of the World." *Psychological Perspectives*, vol. 19, no. 1 (Spring-Summer 1988).

Peek, Philip. *African Divination Systems: Ways of Knowing*. Bloomington, IN: Indiana University Press, 1991.

Pinch, Geraldine. *Magic in Ancient Egypt*. Austin, TX: University of Texas Press, 1994.

Plato. *Works*. 12 vols. Loeb Classical Library. Cambridge: Harvard University Press, 1914-1927.

Plotinus. *The Enneads*. Translated by Stephen MacKenna. Burdett, NY: Larson Publications, 1992.

_____. *The Essential Plotinus*. Edited by Elmer O'Brien. New York: Mentor Books, The New American Library, 1964.

Poncé, Charles. *Kabbalah: An Introduction and Illumination for the World Today*. Wheaton, IL: Quest Books, 1978.

_____. *The Game of Wizards: Roots of Consciousness & the Esoteric Arts*. Wheaton, IL: Quest Books, 1991.

Progoff, Ira. *Jung, Synchronicity, and Human Destiny*. New York: Dell, 1973.

Pylkkänen, Paavo, ed. *The Search for Meaning*. Wellingborough, GB: Crucible, 1989.

Quispel, Gilles. "Gnosis and Psychology." *The Allure of Gnosticism: The Gnostic Experience in Jungian Psychology and Contemporary Culture*. Robert Segal, ed. Chicago: Open Court, 1995.

Roberts, Peter. *The Message of Astrology*. Northamptonshire, England: Aquarian Press, Thorsons Publishing, 1990.

Rossbach, Sarah. *Feng Shui: The Chinese Art of Placement*. New York: E. P. Dutton, 1983.

Sauneron, Serge. *The Priests of Ancient Egypt*. Translated by Ann Morrissett. New York: Grove Press, Inc., 1960.

Schumaker, Wayne. *The Occult Sciences in the Renaissance*. Berkeley, CA: University of California Press, 1972.

Schuon, Fritjof. *The Transcendent Unity of Religions*. New York: Harper & Row, 1976.

Schwaller de Lubicz, R. A. *Sacred Science*. Translated by Andre and Goldian VandenBroeck. New York: Inner Traditions, 1982.

_____. *Esotericism & Symbol*. Translated by Andre and Goldian Vanden-Broeck. New York: Inner Traditions, 1985.

_____. *The Egyptian Miracle*. Translated by Andre and Goldian Vanden-Broeck. New York: Inner Traditions, 1985.

Seligmann, Kurt. *The History of Magic*. New York: Pantheon Books, 1948.

Seymour, Percy. *Astrology: The Evidence of Science*. Luton Beds, England: Lennard Publishing, 1988.

Shah, Idries. *Tales of the Dervishes*. New York: E. P. Dutton, 1969.

Sheldrake, Rupert. *A New Science of Life: The Hypothesis of Morphic Resonance*. Rochester, NY: Park Street Press, 1995.

Smith, Huston. *Forgotten Truth*. New York: Harper & Row, 1976.

Smith, Jonathan Z. *Imagining Religion*. Chicago: University of Chicago Press, 1982.

Sogyal Rinpoche. *The Tibetan Book of Living and Dying*. San Francisco: HarperSanFrancisco, 1992.

Spence, Lewis. *Encyclopedia of Occultism*. Hyde Park, New York: University Books, 1960.

Stevens, Anthony. *Archetype: A Natural History of the Self*. London: Routledge & Kegan Paul, 1982.

Swedenborg, Emmanuel. *Heaven and Hell*. New York: Swedenborg Foundation, 1938.

Talbot, Michael. *The Holographic Universe*. New York: Harper Collins, 1991.

Tarnas, Richard. *The Passion of the Western Mind*. New York: Ballantine, 1991.

_____. *Prometheus the Awakener*. Woodstock, CT: Spring Publications, 1995.

Thompson, William I. *The Time Falling Bodies Take to Light*. New York: St. Martin's Press, 1981.

Thorndike, L. *A History of Magic and Experimental Science*. New York: Columbia University Press, 1923.

Trimmer, Shelly. *Esoteric Astrology*. Unpublished manuscript.

Vaughan, Alan. *Incredible Coincidence*. New York: J. B. Lippincott, 1979.

Voss, Sarah. *What Number Is God? Metaphor, Metaphysics, Metamathematics, and the Nature of Things*. Albany, NY: SUNY Press, 1995.

Weber, Renee. "The Reluctant Tradition." *Main Currents*, vol. 31, no. 4 (March-April 1975).

West, John Anthony. *The Case for Astrology*. New York: Viking Penguin, 1991.

_____. *Serpent in the Sky: The High Wisdom of Ancient Egypt*. Wheaton, IL: Quest Books, 1993.

_____. *The Traveler's Key to Ancient Egypt*. Wheaton, IL: Quest Books, 1996.

Wheeler, John. *At Home in the Universe*. Woodbury, NY: American Institute of Physics Press, 1994.

Wilber, Ken. *The Holographic Paradigm, and Other Paradoxes*. Boulder, CO:

New Science Library, Shambhala, 1982.

_____. *Quantum Questions: The Mystical Writings of the World's Great Physicists.* Boulder, CO: Shambhala, 1984.

_____. *Up From Eden.* Wheaton, IL: Quest Books, 1996.

_____. *Sex, Ecology, Spirituality: The Spirit of Evolution.* Boston: Shambhala, 1995.

Wilson, Colin. *The Occult.* New York: Random House, 1971.

Wilson, Robert Anton. *Coincidance.* Scottsdale, AZ: New Falcon Publications, 1991.

Yates, Frances. *Giordano Bruno and the Hermetic Tradition.* Chicago: University of Chicago Press, 1991.

_____. *The Occult Philosophy in the Elizabethan Age.* London: Routledge & Kegan Paul, 1978.

Yogananda, Paramahansa. *Autobiography of a Yogi.* Nevada City, CA: Crystal Clarity Publishers, 1994. Reprint of the original 1946 Philosophical Library edition.

INDEX

QUEST BOOKS
are published by
The Theosophical Society in America,
Wheaton, Illinois 60189-0270,
a branch of a world organization
dedicated to the promotion of the unity of
humanity and the encouragement of the study of
religion, philosophy, and science, to the end that
we may better understand ourselves and our place in
the universe. The Society stands for complete
freedom of individual search and belief.
For further information about its activities,
write or call 1-800-669-1571.

*The Theosophical Publishing House
is aided by the generous support of
THE KERN FOUNDATION,
a trust established by Herbert A. Kern
and dedicated to Theosophical education.*